TWELVE MONTHS TO LIVE
...AGAIN

///

KAREN DYE-WALKER

Order this book online at www.trafford.com/08-1219
or email orders@trafford.com

Most Trafford titles are also available at major online book retailers.

Back cover photo: Southern Exposure, Hopkinsville, KY.
Back cover photo: Hair and make-up by Sandra Bonner.

Note for Librarians: A cataloguing record for this book is available from Library
and Archives Canada at www.collectionscanada.ca/amicus/index-e.html

Printed in Victoria, BC, Canada.

ISBN: 978-1-4251-7641-9

*We at Trafford believe that it is the responsibility of us all, as both individuals
and corporations, to make choices that are environmentally and socially sound.
You, in turn, are supporting this responsible conduct each time you purchase a
Trafford book, or make use of our publishing services. To find out how you are
helping, please visit www.trafford.com/responsiblepublishing.html*

*Our mission is to efficiently provide the world's finest, most comprehensive
book publishing service, enabling every author to experience success.
To find out how to publish your book, your way, and have it available
worldwide, visit us online at www.trafford.com/10510*

www.trafford.com

North America & International
toll-free: 1 888 232 4444 (USA & Canada)
phone: 250 383 6864 ♦ fax: 250 383 6804
email: info@trafford.com

The United Kingdom & Europe
phone: +44 (0)1865 487 395 ♦ local rate: 0845 230 9601
facsimile: +44 (0)1865 481 507 ♦ email: info.uk@trafford.com

10 9 8 7 6 5 4 3

ACKNOWLEDGEMENTS

JEFFREY, my son, thank you for being my inspiration and handing me the challenge of doing this book. Without your constant love and support, daily phone calls and cheering, this would have not been possible... nor even an idea.

Sandra, my beautiful daughter, thank you for always being "in my face" honest. You have challenged me to look at myself and see who I've been. You've always stood by me and have expected better of me than I have ever expected of myself.

Tammy, my adopted daughter, your tough "hard knock" life has also been an inspiration because of how you have turned out as an adult. You took what you were given and used it as an inspiration to become a great woman and mother.

Dad, thank you for always being in my corner and helping me when I have been unable to help myself. You've always been there for me and we have been close since the day I was born.

Clay and Lily, my precious little ones; you give me laughter, pride, much love and inspiration to do better in life. You are the future. You are my loves.

My friends Ann, Lucio, Sabrina, Joe, Jimmy and John, my church family, and the remainder of my family and friends, thank you for giving me love and support. Without each of you, my life would be devoid of many fond memories.

Will, my mentor, pastor and friend, thank you for your never ending objective to make me better in my faith journey and for your consistency in making me strive to be the best I can be. I admire your strength and focus.

My beloved mother Gloria and my beloved Sister Sheri, your laughter and memories resonate in my heart and even though you are gone, your love still goes on.

Lord, you are my Savior, my peace and my salvation. I love you.

DEDICATION

JEFFREY, I dedicate this book to you, my precious son.

You, along with the Lord's strength, are the inspiration of this work

Always strive for your dreams and remain true to yourself and, most importantly of all, stay close to God.

FOREWORD

IT HAS BEEN SAID MANY TIMES that we learn from our mistakes. For me, this is so true. I have made many mistakes in my lifetime but I am living proof that if you ask for forgiveness, it will be granted. Through much adversity, I have survived and in my constant quest for forgiveness and understanding, I am finally learning who I am: a "work in progress," I have to say...

This is my life! As raw and tumultuous as it has been, it is who Karen is. Do I have regrets? You bet I do, but I also know I am the person I am today because of the path my life has taken. I have lived, I have laughed, I have cried many tears, but the most important aspect of my life is the fact that I have become closer to God through all I have experienced. Without my faith, I would not be here to type these words. I might be a breathing body but I would be devoid of all that matters... peace, love and harmony.

Cry with me, laugh with me, and share with me my many memories of my past and identify with me if you can, through my experiences.. I am not an expert on many things, but I now can now claim expertise in the life of Karen.

TABLE OF CONTENTS

CHAPTER ONE

"I'VE BEEN THINKING!"

1-1-2007   **226 lbs.**

Wow! I cannot believe it is here already. It is the first day of the new year and the first day of the rest of my life. It is the first day of my reinvention and the first day of the writing of this book. It is a whole lot of *firsts* all wrapped up into twenty-four hours. It is almost overwhelming as I sit here with thousands of thoughts running through my head and not wanting to leave out a single one. Will I remember *that* story or the one I thought about last week? I surely do not want to leave anything out. Gosh, I hope I am up to this! Lord, please give me strength! Let my fingers fly over the keyboard as the words come to me like lightning stalking a lone oak in an empty field. Let me face this challenge, day by day, with courage and knowledge, hope and anticipation and eventual victory as I put onto paper my deepest thoughts and most treasured memories, in hope that others will learn from, and enjoy them.

1-2-2007   **226 lbs.**

The phone rang about six, Monday evening, December 18, 2006. I knew it was my son Jeffrey, by looking on the caller I.D. "Hi Mom!" Jeffrey said. "Whatcha doing?" I started with my usual reply of "Not much, watching TV." Jeffrey then asked me what I had done with my day and again I answered with my normal "Well, I went to Grandpa's for coffee this morning, I had a doctor's appointment at one p.m., did a few things around the house; not much of anything really, pretty much an uneventful day!" Jeffrey listened on the other end of the phone while I talked and then I asked him about his day and he replied with his standard answer, "Just worked, made some money today!"

I told him that was great. Then there was a long silence on the other end of the line and I heard those famous words… *"Mom, I've been thinking!"* I thought, Oh my gosh, here we go!

Now, you have to understand the impact of those three words, "I've been thinking" and what they mean to this family. None of us has ever escaped Jeffrey's "I've been thinking" statement without the explanation of exactly what he's been "thinking" about. Trust me I have tried! There have been numerous inventions, ideas, deep thoughts and even deeper questions Jeffrey has run by us since he was a little boy. We have all known about his inquisitive nature. Jeffrey has never lacked ideas and with his entrepreneurial personality, we know that if anyone in our family has the ability to be a millionaire by the age of forty, it will be Jeffrey. At the age of twenty-four, he is just an "I've been thinking" away from making *bank!* Little did I know, however, on December 18, 2006, Jeffrey's famous three words would change *my life* forever!

"Mom, you need to write a book!" There. The bomb was dropped as I heard what Jeffrey said and I immediately started laughing; a gut reflex, I guess. "No! I am serious!" he replied as I continued my outburst. Somehow, I knew with his nervous laugh on the other end of the phone line, that he was serious. "Whoa! Wait a minute here!" I put on my brakes. "Been there, done that!" I thought out loud, quickly remembering years back when I did write a book, when my kids were little and I was *naïve.* Jeffrey then said to me, "Mom, you have so much to tell, so much to say about your life and what you've been through." I listened as my ADULT son told me he thought my story was something that needed to be told. He felt people *would be* interested. I could be an inspiration to others by telling what I had been through in my life, both medically as well as emotionally. Me? An inspiration?. I listened to my son, however, with love in my heart because he spoke with love in his heart, for me, his Mother.

After having a long, sincere discussion, Jeffrey laid out his plan for me about this book. "I want you to write a page a day," he said "And I will hold you accountable by calling you every day to see what you have written," he added. Hmm, nothing like a little pressure to get you excited and wanting to jump right in, not to mention the fact that your youngest child is on the other end of the phone laying down the law, or, as he says, "the deal". *He is really not joking* ran through my mind, trying to sprint past the doubts and leap over the fear I was feeling. However, as I listened to him, my mind started jumping around in at least twenty different directions already focusing on "I could write about this or I need to be sure and tell about that!" Jeffrey and I were still talking but I do not much remember from that moment on about the specifics. Already I was in what I call *"writer's overload."* After a few more minutes, we agreed to talk again the next day. "Think about it," Jeffrey said as we hung up but little did he know, that's all I would do for the next few hours. Forget sleeping; I would not even come close to achieving sleep. My mind raced with so many thoughts and ideas I could not concentrate on one single issue. I was writing chapters in my head and then one very important thought hit me: this book would be an inspiration to others but hopefully, most of all, it would be an inspiration for me!

Let me explain the above theory. I've started the wheels in motion for making a completely new Karen! The first step was the rebuilding of my smile. I used to take great pride in my beautiful teeth and great smile. Because of health issues, however, mainly lupus, my teeth and smile have suffered severely. I have lost a majority of my teeth due to this chronic illness but in the last three months, I've undergone surgery to remove the bad ones. I finally made the very hard decision to go ahead and get full dentures for the top and a partial one for the bottom, saving six of my own healthy teeth. Being only 49 years old, this was a hard thing to do, but the suffering I have been through, not to mention my broken smile, finally won out! In a little over a week, I will have my final surgery and a brand new smile! This will be a great boost to my self-esteem; the one other thing I need to do is lose weight! I can assume I am not alone in this revelation. I know that probably at least half of you reading this book have, in the past or even this year, made the resolution to lose weight during the new year. Our intentions are always GUNG HO at first and a few of us even start a diet on the second day in January. Notice it is never on the first day because there is always that one last family get together on New Year's Day! Some of you may even make it through the first day on the diet, or the first few days, the first month or longer. Notice I said "some of you" because by the end of day one, the willpower <u>I never had</u> is ready for a 364-day nap! And once again, what calms your mind is the famous saying, "You know what they say, there is always *next year!*" Well, for me, *next year* is here!

1-4-2007   **226 lbs.**

What a personal revelation! Why not incorporate the weight issue into the writing of this book? I could incorporate a day-by-day accounting of my impending weight loss into my daily writing and conquer two birds with one stone! My thinking is that someone else might find value in my journey of looking inside myself and giving value back to myself as I shed pound upon pound, peeling back the layers, if you will, to reveal a new slimmer me to go along with my new transformation of self. *Wow,* I didn't know what hit me! Everything was so clear. My outlook on life was coming together right before my eyes. Thought after thought, the outline of the next twelve months was being etched in my consciousness, never to be forgotten! I was getting in deeper and deeper as the hours ticked by, but that little voice; you know the one, the one that always pops up with a doubting tone, saying "Are you crazy? Have you totally lost it?" was right there, chiming in, giving its unwanted opinion! "I am not listening to you!" I yelled back, in silence of course, not willing to give up the feeling of elation I was experiencing regardless of the voice of doubt. This natural high, this joyous feeling of liberation, was much more exciting! "This is it! This will be my *new life!*" On January 1, 2007, I say goodbye to Karen, as I have known her and say hello to my new best friend, the new and improved Karen!

With the weight loss issue coming together in my head, I saw flashbacks of some pictures that were taken of me back in 1985. I feel I was probably the prettiest I had ever been even though I had been a model in the late seventies. These pictures were taken by a close friend of mine for a magazine who was publishing an article about me (I'll tell more of this story later). In the photographs, some poses were taken with me wearing a pair of jeans and a blue jean shirt. These jeans were a size four. I loved them. When I put them on, I felt like Miss America and I knew I looked good. I wore them whenever I could dress casual and would even jazz them up with a great silk blouse or a fancy sweater. These jeans were my most cherished piece of apparel. They were designer jeans and they fit me like a glove. They were long enough to fit my long legs and made as if I was the girl the designer had in mind. As I thought about my treasured jeans, I had another brilliant idea. These jeans would be my daily inspiration to stick with my diet! I would carry them with me everywhere. My purse is definitely big enough to hold my rolled-up jeans. Why not? Lord knows I have everything else in that purse. It would actually give me a reason to remove some things I probably never needed in there in the first place, including six AA batteries, a broken compact and a two-year-old box of breath mints with only two remaining (hey, you never know when you need fresh breath). I'm sure I wouldn't be needing two rolls of film with no camera, or three different kinds of hand lotion, a baby bib and diaper (I am a grandmother), my daily calendar from two years ago, or my passport (I have not left the country since my 1990 my trip to Japan). Then there are three checkbooks (I only use one) and a sewing kit (I don't sew); you get the picture, right? So after cleaning the old purse out, voila... there's room for the jeans. The idea is if they are in my face all the time, I'll be a lot more conscience of what I *put in my face all the time.* What a great plan! I could not wait to share with Jeffrey my addition to our deal. I would call him as soon as I thought he would be awake, which I did.

It was seven a.m. and I couldn't wait any longer to make the call to Jeffrey. I am sure my excitement was jumping out at him over the phone. I laid out my plan and then I heard "That's terrific Mom!"; exactly what I needed to hear from my son. I welcomed his enthusiasm. We laughed and talked, or should I say I talked while he patiently listened. My mouth was going ninety miles a minute as I tried to tell him about the sleepless night I had spent full of ideas, revelations, and resolutions. This was it! I was serious and I think Jeffrey knew it. So now, all I had left to do was clean out my purse... and *find the jeans!* Surely, they were in my closet hanging at the very end where I had always kept them; you know, just in case someday I'd actually be able to fit in them again! I'm sure most of the women reading this and yes, men too, can identify with the "end of the closet" theory. You keep the treasured clothes you once wore in all your glory, at the end of the closet, not to be mixed up with your current "fat" clothes for everyday wear, to be a silent reminder of "Yes... I once looked good!" Your treasured apparel is kept as a subtle reminder of what you *should* be able to wear today, versus what you are actually wearing! And, as they are strategically placed at the end of the closet, when you're really not in the mood to be reminded of what should be, you can shove your ample-sized clothing up against them to cover them up! Out of sight out of mind? Wrong! They always linger at the back of your mind as reminders of the day we wore them with pride, ready to be recalled at an instance when we need to feel good about ourselves. Another time might be when we've made a diet resolution and yet, there we are at a restaurant in the middle of a high-fat, high-carbohydrate meal, shoving it in because we are salivating for the extra large slice of raspberry cheesecake we're planning to devour before we go home. Yet by the time we get home, there is a flashing red light with a loud horn installed over the closet door, leaving it impossible to ignore the fact that your *skinny clothes* at the *end of the closet* are in there yelling, "Shame, shame... we were counting on you!" And your fat clothes? They are in there boasting

"Give me a high five... we are in it for the long haul!" Yup, what can I say? That size-four pair of jeans is embedded in my brain forever, I'm afraid!

The search then begins. Immediately I went to the end of the closet pushing back jackets, dresses, and suits. After peeling back all the clothes, I was staring at a blank space where my jeans should have been. Where were they? They were not hanging in their special reserved space. Hmm... I immediately went to the other end of the closet thinking I might have stuck them on that side, but again they weren't there. Thinking for a second, a sigh of relief came over me as I realized I had most likely left them over at my dad's house in a closet there. I had lived with him for a short time a little over three years ago before I bought my house and I left some clothes there (my skinny ones) in the back closet. I have not been in a big hurry to bring them home because after all, they didn't fit! Surely, the jeans were in his closet, in good company! Later in the morning when I went to his place for coffee, a daily ritual, I went straight to the back bedroom and into the closet. Tearing back pieces of clothing, I held out hope until I got to the end, but the jeans were nowhere to be found. Now what... Oh no... this can't be! Again, I painstakingly went back through the closet but with the same results. I sat down on the bed, bewildered, and started tracing back my tracks for the last four or five years and come to think of it, I could not remember seeing them in that period. I guess I had just assumed they were where they always had been. I quickly went back home and started tearing my house apart for the missing jeans, like Linus looking for his beloved blanket. After the house was completely ransacked, the jeans still did not materialize. It was a good idea while it lasted!

In the process of looking for those jeans, I did find a few other possibilities. There was a pair of size eights, another pair of size tens, and one last pair of size twelve's. The eights and tens had been worn before, yes, by me, but the size twelve's still had the tags on them from when I bought them about a year ago. I remember when I bought them; I had purchased another pair, a size fourteen, that I could actually squeeze into, so I went back and bought the next size smaller to be my inspiration for shedding a few pounds. The sad thing is, I could wear the size fourteen then, but I can't wear now, so they're also in the closet! And the size twelve's are a real example of failure! So, after having myself a good old-fashioned pity party, which I felt quite deserving of, I knew I had to look for the bright side (if there was one) and search my spirit for a reasonable solution. I had it! The first goal would be to fit into those never-worn size twelve's, then the tens and, after that, the eights! There! What a great plan... problem solved! That is, except for one small detail; the size twelve's have more to them then my famous size fours I was hoping to carry in my purse. A whole lot more! Well, you get the picture... they don't fit! After I did all of that thinking, the time came to revise the plan. Giving the issue serious thought, I decided to carry a picture of myself in the size fours and keep the twelve's out in wide open as a constant reminder. There... problem solved... well almost! I could not get the small jeans out of my head so the next day when I went over to my dad's, I spotted a clothing catalog laying there on the kitchen table and I picked it up and started thumbing through the pages. I came across a great sale on blue jeans. My dad had already decided on ordering my daughter something out of the catalog so I conned him in to letting me order a certain pair of jeans, size six, to replace the others. He agreed, I ordered them, and now I am set!

A couple of days before Christmas, I had been driving and listening to the radio. A song came on which I had often heard and liked but I had not paid much attention to its lyrics. For some reason, this time, the words were in my face! I could not believe what I was hearing! This was my theme song, the one for the writing of this book! Music is a very big part of my life so I got really excited once again. When I arrived home, I called my daughter and asked her who the artist was. She told me, and then I called my son and told him about it and he said he would download it and send it to me. I couldn't wait!

1-7-2006   **224 lbs.**

Within days, a package arrived for me at the post office from Jeffrey. When I opened it up, I found two CDs and a letter. One of the CDs was my song, "Unwritten" and the other was a song called "A Song for Mama." I had a meeting to attend so, while driving, I put in the "A Song for Mama" and, needless to say, by the time I arrived at my meeting, tears were running down my face. I had to explain to the ladies at my meeting why my makeup was running all over my face; because of this song my son had dedicated to me. The following is the letter he enclosed with the CDs.

December 29, 2006
Mom,
Well, this is your year. I am so happy to be a part of your growth. We as children of God sometimes have to go through tough times in order to connect with people on a much deeper level. I really believe that your circumstances are not to go unnoticed. There is always a reason for what happens in our life. I feel you can touch people with your amazing story, the good, the bad and the unbelievable. I hope you are committed to making a change for it is time to live your life to the fullest. We only have one life on earth and it would be a shame to leave this world without leaving a legacy. I want you to know I believe in you 100% and I also want you to know I will always be in your corner. You have always been there for me when in time of need. We have not always been the closest but I feel this year can change that. I am committed to you as long as you're committed to our agreement. Along this journey people will probably try to bring you down but don't pay attention to them. You have to develop a thick skin and keep your head straight. Enclosed are two CDs. One being your theme song ("Unwritten"), second a song from me to you ("A Song for Mama"). When you feel down or unmotivated pop in the CDs and get back on track. I love you with all my heart and will help you as much as I can. I will be writing some goals for myself as well and will forward those to you. I trust you will hold me accountable for what I have written. This is no longer mom and son making each other feel good, this is us holding each other accountable for what we want to accomplish and I hope you will not take this lightly. Here is one of my favorite passages out of the Bible. "As a man thinketh is his heart, so is he." Proverbs 23:7. Think it, believe it, feel it and it will be! I don't know what you want out of life, but I know you have a place in this world that is not supposed to go unnoticed. I want you to post this on your refrigerator and read it daily. I also need your goals for weight loss. Make them clear and achievable. We can do a weekly or biweekly check-in to see how that is coming along. I also would like to hear how the book is coming along so we can do a weekly or biweekly reading so I can follow your success. 2007 is the year for a quantum leap. This means one action will turn into many and the actions multiply themselves, leaving you

with more than one individual result. I have no idea how to publish a book, but like they say build it right and they will come. You may not want to take this public but it will help you to get your feelings on paper and clarify your life. I love you mom and here's to a fantastic year...
Jeffrey Walker, Jr.

Boy, there's nothing like laying it on the line for me! Having no idea my son had such a gift of expressing himself, I was truly blown away! My little boy has grown up to be a fine respectable young man and he has never spoken to me with such authority, love and respect. It makes me feel proud and even more determined to make all of this a reality. After all, I cannot let him down. He has to know my convictions are strong and my desires to be a better me are first and foremost on my mind at this turning point in my life.

My new CDs have been played over and over again. I use them both, for inspiration before and after my daily writings of this book. The words of "Unwritten" say it all to me and I can actually apply them to this journey. The last part of the song, "Today is where your book begins. The rest is still unwritten," could almost be my own words; it says everything. I feel this is an anthem for going outside of yourself and taking a journey... destination unknown. You have to take a chance. Chances are not without risk but you never grow if you do not take the chance of expressing yourself. You need to let your feelings be known and to let others in, giving them the opportunity to learn from your wisdom, your experiences and to love you as an imperfect fellow human being. This is powerful! You gain from your release of expression. You learn just how "deep" you really are and also how much you *really* do know! Others gain by your honesty and, possibly, by relating to something you've been through. This is my hope for this project. As you get into it further, you *will* see my life and my heart exposed. It is brutally honest. I have been down some hard roads but, one thing is for certain; I have been down those roads with family and friends who love me. I have been down them with laughter and tears. I've been down them and I have survived by God's wonderful grace. Yes, He has always been with me. *I have never been alone.*

CHAPTER TWO

IT IS NOT WHAT I'VE BEEN EATING OR NOT EATING, BUT MAYBE IT IS WHAT'S BEEN EATING ME!

1-8-2007   **222 lbs.**

I am recovering from an eating disorder. There. I said it. It is now out there for the whole world to know. This is actually the first time I have written or talked about this to this extent. Those close to me have known. By "close", I mean my father, my children, two ex-husbands and a few close friends. It has been one of my dirty little secrets. You know, the ones you wished no one knew but you were unable to hide. Believe me, I tried. Actually, I thought I was doing a good job of it, but the truth of the matter is, my family knew. Those few close friends knew. The only person I was fooling was, sadly, myself. I kept telling myself I was not like those other people. I was not *that* bad. I was in control. I could stop any time I wanted. It was only for a short period. I would stop when I got my weight under control, etc. You know, the excuses any addict tries to convince himself or herself of. The excuses we "junkies" try to use to convince those who love us. The old-fashioned bull... excuses! Well, I was full of them and just plain old full of it!

There is not a time I can remember where I was not conscious of my weight. I was a healthy, robust American girl, well fed and well loved. I grew up in a household where we enjoyed sharing our meals together and both of my parents were great cooks. When I was little, I can remember being at the "family table" for at least breakfast and supper every day. During lunch, we were usually at school, or for my dad, work, but my mother always fixed a delicious supper. Believe me, it never went to waste. Meals were our family's time to discuss the daily events and to reconnect with each other. I have many fond memories of these times. In spite of this though, I was terribly conscious of the fact my mother was overweight. I cannot remember her ever being thin. It was a constant topic around our house. She was always on some sort of a diet. My dad would bring it up constantly even though I am sure he did it with love in his heart for her. He wanted her to be the thin, beautiful girl he married. She was beautiful in spite of her weight but, seeing pictures of her in her late teens and early twenties, showed me exactly how beautiful she was when they met and married. My mother should have been in movies. She was stunning! Her 5'9 ½-inch frame, along with her very long auburn hair and milky white skin, made her a knockout! She would have made some Hollywood movie company millions. However, when my mother got pregnant with my sister, she put on about 70 pounds, she later told me. From that point on, she struggled. It was constant for her. I know her self-esteem suffered terribly. Being a young mother was not easy for her and I now know my mother most likely suffered from postpartum depression. They knew nothing about this condition back then, or at least very little about it, so for her it went unnoticed. I feel she drowned her feelings in food and it became a vicious cycle for her. My mother was a very sickly child growing up, suffering from childhood illnesses, which were common back then. She was in and out of hospitals most of her life. She did not have a strong constitution so the simplest sicknesses would hit her hard. She was ill a lot of the time I was growing up. Exercise was difficult for her so this factor, added with the fact she was an excellent cook and ate what she fixed, did not help her weight.

Looking back at my childhood, I am ashamed to say there were times I was embarrassed by my mother's weight. This is a sad fact. When you are a kid, you want your mother to look like the other kids' mothers, at least somewhat. I have to say now, I probably would have not been quite as aware of her weight if it were not an issue for discussion at home. Eventually, I am sure I would have realized she was heavy but because of her constant dieting and she and my dad often discussing it, unfortunately, I was. I loved my mother so much but I longed for her to lose the weight so I did not have to feel quietly ashamed of her, or humiliated for her, when I know she herself was humiliated. I kept quiet. I never talked to her about the way I felt because I have always felt if you truly love someone, you should never say anything to them that might hurt their feelings. I have had this issue come up in a very important relationship in my life where the other person expressed to me that if I loved him, I would tell him if he was getting fat. I strongly disagree. For me, because I do love them, I do not want to hurt them by telling them something of which they are already aware. What good does that do? You end up with hurt feelings and that person's now-lower opinion of themselves. Does this solve anything? No. The person now feels worse about himself or herself and you have just confirmed to them their problem is bothering you. Of course, anyone with a weight issue knows they need to lose weight. We are not stupid. Believe me, every time we undress and dress, we are fully aware of this simple truth. Every time we see a nice person of normal weight, we are aware. Every time we feel other people looking at us, we are aware. In a restaurant especially, at an all-you-can-eat buffet, where you know others are watching your every move, we are aware. After all, we are fat, not blind!

1-9-2007   **220lbs.**

Dieting is such a hard issue. It takes more willpower than anything else I can think of. It is a lifestyle change to the fullest extent. Being one of millions who struggle with this issue on a daily basis makes me by no means different. It consumes my life. It is the first thing I think of in the morning when I wake and the last thing on my mind at night when I struggle to go to sleep. It has been this way for years. As I mentioned earlier, it is hard for me to think back to the times I was not consumed by my body image. If I had to pinpoint when this all begin for me, it would have to be when I was about 10 years old. My mother was on one of her many attempts to lose weight by a new diet. I am not sure if this was when she joined WeightWatchers or not, but she was on some kind of a diet. I remember vividly that it was in the summer, and I was on school break. I was sitting down in front of my piano practicing. My mother came in to the living room to call me for lunch and before I even made it to the kitchen, she pointed out that "we", meaning she and I, were going to make some serious changes in the way we ate. I was not too concerned about it until she placed something down in front of me, my lunch. To this day I cannot remember what it was, but it was not the usual sandwich and glass of milk I was accustomed to; it was something I recognized as diet food. I sat there staring at it and then my mother spoke to me, saying I could stand to lose some of my "baby fat." She also expressed to me that she did not want me to have struggles later on when I got older. Now I am sure she was well intentioned. For me, however, a very sensitive child, it was received as a criticism and I was terribly traumatized by this experience. Of course, I did as she asked but hated every minute of it. I never said anything to anyone about this experience, especially her. I knew she loved me and only wanted what was best for me but it left a scar on me for life. I know if my mother were still alive, this would hurt her terribly to think she did something that left such an emotional scar. She did love me so very much and unfortunately, we as parents do not come ready equipped with all the knowledge on what things to do or not do. Lord knows I have made more mistakes with my two children than my mother ever did. I know of many mistakes I have made but I am sure my children can name many more things I did which at the time I was unaware of. By no means have I ever blamed my mother for this incident. One thing I do know for sure, however, is this set the stage for many years, 39 to be exact, of being so consumed with my body image that at a very critical time in my life, I decided to do whatever it took to be thin.

Looking back at childhood pictures, I have never found one where I looked chubby. I was always well proportioned. I developed early, meaning by the age of twelve, I was very "well built." Being a very active kid, I was very athletic or at least I tried to be. I rode horses, ran track, did gymnastics on a limited level, roller skated all of my teen years, swam; anything to be in the outdoors. I never stayed inside and watched TV. There was entirely too much to do in the sunshine and fresh air. I remember a turning point for me while I was in the first year of junior high. I had not been too concerned about looking like a girl until this crucial time in my life. I had always been a tomboy. Yes, I did dress up in dresses when I needed to and even wore the occasional one to school, but I was still a little girl until this particular time. It was around Halloween and we were having our usual school fall festival. This meant a good time. For me, it was sort of my "coming out" party. My dad had taken me shopping to get a new special outfit for this occasion and he let me pick it out myself and boy, did I! It was a humdinger! Being from El Paso, Texas, it was still fairly warm outside. The stores were having great end-of-season sales. I knew how to shop! You have to understand this was back in 1969. The sixties scene was winding up, but flower children were still around and so were hot go-go boots! Yes I did! I bought a pair of white patent leather go-go boots, a great pair of black hot pants, a black and white peasant blouse and hair accessories. I am sure I hid the hot pants from my dad, but boy was I set. On that particular Saturday I got myself all dolled up, complete with make-up and I set out for the Fall Festival. I felt *good*! I was a woman; hear me roar! I remember walking to the school and when I approached the building, I saw some of the kids I knew hanging out outside. I walked right past them, them looking; especially the boy, and they did not recognize me. There were even a couple of cat whistles. When I made my way inside, I was the hit of the festival! Not for the wrong reasons, because I was decent and wearing way more than the kids wear today, but because I was all girl and I finally recognized this fact. I was proud to look good and for once to be popular because it was a first for me. I never wanted that feeling to end. Never!

After that experience in junior high, I was completely hooked on being all girl and looking the part. I started becoming very conscious of my body and how I looked, especially compared to my girlfriends. At an early age, I learned my looks would help me in certain situations. Boys started noticing me more and the girls who were not my close friends became more noticeably jealous by trying to make my life more impossible than they had previously done. I liked the attention I got from the male persuasion and, for all of my life, this has continued. While growing up in those teenage years, I knew I was a beautiful girl and continued to become a beautiful woman. I never lacked for male attention. What I did, however, was self-esteem. I was not by any means the most popular girl in school. Yes, I had close friends but I did not fit into the 'clique' as we called it. Going on about my business, I had few girlfriends who I considered close friends. I did however have many, many guy friends whom I adored and really felt closer to than most of the girls. Maybe it is because they showered me with attention, on which I thrived. I always thrived on looking my best and accentuating what I was born with to do so.

There was never a weight issue for me until after I got married, at about 18 years old. Weighing in at 128 lbs. on my 5'8" frame, I was actually very slim. After I got married, which I wanted to do more than anything else in the world, we moved about 45 miles away from our families. This was difficult for me because I was very young and had never been away from my mother and father before. We were living out in the country, which was again very new to me because I grew up in the big city. Suddenly, I was a housewife, kind of isolated, and I had no friends where I lived. It was a long distance call home and we were on a tight budget so I could not just pick up the phone and call. We were trying to have a baby but that was not in the cards for us. I thank God for this fact now because I was just a baby myself but it was very disappointing at the time. I do not know exactly when it happened but I turned to food for comfort. This is what I had to do to get me through a lonely time in my life. Before I knew it, I had escalated to about 160 lbs.! It seemed to happen overnight! Being very frustrated with myself and after a comment made from my then father-in-law, I went on a crash diet to lose the weight. This is also when I was introduced to running. My dad ran every day so after moving back into the city I incorporated running with my crash diet and dropped down to about 140 lbs. It was brutal. My diet consisted of a granola bar and a can of nectar for breakfast, lunch and dinner. When I reached the 140 lb. mark, I was burned out and was finding it difficult to continue. Granted, I looked fine, but was not as slim as I once was. One thing I was aware of though, the opposite sex still paid me much attention so this made it okay. During this time, sadly, my marriage was on the rocks so I made myself as busy as I possibly could. I worked at a hospital as a pharmacy technician, went to classes, trained as a lifeguard, sold jewelry and was introduced to modeling. The few extra pounds I could not seem to lose did not much matter. Men of all ages paid lots of attention to me. This was how I valued myself.

During a separation of over a year, I continued my modeling career and dated about three different men, including my second husband, Jeff. We were married in May of 1978. On March 17, 1979, I gave birth to our daughter Sandra, our first born. I was twenty-one. My pregnancy was great; there were no complications, no morning sickness and I continued to model. I was not gaining as much weight as the doctor wanted, even though I felt I was eating healthy. I actually modeled in a swimsuit while very pregnant with no one knowing except my family and the photographer. At about six-and-a-half months along, my doctor put me on a very high-protein diet because he felt my baby was not growing as much as she should have been. Well, this became my license to eat anything and everything! After all, I was eating for *two*! It did not matter how much I put in my mouth as long as I was nourishing my unborn child. I was falling right into my mother's footsteps. I cannot really say I did it without knowing it, because I was aware I was gaining five pounds a week, but I just did not care. The only thing I was focused on was the fact I would lose the excess weight after giving birth so it was okay to indulge, and boy, did I. Before I knew it, I had packed on about 55 pounds. When I weighed in at the hospital at the time of delivery, I was a whopping 195 pounds!

1-11-2007 **218 lbs.**

After my daughter was born, I lost about 20 pounds in a week. Of course, this was the baby weight. I was left with a 175-pound body! The first couple of months the excitement of having a new baby outweighed the worries of losing the extra weight. I do not think I really paid much attention to it at that time. Possibly, I was just waiting for it to miraculously vanish, just like the first 20 pounds. This did not happen, however. A few months went by and I was stuck with the weight. I hated it. My self-esteem started suffering more and more. I was a happy new mother but a very unhappy woman. I tried to diet. It would last for a day or two. I then would pour myself into more of a depression by eating anything I could get my hands on. The "Next Monday" theory ruled my life and unfortunately has ruled my life for many long years. The "Next Monday" theory is when you justify your eating actions by telling yourself it's okay because you are going to knuckle down "Next Monday" and start that diet, come hell or high water. I have spent years trying to live up to the "Next Monday" theory. However, something is different this time. I did not start this diet on a Monday. Instead, I started on a Wednesday. This is just the way it worked out so, just possibly, I am through with my ""Next Mondays!"

After a about a year of my daughter's birth, I was still no thinner. My family, including my husband, started making obvious comments about my weight. Thinking back to when we were dating and when he had met my mother, I can remember a few comments he made to me having something to do with the fact that he hoped I did not ever gain weight as my mother had. This became set in the forefront of my mind and I resented it because not only did I take it as a putdown of my mother but I also had to question the fact that if you love someone should their weight matter? My husband was becoming more and more vocal about it, especially when I would turn away from him in bed crying because I was ashamed of my body. He was never mean. He always told me I was beautiful regardless of my weight but I knew it bothered him. Of course, the vicious cycle continued. I would try to lose weight. I would fail. Repeatedly, this was my life. I just could not seem to get a handle on it. Then, I needed to go back to work and my father offered me a position in his company. He wanted me to look professional so he agreed to send my mother and me shopping for a wardrobe to wear at the office. He did, however, stipulate his wish for me to lose weight, which I took as a condition for my new job and wardrobe. I once again felt defeated. I went to work at his office, which was a total nightmare because of two witches who worked for him and resented the fact he hired me to work there. They made my life a living hell and were very good in making sure I heard the "fat" jokes they would tell in my earshot. Then, something else happened; my love for modeling crept back into my head. I always read all the fashion magazines. One day I came upon an advertisement for a beauty contest that was coming up within a few months so I made it my goal to enter this pageant, and enter I did. I would travel to Houston, Texas, with enough time beforehand to drop at least 25lbs. if I crash dieted. Well, I tried. I did every type of crash diet someone put down in front of me or told me about, and each time I set myself up for failure. At the time of the pageant, I had not lost any weight. I was still my fat old self but now with the pressure of being seen by other contestants and, worse of all, I would be judged.

The Cover Girl USA Pageant was almost upon me, and it was perfectly obvious I was not going to slim down, so I dedicated myself to the talent portion of the contest. I knew I could sing and play guitar and there was a scholarship offered for modeling school and/or music studies. I still had to compete in the beauty part of the pageant but my focus was on winning the talent prize. Therefore, after planning my wardrobe carefully and spending hours rehearsing my act, I took off to Houston for the state pageant. It was exciting. I went by myself, stayed at a great resort and it was glamorous. The evening I got there, I had free time because the pageant was not starting until the following morning. I decided to go to one of the hotel's many nice restaurants for dinner. While seated alone, a pilot from a major airline was sitting alone across from me. He started a conversation with me and even though I told him I was married, he told me I was beautiful and definitely deserved to win the pageant. This gentleman made my whole trip. He set my doubts about myself into place and even though we only engaged in harmless flirting, I stood up and paid attention to the fact that I was still beautiful. Sometimes it takes a stranger to point out to us what others close to us have been saying all along. I think we are more sensitive to their opinions because, after all, if they really loved us, would they say anything to hurt our feelings? For me, I would take their words and let them fester inside of me, building hurt and making my opinion of myself worse. This occasion, when a total stranger wanted to go out of his way to tell me I was beautiful in spite of my weight, was possibly a little voice of encouragement which I heard loud and clear.

1-12-2007   **219 lbs.**

I competed in the pageant the next day and I took the talent competition. I wore my "Marilyn Monroe" dress and sang Patsy Cline's "Crazy." I was thrilled! The pageant invited me to compete in the national competition, which was held two months later in Ft. Lauderdale, Florida. Again, I tried to lose some weight and was unsuccessful. I threw myself into my "act" for the competition because I felt at least there, I had a chance. What I did not know was the fact that I would be the oldest girl there at the age of only 22. The rest of the competitors were in their early teens with the exception of two other girls who were in the 18 to 25 category. They had both just turned 18. They were gorgeous. When I laid eyes on them I wanted to walk right out of there and never look back. My nerves got the best of me and I think I placed third in the talent competition. It was a revelation for me. At the ripe old age of 22, I thought I was over the hill! Anyway, my humiliation was worse than ever before and I went home crushed.

Something did come out of that experience, however. After getting home, I had some photos developed that my husband had taken of me before we left for the pageant. It was of me coming down the stairs of our home, all dressed up in one of the outfits I was to wear in the competition. When I picked up the pictures from the developing store, I immediately took them out to look at them. What I saw totally blew my mind! There was this once-beautiful model standing on the stairs, all blown up. I looked like the Pillsbury Doughboy. I knew what I looked like in the mirror, but for some reason, seeing myself in a photo looking so heavy hit me in the gut. This was not me. This was not Karen in those pictures. Being so use to seeing myself in print due to the modeling I had done, I was ashamed to see this "fat person" staring back at me. Something clicked right there and then. I quickly hid the pictures and made a pact with God. If he would help me be strong and stick to a diet, I would try to do better and be a better person. This time I was serious. Nothing was going to stop me now. I was on a mission to become thinner and healthier.

It actually took me about two months to pull myself together and devise a plan. I would diet seriously but, more importantly, I would start an exercise routine and stick with it. I became very determined. Even though I hated it at first, I decided to start running. After all, I ran in school and my father was a runner. So, I devised my own plan of attack. Instead of going to eat lunch at the local deli next to where I worked, I would go to a nearby high school and run on their track during my lunch hour. Starting slow at first, I ran about a mile a day. I started to feel better and my body started changing. I could see the results so I increased my running to two miles a day. Unfortunately I did not pay close attention to my diet at first, not making sure I got the proper amount of nutrients. After suffering extreme leg cramps at night and talking to others who ran at the high school, I adjusted my diet accordingly. I had more energy and no leg cramps, and after about two months, I had worked up to five miles a day! I started to live for running. I loved it. The natural high it gave me was fantastic. My muscle tone was getting better and better. I was getting stronger and stronger. Most importantly to me, I was getting thinner! I set goals for myself when it came to my running and I wished to be able to run 10 miles a day! Continuing this path and finally looking good, so long after my daughter's birth, I poured myself back in to modeling. I taught modeling at a local modeling school and even worked with a close friend to start his own modeling school with me in charge. My life was becoming good again because I had gained back my confidence and my self-esteem was improving. My outlook on life had changed and my husband and I were getting along better than we had in the past because I was not so ashamed of my body. I realized my body image affected every part of my life and ruled over me but at least at this moment in my life, I had a partial handle on it. I said "partial" because even though it did not matter if I was at an okay weight, somewhere inside my consciousness I would still feel I was never good enough. My own self-doubt was also ruling my life, from within. I felt better about myself but I would never feel completely good about myself.

1-13-2007   **216 lbs.**

Continuing on the path I set out for myself was hard but I did get some rewards from it. Physically, I was feeling better, but mentally, I still longed to be 128lbs. Working with other younger models kept my weight in the forefront of my mind. I would try to ignore it, but it was always there. Other people told me I looked great but that was not how I felt. Then, in 1981, exactly three days before Christmas, I got the shock of my life! It started with my two-and-a-half-year-old daughter announcing to her grandfather that morning that mommy was having a baby! I didn't hear her announcement but when I went down my stairs to the living room where my father-in-law was sitting, he asked me if I knew something he did not know. I had absolutely no idea what he was talking about. He then told me what Sandra had said. I laughed! There was no way on God's green earth, I assured him.

It was a complete coincidence I had a doctor's appointment that very day for my annual physical and my birth control refill. I went to my doctor, forgetting the earlier conversation at the house. During an annual physical they usually make you pee in a cup, which I did. I waited in the examining room for the doctor to come in. Boy did he! Walking into the room, he met me with a big "Congratulations!" I looked at him funny. He then asked of how I was feeling. I said "Fine." Then the shocker came! "Any morning sickness?" Again I laughed. "Very funny!" I replied. Then I watched the color in his face became an unattractive shade of gray.

"What are you here for?"

"I'm here for my annual physical and birth control."

Then my doctor started laughing almost uncontrollably. "I'm afraid you might be a little late for the birth control," he said between guffaws. "I thought you came in for a pregnancy test," he added. "You're very pregnant!" I didn't hear him. Actually, I thought my mind was playing tricks on me. He then said, "I figure about eight weeks along but I'll have to examine you to make sure."

From that moment on I was in a complete daze. He talked while examining me and I just blanked out. I was not in my body. Then he told his nurse to give me some prenatal vitamins and set up monthly appointments for me.

"It looks like your going to have summer baby," he continued. "But you're a pro. After your first pregnancy and easy delivery, this one should be a piece of cake."

"But doctor... how can I be pregnant again on birth control? We changed the pill to something else so this wouldn't happen again!"

He shook his head with a slight smile on his face and then reminded me I obviously fit into that one percent of women who still got pregnant while on the pill. *Oh my gosh*, I thought. *What is my husband going to say? How will I break the news to him?* We had planned to wait about another two years before trying for a second baby. This news would be as big a shock to him as it was to me. How did my daughter pick up on it? I left my doctor's office thinking about all of this and then I called my mother and broke the news to her. I needed my mommy!

It was three days until Christmas so I decided to put three blue booties in the Christmas tree with a little note inside each one. One was for my husband, one for his dad and one for my dad. The note announced the news! My husband was shocked! Both grandfathers were elated! After the initial shock wore off, my husband was very happy; we were both very happy. You might ask why I put blue booties in the tree. I knew we were having a beautiful baby BOY! My instinct, my sixth sense told me so!

The next few months were great! I was healthy, I had no morning sickness, and I continued to run every day. The doctor told me I could continue my physical activity because I had been doing it for so long. I continued until my eighth month of pregnancy, when my doctor made me quit because he was afraid I was going to have my baby on the running track or street somewhere! My diet was closely monitored. I only gained 28 lbs. during this pregnancy. I was on the right track! I even ran a 10k race in my seventh month!

We ended up buying a bigger house and life was pretty good. Then the time came for delivery. I saw my doctor on August 11, 1982 and he advised me he was leaving town for the weekend so he decided to admit me to the hospital the following morning and induce labor. All was well. We both expected a quick labor and delivery. We were all set.

1-14-2007   **216lbs.**

We arrived at the hospital the next morning and they induced my labor. It was a very hard labor; nothing like my first one. I actually had to take pain medicine to get through it, which I did not do for my daughter's birth. My son was born at 3:12 in the afternoon. I thought I'd never survive the labor but I did. My husband and

I had decided a few months earlier that if the baby was a boy, I would have my tubes tied the morning following delivery. We only wanted two children, a boy and a girl, so this was not a hard decision. The surgery was scheduled for the following day. After my surgery, I suffered deadly complications (in a later chapter, I will go into full detail about this). This experience left me broken, both physically and mentally. Months later, when I was able to care for myself, my self-esteem suffered yet another blow. Not only did I have many physical scars on my body, but also I had even deeper emotional scars. My body was ruined and I knew I'd probably never model again. My self-image was worse than when I weighed in at my heaviest. I felt guilty, and my family suffered right along with me. Before I knew it, whenever I looked in the mirror, I saw this hideous woman. How would my husband ever love me the same way? I was so embarrassed to be seen without my clothes on that I thought I would die every time he saw me. Before I knew it, my whole personality started to change and my disgust carried over to my exterior. Even with clothes on, in my eyes, I looked horrible. Before I knew it, this translated to "I look fat." Granted, I was not in the shape I had been before I got pregnant, but I was not by any means large. With me being in this frame of mind, unfortunately, something happened which would change my life forever.

One day I was watching a movie on TV. I don't know what it was called, but it was about someone with a sickness called bulimia and it caught my attention, but not in a good way. For me, it was an education on how to *control* my weight. I'd never heard of such a thing before and I soon ignored the main focus of the story. I zeroed in on what bulimia might do for me; after all, I'd do this and lose a few pounds, get back down to 128lbs., and I would stop. WRONG!

For the first month or so, I would eat, not excessively, and then go straight to the bathroom and make myself throw-up. In no time, my hands started showing the signs of teeth marks on them. I couldn't have this. After all, *this was a secret! My dirty little secret!* There's no way I could let anyone in on it, no way in hell! And it ended up *being* hell! I had to find a new plan; some other way to accomplish my purging without using my hands.

I remembered going on a camping trip up in the mountains of New Mexico and before I even got there, I was totally stressed out! How would I get through three days without a bathroom? My worry about outdoor bathrooms was not because of the usual reasons. After all, I had "gone in the woods" many times before. My worry stemmed from finding a way to hide my bulimic ritual, but hide it I did. After eating a big campfire meal, I would exit the group I was with and take "a walk" to be by myself. Then I would purge, my hand down my throat. I always made sure I had plenty of toilet paper with me so I could wipe my hands clean. I also went to the trouble of digging a hole in which to throw-up so I could cover it up and be secure no one would be the wiser if they happened upon my undigested meal. I made it through that weekend without anyone finding out. My hands were looking worse, though. After I got home, I tried several new ways to rid myself of the food I consumed,. I tried shoving different objects down my throat to see if they would bring on my gag reflex. Most did not. Then I tried a simple kitchen spoon and it seemed to work. After a while, though, my throat started getting sore and I found the spoon was not quite long enough. Little did I know, I was soon to find my "best friend" and this "friend" stayed with me for many years.

1-15-2007   **216 lbs.**

One evening, a close friend of ours came over to our house. When visiting, he always wanted me to fix him a cocktail, which I would do. This particular evening, I was mixing his drink at our home bar and was using the bar utensils I had used many times before. As I stirred the drink, I noticed the spoon. The scoop part was much smaller than the kitchen spoons I had tried to purge with, and also, the length was twice as long. A big, bright light went on in my head; this was it! I excused myself and went straight to the bathroom. I then gave that bar spoon a trial run! It worked and I was in business! Sadly, it worked *too* well!

This simple bar spoon never left me. It went everywhere I went and it fit in my purse just fine. Or maybe I should say, I never bought a purse it would *not* fit in. Then, after getting tired of always having to take it from my purse to the bathroom at home, I got another bar spoon. I had one for the bathroom, and one for my purse. After all, it would have looked pretty stupid taking my purse to my bathroom at home!

These two spoons were a vital part of my existence. Wherever I went, I made sure they were with me before anything else. I would make sure I had them packed before I would plan my wardrobe, before I had my toothbrush packed and before I actually cared about anything else going with me. It was sad, but this is how I lived. This was my reality.

After about three months of purging, my body started slimming down. I was losing the weight I thought I never would, and everyone around me started noticing complimenting me. I was still sick, however, from the medical complications from before, over which I had no control. My eating and throwing-up however, I did have control of; at least so I thought. *And remember, I can stop any time* I kept telling myself, but as I started seeing the weight I had longed to lose for years melting away, and with me getting down past the 140lb. mark, I couldn't give up. I had to keep going. This was working. Why had I not known about this secret years earlier? I had hit pay dirt and I now knew the best diet in the world. I would keep this diet totally to myself and only I would have the secret of weight loss that people had searched for centuries. You see, I had forgotten the movie on television I had seen not long ago. At this point in my life, I thought I had invented it and no one else knew. No one else was the wiser, or so I thought!

One Sunday, friends of ours came over to our house for a meal. I remember fixing a big turkey dinner for them because they had requested it. These friends were entertainers. They sang at a local hotel, which is where we met them, and we had instant chemistry and became fast friends. As they were in the public eye, my girlfriend was always conscious about her looks. She worked out daily and she had a great body. She never even had to wear a bra. She was well built, to say the least! On this particular day, however, after we ate dinner, she excused herself to go to the bathroom. Thinking nothing of it, I happened to walk past the bathroom on my way to another room in the house. Then I heard her. She was throwing up! I was shocked! This couldn't be because only *I* knew about this!

1-16-2007   **215lbs.**

The day I found out my friend binged and purged, I was shocked. She was always in control. Why was *she* doing this? When she found out I knew, she told me she only did it once in a while. Normally, she was so careful about what she ate. She was such a health nut on the outside but she had my same dirty secret. She begged me not to tell her husband. Of course, I agreed to keep it between us. If the tables were turned, I would have begged her to do the same. Do you know what the sad thing was? I didn't share with her *my* behavior. Know one could know – not even my friend.

Months passed with me continuing my behavior. I was obsessed. My stomach became accustomed to not having much food in it. I really did not consider myself the binging type of bulimic. I did not sit and consume great amounts of food at one sitting and then purge. In truth, I ate normally because I was so scared of my weight. I even tried to eat a lower-calorie diet. The problem was, even though I was watching my calorie count, I would still purge. This went on and on and before I knew it, I really did not care about eating at all, and the fact people around me were so amazed with my physical transformation did not help. My mind was all jumbled up. The compliments I was receiving just reinforced my behavior. After a while, I just stopped eating. I didn't miss it; it actually gave me a reprieve from purging. I would go two or three days and only drink liquids. The hunger pains left, and the only thing that would get me to eat was when I got so weak or light headed, I knew that if I didn't feed my body, I'd end up in the hospital (then everyone would know what I doing to myself and I couldn't have that!).

Months turned into about two years. During all this time, I had become a partner in my father's construction company. Working for him on and off for years had been a part of my employment history. I had now grown into a position that utilized my public relations skills. I was great with the public. Making friends was easy for me and looking good didn't hurt either! A majority of the construction industry back then was men and this was to my advantage because I've always gotten along with men better than women. Men always became better friends for me, and when it came to business, my greatest accomplishments came from relationships I had established. Professionally speaking, this was the greatest, and my fondest, accomplishment of my working history.

1-17-2007   **214 lbs.**

Working in the public eye made it difficult to maintain my eating habits. I ate out in restaurants one or two times a day, sometimes with the same people. I could get by with eating just a little bit at one meal but twice a day made it a little more difficult. If I knew I was going right back to my office after eating, I'd wait until I got there to do my deed, but when I knew I would be out and about for an hour or two, I'd excuse myself and go into the public restroom. Looking back on this, I truly realize just how disgusting it was. I would have to wait until there were no other women in the restroom before I could wretch. After all, how gross would that have been? I know I wouldn't want to listen to someone puke their brains out! As I would have to wait until the coast was clear, sometimes I'd be away from my associates for 10 minutes. Doing this on a daily basis must have made them suspicious, but none of them ever said anything to me. If they had, I would have made up some excuse or totally denied it. What they did say to me though was how great I looked. That was, until I got down to 107 pounds and my friends and associates started making comments to me about how frail I looked. They knew I was still suffering from medical complications that had occurred in 1982, so I blamed my frailty on that fact. I was still in and out of the hospital many times. Even the doctors were none the wiser and my nightmare of a life continued on.

In 1985, after attending a convention in Nashville, Tennessee, a friend gave me a picture he had taken of me one evening wearing a new outfit I had bought that day. We were on our way to dinner with some other friends when he snapped the picture. I remember being so jazzed because I had bought a size one suit and I actually fit it. That was a proud moment for me. Then, I saw the picture. It was horrible!! I looked like a skeleton! I was so bony; it didn't even look like me. My face was so sunken, with my particular profile, I looked like a witch. This shocked me; even scared me. This thing staring back at me couldn't possibly be me. Sadly though, it was. I knew my patterns and practices had to change right then because I was killing myself, one puke at a time.

After I was hit by the realization I was starving myself to death, I started to eat more. Of course, I'd still make myself sick, but I made sure I ate some high-calorie item once or twice a day when I didn't purge. After a while, I ate anything I wanted when I went out, throwing calorie counting to the wind. Most of the time, however, I'd still throw-up. I was very sick and I knew I was very sick. This disease was much stronger than I was but I was still lying to myself. Thinking all I needed to do was nourish my body a little bit more, I would get back on track and then I would be just fine. Yeah, sure... just fine.

I did put on some weight though and this made everyone else happy. I was looking healthier. If my weight got up to about 130 pounds I would then "put on the brakes" and force myself to go down to about 120 again, then the next time I would let my weight escalate to 140 pounds, feel fat, suffer through that, then lose the weight again. My life was a constant roller coaster that never ended, and this behavior went on for years. Sometimes, I would literally get so tired of the ritual, the hiding and the lying, I would quit altogether for a while. I would then escalate up to 160 or 165 pounds and have to start all over again to bring my weight back down. My whole existence was based on what Karen ate, or what Karen didn't eat, along with how Karen could get the weight off. There's another thing I haven't mentioned that I was doing as well as purging; the laxative abuse that went right along with it. There were times I took up to nine laxatives a day. You can imagine what this did to my system. Looking back, it's a miracle I ever got anything accomplished because of the time I spent in the bathroom.

Sadly, up until a few years ago, this lifestyle, the dirty little secret that had controlled me for most of my adult life, continued. Even more sadly, those closest to me knew about it. There were comments made to me, but I'd cover it up with the "I'm just sick to my stomach" lie. My mother, my father, my sister, my children all said something to me. They would try to talk to me but I would never fess up, and I never sought professional help either. I was "too good" for that! Eventually something happened that made me stand up and take notice of my destructive behavior. That "something" put so much fear and guilt on me that I was scared straight. It started the summer of my daughter Sandra's sophomore year in high school. She and her friends were constantly on the go. She was gone so much I hardly got to see her, let alone feed her. They'd take turns spending the nights at each other's houses so I didn't get to see her eat dinner much. One particular afternoon, she was home and standing in our kitchen getting ready to get a snack. She dropped something on the floor and bent down to pick it up. When she did, her shirt lifted up on her back and what I saw frightened the hell out of me. I could see every rib, every bone in her back. She looked like a skeleton! In shock, I asked her what happened! She told me she was so busy with friends and activities, she hardly took the time to eat. I wasn't buying it! After all, don't kid a kidder! She swore to me this was all it was and she promised to do better. Needless to say, the next day I had her in to see a doctor. Thankfully, it was nothing serious. Once she got back into school, she leveled out and was healthy and strong. After that experience, it made me take a good long look at my destructive behavior as I didn't want my daughter to slip into the same fate.

Facing my shame was difficult. The guilt will always be with me and I will always be recovering from an eating disorder. I know my life will always be one episode away from falling right back into the trap. It is like drug abuse, alcohol abuse, or any other type of addictive behavior. I will never recover from the things I've done to my body; that's a fact. Yet there is a power stronger than my addiction. It is my life force. It is how I get from one day to the next and it is the reason I'm alive to tell my story. It is the driving force behind my will. "It" is the power of God! The Lord has seen me through so much adversity and I know His immense love for me exists because I'm still here! I know I test His love for me on a daily basis but He always carries me through. *He loves all of us.* Sometimes, we just have to LET GO AND LET GOD!

Those who live according to the sinful nature have their minds set on what that nature desires; but those who live in accordance with the Spirit have their minds set on what the Spirit desires.

Romans 8:5

CHAPTER THREE

THE HILLS ARE ALIVE IN THE LAND OF ENCHANTMENT

1-18-2007   **218 lbs.**

When I started working on the draft of this book I wanted to make sure I was able to tell my entire story, both the good and the bad. I did not want to focus on the things that have gone wrong in my life, without giving a fair shake to the wonderful things that have also happened. After much thought on how to accomplish this, I decided to try and follow a "get to the point" and "down and dirty" chapter with a story of something that has truly made me happy in life. This is why I chose to make this chapter about a place very dear to my heart.

Some of my greatest memories were formed at a little farm up in the mountains of New Mexico. This was a place I spent a formative part of my childhood, on the weekends and during most of the summers until I turned fifteen.

Mayhill, New Mexico is a place hardly on the map. A place where the air is clean, the mountains are covered with pine trees and the ski resort at Cloudcroft was fewer than 10 miles away. It's a place, unless you were looking for it, you would likely miss and never know it existed. A place where nature was all that mattered and people were only allowed to share it with Mother Nature, by her rules. It's the place where I left a big part of my heart and the place where, in the late 1950s, my parents purchased a small run-down house sitting on 180 acres of property.

I don't know the exact date they bought what we referred to as "Mayhill", but I do have memories all the way back to when I was only two years old. These are the best memories ever! These memories are all happy ones! I know I speak for my whole family when I say this because I personally only remember two incidents that occurred at the farm that brought any sadness to us. The first was when my father almost cut his index finger off while working with a piece of farm equipment, and the other being when my mother and I were at Mayhill alone, awaiting my dad's arrival from the city and getting worried when he was very late. His lateness turned out to be due to a catastrophe that had occurred at one of his construction sites that same day. You see, we had no telephone at Mayhill and never did the whole time we owned the place. If we needed to make an urgent call, we'd travel to the closest neighbor's house to do so. I think the whole reason we never got a phone there was because it was a mountain retreat – the one place you could escape the city and its big city ways. My parents never wanted to diminish its quaint uniqueness. This was the hills... and *the hills* it was!

Running through memories in my head, one of the first things I remember was the fact we had no indoor plumbing! It was this way for a few years! Hey, you make the best of it! We did, however, have an outhouse; not just any outhouse, our *own* outhouse! To this day, I can still picture the outside, the inside, the whole darn thing. Each one of us became very familiar with its rustic charm. The funny thing was I don't think I was ever allowed to go in it by myself until I was about seven years old. At night, going to the outhouse was a family affair; if one of us had to go, all of us had to go! You see, it was so dark in those mountains at night, you could not see your hand in front of your face, so to be on the safe side, we all went to scare off any bear, snake, porcupine, skunk, or any other creature of the night. It was quite comical, actually. We would form a single line with my dad always leading, flashlight in hand, followed by my mom, my sister then myself. This was only if we didn't have people visiting! If we did, they followed right along also. Then when we got there, we went in one at a time, except for me. I had to be in there either with my mother or my older sister so they could be on the lookout for any big spiders that might be lurking around. That was just fine with me! I wasn't modest!

I have to tell you a little bit more about our famous outhouse. It was not placed close to the house like most self-respectable outhouses! No, it was about fifty yards away, down a trail, by a pear tree! (Incidentally, that pear tree produced the best pears I've ever tasted and did so, year after year! Hum, I wonder if its location had anything to do with it!) Sorry, just drifted off there for a second! Anyway, back to the story.

One thing I remember the most about the outhouse was the BIG HOLE! For years, I thought that HOLE was going to swallow me right up! It was the darkest, scariest thing in my life, at that particular time of my life. What lurked below, I did not want to know! I know for a fact my mom never had to worry about me wasting any time doing my business! I was in and out of there, lickety-split! This routine went on and on until my dad finally knuckled down and installed indoor plumbing, much to our approval, of course.

1-19-2007   **212.5lbs.**

Before starting to write today, I asked my father just how bad the house at Mayhill was when they purchased it. His exact words: "A wreck!" We both got a good laugh and then he reminded me of some things I had forgotten. To give you a picture, the house had been unoccupied for some time, the exception being the few animals that had traipsed in and out for some shelter now and then! You can imagine what the inside looked like with these types of trespassers! My dad told me the walls of the house were insulated with newspaper and a few old Sears, Roebuck catalogs! I still remember the old Sears catalog pages remaining in the outhouse for years, just in case you wanted reading material! We also used newspaper to insulate the walls! That's what I call primitive! Nonetheless, my dad had a lot of work ahead of him. He labored weekend after weekend to make our little hideaway the best he could make it. We were all there for moral support, if nothing else! Truthfully, we were probably in the way more than he ever admitted!

My dad is an excellent carpenter. He was telling me today how he went up into the forest and chopped down pine trees, scraped the bark off, and then finished them into pillars on the bar area that divided the dining area from the living room. Those pine columns were beautiful, reaching up to the ceiling! My mom decorated them with ceramic squirrels that looked so natural; you would do a double take each time you walked by, just to make sure they weren't alive! Those squirrels even became a part of the family!

My dad's great work on the inside of the house started winding down after a few years. I say a few years because while he worked on the inside, there was plenty to be done on the outside. After all, he became a "weekend farmer" when he bought the place. This is why projects took so long. He had six or seven going on at the same time! There is one particular project inside of the house I remember, however. It was when my mother insisted on a having a bay window in the dining area. She wanted to be able to sit in the morning, drink her coffee, and look out on the beautiful mountains, the wildlife and even our own many animals grazing lazily in the field. She and my dad argued about that window, back and forth, only because I think my dad really knew what he was getting himself into! This was not an easy job!

The first set of windows he bought were not the right size when he got them up to the farm. This was not a good thing! He had to reorder them, and this took weeks. These were not your everyday, in-stock windows. They had to be custom ordered. Then, when he finally received the right ones, the installation was not a "hurry and knock it out" job. I think I remember a few choice words being thrown out by my dad, and my dad didn't even cuss, but it was all worthwhile in the long run. Those bay windows provided many happy hours of nature watching from the inside. They were beautiful, and to this day, I miss sitting at the dining table, with that old oil cloth covering it, eating meals and looking out at the beauty this country had to offer. It was totally breathtaking! That dining table and those bay windows became the focal point of our mountain home. Oh, to be so lucky and sit there once again, sipping on a cup of hot chocolate, sharing family stories or simply just gazing out on the majestic mountains. What a dream come true this would be!

There are so many stories to tell about Mayhill, it's difficult deciding what to tell first. When you have so many happy and funny stories, you want to be able to tell each one quickly. After all, they are all worthy of being first in my writing but I guess I will have to start with stories of my horses and how I learned they were sometimes, if not all the time, smarter than me!

My grandfather, who I called "Papa", had me on horseback when I was only two years old. I still have pictures of myself sitting on a big brown horse named Brownie when I was so small my little legs hardly covered his back. They couldn't even hang over on his sides, I was so tiny!

Let me tell you about Brownie! This had to be the most stubborn nag on the face of the earth! The only thing more stubborn than that big hunk of horseflesh was ME! The two of us were a match made in heaven! Brownie became my horse the first time my grandfather put me on his back and he remained mine until I was old enough to ride something that would actually move when I got on it! Therefore I rode him until I was about six. Brownie and I had a real understanding between us. I'd try to get him to do what I wanted him to do and he would do whatever he wanted to do! Yep, this worked! I'd get up on him and kick his sides trying to get him to at least trot, but he would usually stand there, not interested in breaking a sweat whatsoever! This infuriated me! I would get mad and start yelling at him and kicking the heck out of him but most of the time, he just didn't care! This is probably why my parents never really worried about me when I was riding him. They knew we weren't going far!

Sometimes though, when Brownie got a notion, he'd actually get some spunk! These episodes of course were few and far between in the beginning, but after I got a couple of years older, he started getting a little more loose with his movements. Of course, he always let me know he was in charge even though I argued with him about that fact! He finally got to where he would actually gallop for me, and when this started happening my mother reeled me in! She would make me stay in the yard area where she could keep an eye on me through the windows of the house. The yard was big. I hated this but it was the only way I was allowed to ride without someone else riding beside me. So I obeyed, almost! Brownie and I would walk past the windows all sweet and innocent but as soon as we got past them, I'd kick Brownie and we would trot or gallop to the next window then I'd pull him back. We did this routine many times until, one day, Brownie got tired of me and decided to take matters into his own hands, or hoofs I should say!

We had been around the house several times, but Brownie was getting tired of me so he decided to take me under a big willow tree with its branches hanging down. I tried to guide him away from the tree but he wasn't having it! He was tired of me and he was going to make sure I knew it! Make sure he did! I saw a huge branch coming at me, right for my head. I yelled at the horse but he wouldn't budge. Realizing I was going to hit the branch, I reached up and grabbed it to push it out of the way. About that time, Brownie lunged forward, leaving me hanging about six feet off the ground! I was screaming at him, at anyone, until I lost my grip and went tumbling down to the ground, landing on a big rock! Fortunately, the only thing that was hurt was my pride. My mother came running out to retrieve me, me crying and yelling, "That stupid ole horse... I'll never ride him again! I hate him!" Then, within about thirty minutes, I was back on him, riding around the house several more times before the day ended.

1-20-2007   **212 lbs.**

Not too long after this, I outgrew Brownie, or maybe I had just worn him out! It was time for me to graduate to a horse with a little more spunk. My big sister's horse, Trip, was the next likely choice. Trip was a retired barrel-racing horse. My sister was a more experienced rider than I was and when she got on Trip, he flew with her. When I got on him, however, he was gentle and calm; he sensed the difference between an experienced rider and one not so experienced. My sister rode sometimes, but she was more into high school and friends when Trip was handed down to me. Riding was my life. From the time we arrived at the farm on the weekends until we left, I was on horseback. My parents would have to drag me away from my horse in the evenings. Because I spent so much time with my horse, I was constantly thinking of new and exciting things for us to do together. I had no fear when it came to riding. I remember being a small girl and wanting to be just like the girls in the circus who stood up on the horses' backs while they paraded in a circle under the Big Top, so I would sneak somewhere out of sight of my family, and try to stand up in the saddle! Of course, I'd slip within seconds or when Trip got tired of me fooling around.

One day I came up with the idea of all ideas; I would make a chariot to ride in while Trip pulled me behind him. What a great idea, don't you think? I thought it was, especially for a six year old. Off to work I went. I pulled Trip into the old barn where we stored almost everything. After spotting my bicycle in there I thought to myself, *hmmm, this might work.* Now, all I had to do was find some way to attach the tricycle to Trip. I looked around and found two old ropes. Good! They would work just fine. Diligently, I went to work and before long, I had created the perfect ride; I was all set. I tied the ropes onto Trip's bridle and then brought them back to the tricycle and tied them to the handlebars. Remember, we were hidden inside the barn so know one could see what a bright idea I had cooked up; and those famous bay windows I talked about earlier? Thank God for them; they probably saved my life that day.

My mother and sister were inside the house sitting at the dining table looking outside. They saw Trip suddenly lunge out of the barn with something dragging behind him. Within seconds, they realized it was me on the tricycle! I had given him a loud "giddyup" and when he lunged forward, the bars on the tricycle turned, flipping me over on the ground and spooking him. He was dragging me behind him and I was pinned under the tricycle! Trip started heading up the steep embankment directly to the highway above. My mother and sister went running out to stop him and watched in horror, knowing he might spook even more with them yelling and running towards him. Suddenly, by the grace of God, Trip stopped on a flat spot before going any higher up the hill! The next thing I remember was lying on the bed with my mother frantically removing pieces of gravel that had embedded in my back and legs. I had blacked out for a short period of time, but the only injury I suffered was the extreme gravel burn I got on my back and on my legs because I was wearing shorts. I also suffered because of the trouble I was in once my mother knew I was okay. I think I was grounded from horseback and horse contact for several weeks. What could have killed me just got me in serious trouble, thank the Lord! He watches out for little children and I truly kept him very busy when I was a kid.

1-21-2007   **211 lbs.**

Back then, my horse was my best friend. We spent countless hours exploring those mountains of New Mexico. On our farm, we had three mountaintops; each had something unique about it. I would ride up to those mountaintops and find all kinds of things to do. For instance, between there were some great ravines to explore. I would ride my horse as close as I could get to the edge of the mountaintops, then I would tie Trip to a tree and start down the cliffs to see what great adventure I could find below. I was pretty much of a loner and had no problem spending hours by myself. Looking back now, if it were my kids wanting to do the some thing — spending hours gone on horseback and alone at such early ages — I don't think I would have ever allowed it. My parents let me, but I think times are different now.

I also spent many hours up on the middle mountaintop, which we referred to as "Arrowhead Mountain." At one time, this site had been an Indian campground and we found so many artifacts there throughout the years that friends of my parents would come stay for the weekend just to go up there and hunt for artifacts. For me, it was great fun to go up on horseback and pretend I was back in time and I was a Native living off the land. Even though my horse was bay, or reddish brown, in color, in those times he became buckskin! The memories I have of that mountaintop are never ending.

One time I remember riding up on the third mountaintop. It was late in the afternoon and the sun was starting to go down. From where I was, it would usually take me about 10 minutes to get back to the stables and barn. I knew I had to start back soon because up in the mountains, it started getting dark by about four. I was at a point where I had rarely ridden before, and I just had a little further to go until I reached the fence that separated our property from the national forest. For as long as my family had owned the property, we had been warned about bears being in that part of the country. There were mountain lions there as well. The mountain lions we had seen, but never any bears. My grandfather claimed that one day, when he was riding along that same mountaintop, he saw a big bear in the distance; he did not stay to see just how big the bear was , however! This one afternoon when I was up on the mountain, something happened. Trip and I were almost at the fence line when he suddenly put on the brakes and almost threw me over his head. He then snorted loudly and, at the same time, wheeled around and started running down the mountain towards home. He was uncontrollable and all I could do was hang on for dear life! While coming down the mountain, there were times when he went down to the ground on his rump to keep from falling. We were back at the barn in about four minutes! My dad was out in the field working when he saw us running quickly by. He ran up to me, asking, "Where's the fire!" When I finally collected myself and could actually speak, a few seconds later, I told him what Trip had done. I was angry, scared and puzzled, all at the same time. "He could have killed me!" I cried out. About that time my grandfather, who heard all the commotion, came out from the barn and said, "That horse either saw a bear or smelled one, you can bet your life on it! He was getting you to safety! You need to be thanking old Trip, not fussin' at him!" When those words passed my ears and after the shock wore off I realized just how close I had come to extreme danger. I hugged Trip's neck and made sure he got extra sweet feed for the night!

1-22-2007   **211 lbs.**

When I started getting a little older, my usefulness on a horse was starting to become more apparent to my dad. My sister had moved on to college so it was just me and him there to get certain things done. My sister and I were the sons my dad never had. We did almost everything boys could do and most of the time, we did it better. Because of this, it was no big deal for me to be involved in rounding up cattle on the mountaintops and bringing them in to be branded or vaccinated. My dad and I would work together as a team. On one particular occasion though, our teamwork proved to be a little more than effective.

We had rounded up the cattle and were bringing them down the mountain; at the bottom, there was a dirt road to follow until it reached a bridge. At the bridge you had to make a right turn and then follow a lane that ran between a fence line and the Penasco River, which cut right through the property. Usually, once the cattle were forced to this point, they would continue running to the barn. The plan was in action; we were almost to the bridge when my dad yelled for me to rush ahead of the cattle and duck into the barn area so they would follow me and not crash into the fence line at the end of the lane and he would run them in from behind. I did as he said, getting in front of the herd, leading them, then I ducked in. Most of the cattle turned into the barn as I did. There was one outlaw, however, who had other ideas; and so did my dad when he saw him! My dad was riding our filly, Dolly, who had some roping experience, and my dad was riding with a rope. The natural thing to do at this point was to try and rope the stray before he got too far past the point of no return. My dad set his feet firm in the stirrups, took a good firm hold of the rope, swung and then released with perfect execution… almost. He didn't rope the steer; instead, he precisely roped the fence post on the corner, right at the turn! Of course when he roped something, anything, Dolly made a dead stop, but the fence post he roped was not giving at all. Dad went over Dolly's head, hit the ground hard, and I thought he was dead! He wasn't moving, so I ran screaming for my mother. Then, dad finally yelled out to me. I turned around and he was staggering towards me. "Gosh dang that stupid horse! I just hit the hardest piece of ground in all of Otero County" he fussed. "Are you alright?" I asked. "Heck no I'm not alright! What do you think? I told you I just hit the hardest piece of ground in Otero County!" he grumbled back at me. Then we broke out in laughter. My mother looked on in total confusion. Then, when she realized dad was okay, she turned back to the house, leaving us to it. My dad dusted himself off and as we turned around, we found Dolly still holding on to her "cow" with total dedication!

Another funny story comes to mind. This story involved my dad, another horse, a herd of sheep and the pear tree by the old outhouse. We had this huge, black "jug head" horse named Dan. Dan was one-of-a-kind, to say the least. He stood about 18 hands tall, was ugly as sin, but had a decent disposition about him. He was a stallion and at this point, we had not gelded him yet. He was not the typical hard-to-handle stallion; he was more laid-back and easy going. One fault he did have, however, was his love for pears! He would stand under that pear tree and eat all the fruit he could reach. With his size, he'd clean the whole bottom half of the tree out. Getting a clear picture of this, you'll better appreciate the story I'm about to tell.

One day, when my dad was up at the place by himself, he decided to bring our herd of sheep into the barn for some reason. He saddled Dan up and headed out. He located the sheep, rounded them up and started back in. The sheep moved right along, as my dad tells it. Everything was going well until they were heading down the lane to the barn. My dad was right on them, rushing them in. They were making the turn and by this point Dan and my dad were at full speed. Then it happened! One lonely pear, hanging from the very top of the tree — a pear Dan had failed to reach — came falling down a long way out in front of them. My dad didn't see it fall — heck no, he was watching the sheep — but Dan saw it fall. With my dad totally unaware of the situation, Dan hit his brakes hard, causing himself to sit to the ground with his front legs stretched forward, skidding on his rump up to that single pear, while my dad, once again, hit the "hardest piece of land in all of Otero County!" Needless to say, Dan was taken to El Paso, Texas the next week so he could pay the veterinarian a visit and be gelded, whether he needed it or not!

1-23-2007   **210lbs.**

I don't want to forget this other story about Dan. This crazy horse was quite a puzzle from the very start. We had a big Morgan filly named Ginger and we were fortunate enough to have the opportunity to breed her to a champion Appaloosa stallion. This stallion was owned by Dan Blocker, who played Hoss in *Bonanza*. Mr. Blocker had a ranch not too far from us in New Mexico. My grandfather made friends with him and convinced him to let us breed our filly to his prize stallion. I think the stud fee ended up being only $200, which was unheard of for a champion. I believe his regular stud fee was around the $5,000 range. My grandfather arranged for the "meeting" and soon we knew we were having a baby! The anticipation was almost more than we could stand, waiting for the blessed day. As the time came near, my grandfather made it a point to stay up at the place during the week when we could not be there. That way, if the mare had any complications with the birth, he was there to lend a helping hand. Soon, it was just a matter of days and we were all awaiting a phone call from my grandfather; from the neighbor's phone, of course.

Then the day came. It was a Thursday when he called, and he was so excited he could hardly contain himself. We were all the proud owners of a little stud colt. As my grandfather put it, "He was blanketed all across his rump... spots everywhere!" We were all so excited and could not wait to see the new baby! Due to it being Thursday, we would have to wait until the weekend. Time went by very slowly.

Friday evening came, and we were off to the mountains. We knew we would get to Mayhill late in the evening and would not be able to see the new colt until morning, but it did not matter because we were just that much closer. Excitement was full strength all through the night; morning could not come fast enough! On the other hand, I would have to say, the time came a little *too* fast! Until we could see him, we at least had high hopes. Then reality came up with the sunrise; the morning sun brought us all a big shock, to say the least.

All of us except my grandfather, who had gone back to the city the day before, made the journey out to the barn to see the new "champion". All we had was his word that the new colt was a beauty, and boy was his word a dirty one! When we went into the barn, what we found was our Ginger, with the longest, lankiest, ugliest, coal-black spotless, jug-headed stud colt we had ever seen. Not one single spot, not one single speckle, just plain black and ugly! What he did have, on his rump, was some dried mud. Evidently, in the excitement of it all, my grandfather assumed the dried mud was actually spots. The mare had not given birth in the barn; she was out in the pasture and it had rained the day before. Being optimistic, he "imagined" the mud as a full blanket of Appaloosa spots! Anyone in the same situation might have made the same mistake. Nevertheless, do you think we ever let him live it down? Never; not in a gazillion years! Why do you think we named the horse Dan? Coincidence? I think not; after all, we felt it only fitting Mr. Dan Blocker got full credit for the "champion" we had the pleasure of owning!

When Dan was old enough to start breaking, my dad didn't feel it would be such a big deal. After all, Dan was so gentle you could slap him all over his body, touch him on his belly, and walk behind him without the fear of his hauling off and kicking the heck out of you. He would let you do almost anything to him including hanging all over him. Obviously, the next step was to put a saddle on Dan and jump aboard. Unfortunately, my dad decided to do this on one of those weekends my mom and I were not there with him. As he tells it, he took the saddle blanket and rubbed it all over Dan; the young horse seemed to be okay with it so my dad put the saddle on his back. So far, so good. My dad then walked Dan around a bit, so Dan could get used to the feel of the saddle. Then my dad put his right foot in the stirrup and gave it a good tug so Dan would feel his weight. Again, so far so good! My dad tested the saddle to make sure it was a tight fit and when he established this, he swung up and over onto Dan's back, but he did not stay there for long; he became a human rocket before he had a chance to get a good firm seat. He was airborne! Yes, he did hit that "hardest piece of land" once again and lived to tell about it. I am still amazed, however, that Dan lived through it!

As you can see, our horses were a great source of pleasure to us. Nevertheless, the horses were not the only animals we had extreme pleasure with. We had cattle, chickens and, some of our favorites, the sheep; what started out to be a herd of four or five ended up to be about thirty! This all came about due to my sister Sheri's involvement with the 4-H club while in high school. Sheri decided she was going to show sheep for her 4-H project the first year she was involved. Both my parents were of course heavily involved in 4-H as leaders, so I am sure she was somewhat coerced into it. With her love for all animals, I know this coercion was not hard. Sheri and her best friend Roberta both ended up with lambs to show. They worked very hard and their hard work paid off with them both winning prize ribbons. Then the time would come for the lambs to go to market. They had to be sold at the Southwestern Livestock Show where the girls showed them; the auction was inevitable for the animals. The girls, however, had different ideas! They made sure my dad was in on the auction so he could repurchase the lambs he had already once paid for, and save their fate. Of course, he did it. He was such a big softy and the girls knew the lambs were safe in his hands. This is how it all got started; all the kids who showed lambs and became so attached to them they could not think of their babies being slaughtered went to my dad for reassurance and salvation! His sheep herd grew and grew and they all became our family's babies.

1-24-2007   **210 lbs.**

The cattle we had were also entertaining to us. There was always something going on involving one or all of them. They would hang out in the mountains and when we got up to Mayhill on the weekends the cattle, along with the horses, would hear us drive up and they would start running down the mountain to make it to the barn for their feed. This was a treat for them after living off the land during the week! They were all big pets; they had their ups and downs, however. Several times we would find a calf or a cow that had come into contact with one of the many porcupines who inhabited the area. These poor cattle would show up with snouts full of quills, making it impossible for them to feed. It was a delicate operation removing the quills from their noses. My dad would have to tie them down and then snip the end of the quills off to release the grip. Then he would have to use a pair of pliers to pull them out. It was not a pretty picture and I hated to witness the process.

There were other moments I remember with the cattle. The first one that comes to mind involved a bull we had nicknamed "The Escape Artist!" This darn bull could get out of any fenced area he wanted and we could never figure out how he did it without leaving any trace of destruction. The fence would be perfectly fine; no holes or breaks in it but we would always find him on the side where he was not supposed to be. Finally, my dad actually had a chance to witness exactly how "The Escape Artist" managed his capers!

My dad had put the cattle in the closest pasture to the barn and closed the gate. The bull moseyed over to the gate and tried to push it open, with no luck. Then, with my dad watching, the bull placed himself parallel to the entrance and then made a jump straight up in the air and twisted his body up and over the gate with my dad watching in disbelief! Dad thought his eyes were playing tricks on him, but they were not. "The Escape Artist" had a definite talent that he proved over and over again in the years we had him.

The livestock at Mayhill shared the place with much wildlife. There was an abundance of deer and wild turkey in those mountains. My parents protected the wildlife on our place but that did not mean my dad did not hunt from time to time. Being a big hunter, he would always hunt deer in season, but after he got his first, that marked the end of his deer hunting season. We would then eat the meat throughout the year. To my dad, hunting was never just for sport. We loved venison and looked forward to the annual deer. As I have gotten older, I still love venison but the thought of killing a deer in order to have it makes me very sad. Deer are such beautiful creatures.

One day comes to mind in regards to the deer. We happened to look outside and there stood a young deer drinking out of the water trough. He was not alone; right beside him was a half-grown German Shepherd drinking right along with him! When they got through drinking, they walked off together like Mutt and Jeff. Somehow we knew they were traveling buddies as we watched them fade into the distance with no other deer or dogs in sight. What a great picture it was!

As I mentioned, the turkey were plentiful at Mayfield. One year my dad decided he was going to get a turkey for our Thanksgiving dinner. There was one problem; it was not turkey season! My dad always obeyed the hunting laws but for some reason, this time, he decided to cheat just a little There was turkey everywhere. He decided to go up into the pine trees and hide himself from view, making sure no one could see him. After all, we did have a busy well-traveled highway up above the place and he did not want anyone, especially the game warden, to see what he was doing. As he sat, perched in the tree, the turkeys came out in front of him. He positioned himself and then took his shot. Bam! He hit a giant bird! Wouldn't you know it, the turkey rolled and rolled, straight down into the field, in plain sight of anyone driving by. I know for a fact he never did that again! Unfortunately, that darn old bird he shot was dry and tough to eat for our Thanksgiving dinner... or at least my dad thought it was.

I have talked about all the animals at the farm but have failed to mention the most important animal of all. I wanted to save a special place just for her. The fifth family member of ours, who went with us everywhere, was a little red dachshund named Priscilla. "Prissy", as we called her, was as much a member of our family as any of us. She was purchased for me after I was born and she grew up with me, right by my side. Prissy was a true character! She thought she was as big and tough as any large dog and she did not back down to anything. She loved the farm at Mayhill. She could go out and explore and it was much more interesting than the city yard she had in El Paso. Even though she was a housedog, she loved the outdoors, but when you weigh only about 20 pounds and have short little legs, you can get into some pretty serious "big" Trouble with a capital T! She had to depend on us to keep her safe. This we tried to do.

When we would get ready to leave the city to head for the mountains, Prissy felt the anticipation. She would become so excited! Then, when we got into the car, she would take her place between my sister and me and settle in for the 90-minute drive. As we started approaching the farm, her radar went off and she would wake out of a dead sleep and start wagging her tail. My dad would pull into the drive and start down the hill to the house and it was all we could do to keep her contained. As soon as we stopped, she was always the first one out of the car. There were a couple of occasions where being the first was not the best thing to be! Once, she jumped out of the car and started running towards the house but soon realized she was not the only creature out in the dark. It just so happened we had a porcupine that lived in the big tree by our gate into the yard. This particular evening, he was on the ground and Prissy, being the busybody she was, went straight for him to check him out. The porcupine had the upper hand, with his many quills just waiting for Prissy's snout to touch him. Prissy got it bad! Her poor little nose was completely covered with the very unwelcome presents the porcupine left behind. It was torture for her having to sit while my parents worked to get the quills out; the poor little dog was hurting. You'd think that experience would have put her off further curiosity but it did not. We just had to keep a better watch on her after that.

Something funny happened with Prissy one winter. We had just arrived at Mayfield after a snow of about sixteen inches. My dad stopped the car, my sister opened the door to get out, but Priscilla beat her to it and went down to the ground. The problem was, when she hit the powdered snow, she sank straight down and disappeared! She was buried and all we could see was the snow "rolling" as she made her way through it for about twenty feet. It was the funniest sight; I still laugh with when I recall the incident.

1-25-2007   **209 lbs.**

The years that I spent my weekends and summers at Mayhill are embedded in my soul forever. There is nothing that can compare to Mayhill's beautiful land and fresh air. It is the closest I have ever been to what I imagine Heaven to look like. This beautiful place kept my family captive to its charm for 11 years. During that time, my sister and I grew up with an advantage not many city kids had; but the escape from the city smog, traffic, and all the people in the big city was something we *did* have the chance to share with many of our friends. My parents often invited their friends there for a visit and we had many good times entertaining them. My sister and I also had chosen friends we took with us on weekend outings. I can remember being about 10 years old and having one or two of my girlfriends go with us. When we got there, we would stay busy the whole time exploring. There was a waterfall on the property and my friends and I would spend hours playing in the river underneath it. The river was only about two feet deep through our place but we would splash and frolic in it on hot summer days. There was also another part of the property, across the highway, we called the "Gravel Pit." This was an old gravel pit containing a huge amount of blasted gravel and aggregate once used to build the highways in the area. It was abandoned and was now part of the acreage of our place. We would hike up there and look for seashells and fossils; the remnants of much earlier times.

I mentioned before that Arrowhead Mountain was one of the areas most visited by us and friends of my parents. I remember once my parents invited all of their friends to the place. These friends belonged to a club to which they all belonged. When their friends arrived, they had to follow humorous, silly signs up to the mountaintop to have a big breakfast campfire feast! This party was a tremendous hit and was the favorite topic of many cocktail hours for years to come. This place, nestled in the mountains of New Mexico, was magical to everyone who visited it.

As I try to wind down this chapter, I keep thinking of things I have failed to talk about and it is hard for me to find an end. There was the time my dad was raising corn and the porcupines kept going in at night, stripping or breaking down the stalks. There was many a night we would form a single line with my dad and his .22 rifle, my mom with a flashlight, my sister, Prissy and me, and then head out to the field looking for the culprits to catch them in the act! Then, when the corn crop did come in, I would fill my little red wagon with some of the harvest and go up to the highway. I would spend the whole day peddling the ears of corn to passing cars. I was saving up the money for a new horse I had my eye on!

I have not told of the time my dad took my sister and me up on a snowy slope with a homemade sled and almost killed himself in the adventure! He had made the sled out of corrugated roofing tin. Sheri and I would get on it at the top of the slope and then he would release the rope he dragged it up with. We would go sailing down the hill in great delight! After witnessing the good time we were having, my dad decided to get on the sled with us and we would all go for a ride. There was one thing he had not counted on;

with his weight added to ours, the homemade sled traveled much faster and much further than it had before! I fell off immediately, leaving Sheri sitting behind my dad. Then *she* bailed off, leaving Dad traveling at "light speed" to the bottom of the mountain! There, in front of him, was a barbed-wire fence approaching much too quickly for comfort. In the split second before he hit the fence, my dad sat back and extended his feet out in front of him, hitting the barbed wire with his hunting boots! The fence snapped, allowing him to go through it safely. It could have slit his throat, broke his neck or decapitated him! Thank the good Lord once again.

We spent many a Fourths of July firing off fireworks into the jet-black sky. Then we would enjoy the crisp, cool watermelon my dad had been soaking in cool water all day. He would place it under a wet brown feedbag under a trickling stream of cold water from the faucet by the house (our water supply came from a natural well close by and it was always ice cold). To this day I have never had another watermelon taste as grand as those we enjoyed there; the sweetness and juiciness of those melons makes it hard to enjoy any store-bought melon the same way. Then there were the fresh vegetables from the garden; no other vegetables have compared to the ones grown in that black soil. It had something no other ground had; anything grown in it just tasted better! My mother canned everything from the garden so we always had our homegrown veggies to enjoy year-round.

This was indeed God's country; there is no other way for me to explain it. Sadly, in the early 1970s, my dad made the decision to sell the property because it was getting to be too much for him to take care. He was the president of a major construction and development company and the time he had during the weekends was not enough to keep up with the farm. He came to us and talked to us about selling and we were all totally against it, but our reasons were purely selfish. We knew he worked himself very hard keeping up with both his business and the farm. Being an executive and a farmer are two full-time careers. It did not stop us from being upset though; I stayed angry for a long time. I was 15 years old and it felt like part of my life was being snatched right out from under me. Actually, it was! I can honestly say I have never gotten over the disappointment. My sister felt the same way. She and I made a pact that we would buy the place back someday and retire there in our older years. Of course, this has not yet happened. My sister is now gone, but I still have hope that I can call my beloved Mayhill "home", someday.

Mr. and Mrs. Pyle, the couple who bought the place from my parents, loved it so much they refused to change anything about it. The dilapidated barn; the mailbox with our family's "Dye" name on it; even the way my grandfather used to lay apples along the bar; this all remained the same. This was the magic of Mayhill. If they had changed it the slightest bit, the magic would have been revealed to be nothing but smoke and mirrors!

Several times, we were fortunate enough to travel back to that little farm and spend time there, just remembering the many good times. The last time I was there was in 1997 when Sheri and I made the trip from Phoenix, Arizona, where she was living at that time. She had just been diagnosed with breast cancer and was facing some tough choices. I traveled to Arizona from my home in Kentucky and she and I decided the closest place to God we knew of was Mayhill. At this time in her life, she needed to feel as close to Him as she could. We set out on the trip, and the journey was one of the most beautiful times I spent with my sister as an adult. As we started approaching the place, we laughed, cried, and talked and laughed and cried some more! Even though what we found when we got there was disappointing, we found the connection between us we both desperately needed.

The house was vacant and animals had taken over. My parents' hard work was in ruins, but amongst all the destruction of the house, something caught our attention almost immediately. There in the kitchen area, in front of the bay windows that were wanted so much by our mother, stood the dining table my parents had placed there so many years earlier. Covering the table was our same red-and-white oilcloth table cover that served as protection to the wood surface below. Yes, it was tattered and torn, but it was still there, weathering the storms and proudly serving watch over the many, many memories that were made in that incredible mountain home. Somehow, we knew that place would always be ours, no matter what. Now, I smile when I think of my beautiful sister being in Heaven and gracing Mayhill with her angel wings, keeping watch over our "Land of Enchantment."

///

REFLECTION 1

1-26-2007   **205 lbs.**
Before I move on to the next chapter, I would like to say a few words about how the last few weeks have gone for me. I am nearing the end of January, and a lot has been accomplished this month. To start with, I have undergone my second surgery on my mouth and came through it with flying colors! I had my surgery on January 16, 2007, to remove my remaining upper teeth. The surgery was a piece of cake; I went through it without any pain whatsoever. I was fully awake during the procedure because I do not do well with general anesthesia. It was over so quickly I could not believe it! Then, immediately after, my surgeon placed my new upper dentures and my new lower partial in my mouth and sent me home. I thought I might have some pain after the numbness wore off but I didn't. My new teeth felt so good and natural I was elated. The following morning, I went to see my dentist so he could make any adjustments needed. There was only one adjustment I asked him to do. He was amazed how well I was doing! He also told me I would most likely need some more adjustments after a couple of days but, to date, I'm doing great! I have to tell you that on Sunday, January 21, six days after surgery, I ate a nice big steak dinner! This is unheard of, I'm told. You see, I went into the surgery with a completely positive attitude and never faltered from that frame of mind. I believe in my heart being positive is ninety-nine percent

of the battle and I think I have proven this. Most importantly, with the help of God, all things are possible. I have had my share of friends praying for me and I always ask God to see me through each day. At this time, I would like to thank the two wonderful doctors who took care of me during this endeavor: Dr. Terry Ellis of Clarksville, Tennessee, my oral surgeon, and Dr. James Stokes of Hopkinsville, Kentucky, my dentist who made sure my new teeth are perfect. They are my knights in shining armor. These two doctors were so kind to me and their expertise should not go unmentioned. They gave me back my smile; my whole life is a much brighter place knowing I do not have to be embarrassed when I smile. I knew my crooked smile affected me but I did not know the extent until I realized that now I can't help but to flash my smile so proudly!

I have religiously been sticking to my diet plan and, as you can see from my daily weight log, it has been a great success. I feel so fantastic I cannot contain myself! I weigh every morning with a sense of pride. It has not been a struggle for me this whole time. I think the reason being that my mind was so ready to make this change in my life, I don't miss my old eating habits. I look forward each day to what I am going to do to make myself happy and continue on the path of healthy living and healthy eating. My energy level is through the roof! I went to my regular doctor today for my monthly checkup on my lupus and she was amazed at how I looked. She expressed how proud she was of me, which felt good, but the most important thing is how proud *I am* of myself! This is my swan song and I will sing and dance it for the rest of my life!

In writing Chapter 2, I touched on feelings that I have never expressed before. As I sat down everyday to write, I learned more about myself than I ever wanted to admit. This was the most therapeutic thing I've ever done. Seeing those feelings and behaviors in print staring back at me made me face some demons I had not faced before. It felt good to finally get things out in the open and not hide behind secrets any longer. Even though some of the things I talked about were a bit graphic, my wish for anyone reading it with a similar, or even someone who is in recovery, is to let these individuals know they are not alone. I have been there and I have survived, and I think am a better person. Sometimes our weaknesses of the past make us better and stronger for the future. They also allow us to teach faith and perseverance by example.

Telling my cherished memories of the place in the mountains that meant so much to me was like giving each of you one of my most cherished presents. My goals for this chapter were to show just how beautiful many parts of our country are, and to share with you the bond of a close family. Happiness can come from anywhere you may be in life, and for me these childhood experiences were happy memories of our family sharing something very special through the years. It just so happens we were fortunate to spend those cherished moments at one of the most beautiful places in the United States. I hope I succeeded in painting a picture of those magnificent mountains, but even the most talented writer and painter in the world could not capture the wonder of it all. Yes, it was the Dye family experience, but I hope you found enjoyment in the stories and I hope it made you look back to *your* special place in life, the time that made you the happiest while being there.

It's time to move on to another chapter in my life. I will continue to be as honest as I can and I hope you find something *you* can relate to in the words written ahead. If I can touch even one person through my experiences, my work is complete and I will have succeeded in my reasons for wanting to write this book.

"Do not ever look back without first looking forward!"

CHAPTER FOUR

SCHOOL WAS NEVER MY CUP OF TEA!

1-27-2007   **208lbs.**

From the time I was a little girl starting first grade, I hated school with a passion. Because of my birthday being in October, I actually had to start first grade at the age of five. We did not have public kindergarten at the time and because my mother did not work, there was no reason to send me to a private kindergarten. With my sister being 10 years older than I was, I was by myself with my mom during the day. I had few friends to play with my age, so I was not use to being around a large group of kids. I was also very shy and a mommy and daddy's girl. Never wanting to let them out of sight, the concept of being left at a strange place for most of the day was overwhelming for me. I remember the first day of school, crying the whole way there, as my dad drove me to my new life. I was petrified! My dad walked me up to my classroom and opened the door. What I saw inside was so scary; I started clinging to his leg so he wouldn't leave me there. The teacher greeted us and assured my dad I would be fine. I started screaming and begging him to take me home. He tried to talk to me but I was not listening to him. All I knew is I was being "dumped" in a place of total strangers with no idea if I would ever go home again. In my five-year-old mind, I was being abandoned. After pleading with my dad for so long, he had to leave me there with the teacher assuring him once again, that as soon as he left, I would be okay. When he left me, I still remember looking out the window and seeing him disappear. I was all alone without my family and so scared that I cried all day. I had never been separated from them before and

I did not understand why I was put in this strange place, with a bunch of total strangers, to fend for myself. Almost immediately, the other kids dubbed me "cry baby". Most of them had brothers and sisters close to their age who also attended the same school so they seemed to adjust better. Another thing I noticed was the fact I had blond hair and light skin while all of the other kids had dark skin and dark hair. They also talked differently than I did and I did not understand why. Half of the time, I could not make out a word they were saying and they would talk amongst themselves and then point and laugh at me. I became totally withdrawn; I did not like this new world. I grew up in an area that was almost all Hispanic in population. Being a border town, El Paso's Hispanic population was prevalent. The Anglo kids in school were few; we were the minority and this became very obvious when you looked in a classroom and saw one or two Anglo children and twenty-five Hispanic children. The difference in our language was hard for me to understand because I had never been exposed to people who talked differently than me. With my insecurities of being away from home, this just made the whole school situation even stranger. I never wanted to go back after that first day! Again, I begged my parents to let me stay home, and of course, they told me I had to go to school because it was what "big girls" did! They explained to me that I would be learning all sorts of great things like reading and my ABCs. I was not the least bit interested in this whole concept. Why couldn't I stay home and learn the same things? They then told me it was the law: all kids my age had to go to school, period! I fought with them every morning as got dressed and ready. It did not matter how much trouble I was getting in as long as I stalled the trip to school. Then, my dad started using bribery as leverage to lessen the morning fights. Sometimes parents have to do what they have to do to get through situations without losing their minds in the process. The first bribe was based on me only having to approach the school without crying, and if I did, I would get a treat in the evenings when my dad got home from work. I'm sure my mom never knew about this arrangement! It took several times before I actually did not cry on the way to school. Then, he followed that by offering me another bribe if I would actually walk to the classroom by myself. Each day I promised to do so and each day I'd breakdown and have to have him walk me to the door. This went on for weeks. My dad was such a pushover when it came to me. He tolerated by behavior, until one day he reached the end of his rope! Very rarely did my dad ever raise his voice to me, but he had reached his limit. I remember him telling me before we ever left home one day, that he was dropping me off in front of the school and I was going to class by myself, period! I fretted, but he did what he said he was going to do, leaving me at the school to watch him drive off as I stood there in total horror!

As you can see, the whole school experience for me got off to a rocky start. The sad thing is the fact I spent most of my school years with the sinking feeling I never belonged there in the first place. School was a total struggle for me most of my academic years. I never felt that I fit in with other kids and I felt dumb in so many ways because I had a hard time understanding on so many different levels. I could not grasp my studies those first years of school. My concept of what I was supposed to be doing was foggy, to say the least, and it showed up in my grades. My shyness and fear of others thinking I was stupid overshadowed my learning. I just didn't get school at all! Why was it so hard for me and so easy for other kids? I felt so alone.

1-29-2007   **208 lbs.**

While in the first grade, I somehow got it into my head that if I was the first one to hand in my assignments, I was doing a good job and would get a good grade. It did not matter if I did the paper correctly, all I had to do was beat the other kids to the teacher's desk! Of course, my work was sloppy because I rushed through it to get it done, resulting in poor marks. At the end of every day, the teacher would give me back the papers I turned in and the next day there would be red writing all over the papers. I was supposed to take the papers home and let my parents read what the teacher had written, have them signed, and then return them to the teacher the next morning. Because the teacher was kind enough to write on my papers with such a pretty red color, I thought that I was doing something special! My parents quickly explained that this was not at all the case; they tried to get through my head the fact that being first was not a good thing unless I did my assignments the *right* way. I did not comprehend this at all. I struggled with wanting to rush ahead. Because the work was hard for me to start with, what was the point?

From the first day of school, I was an outsider. I looked different, dressed different, talked different and was raised different than most of the other kids. I stayed to myself a lot of the time. The only thing I did like about school was the 3:30 school bell! But then, I would have to endure the school bus ride home. Never feeling safe on the school bus because of someone always threatening to beat me up made the whole school experience even worse. I had no older sibling there to watch out for me because my sister was in high school. So, day after day, I would try to come up with some excuse to stay home from school. I always had a stomachache or a sore throat; my head hurt or I thought I was running a fever. Sometimes I would even lay my face on my mother's heating pad so when she felt my forehead, she knew I was "burning up!" Sometimes she bought into my act but most of the time she did not. The times I really *was* sick, it would be something serious like German measles. Missing a lot of school did not help me keep up with the other kids; I was always lagging behind. Other kids zeroed in on this fact, which gave them another reason to pick on me. Looking back on this now, I don't think my parents ever really knew the terrible things I went through at school. Never telling the adults in charge the things that had been done to me, made it even easier for the cruel kids to continue their bad behavior. We had major gang activity going on all around us, and these behaviors were brought into the schoolyard. I was never a fighter; I would cower down to anyone who looked cross-eyed at me. Some kids can be mean if they sense the least bit of fear from someone they are threatening; it makes it that much more fun to continue on. This made for an extremely difficult time in my life and I would not relive those school years for a trillion dollars!

I can't say I blame my miserable elementary school years only on cruel children. A few teachers contributed to some of my anguish as well. It is sad to say that there were educators in my school who had absolutely no business being around children. Today, if a teacher were caught doing some of the things I witnessed as a child, they would be put in jail. For instance, we had a boy's coach who would wait until the little girls "suited out" for P.E., then come around and pat us on the backside. What was worse was the fact that the girl's coach was engaged to the boy's coach and she thought it was so cute the way he "adored her girls!" When I think about this, it literally makes me sick to my stomach. I knew something was not right with that whole situation but I also knew these two coaches were popular with most of the older kids so I never said anything to my mom about my uneasiness, for fear of more bullying. My mother had taught me that if something didn't feel right in my gut, it usually was not. I am sad to say I never spoke up about this situation; if I had I might have saved other girls from the same humiliation.

1-30-2007   208 lbs.

When I was in the fourth grade, I had a teacher I was completely afraid of. She was mean and gruff; she went out of her way to ridicule children whenever she got the chance. No one liked this teacher. Sad to say, for those of us who needed extra help, she made it well known to the other students that we were not as smart. With my natural shyness and her attitude, I fell way behind; not because I was not trying. I *did* try because I did not want this teacher to spend any more time ridiculing me than she already had. If I worked hard, possibly she would lay off me for a while. Unfortunately however, that was never the case. Because of her lack of ability to teach and my struggles, my parents decided to hold me back in the fourth grade for a second year. I was upset at the time but later realized it was the best thing they could have ever done for me.

I have to share something with you that happened in this particular teacher's class. This particular event has stuck with me through my life and upholds my theory that some people have no business whatsoever being educators! The incident scarred me and made my dislike for school even stronger.

During the school year, we as fourth graders were encouraged by our principal to bring new and interesting things for show and tell. All three of the fourth grade classes would participate together in this assignment; it was part of our Science grade for the year. When it came time for my class to have its turn, I was more than excited to share my knowledge with my classmates. As I am sure you know by now by reading the previous chapter, I had an extreme love for animals. I shared this love of animals with my uncle Charlie, my dad's oldest brother. Uncle Charlie lived on a ranch in central Texas and we would visit him whenever we could. Charlie had all kinds of animals on the ranch. When I was there, he and I would spend lots of time together with him introducing me to his newest critters! He loved animals just as I did and the special bond we shared revolved around this mutual love. The summer before my fourth grade in school, we visited my aunt and uncle at their ranch. When we got there, Uncle Charlie could not wait to show me his new "special chickens!" We went out to the chicken house and he told me how he had ordered these particular chickens from far away. There were very few people in the United States who even knew about their "special talent." As we approached the henhouse, with all the chickens running around, he pointed out the new ones; they pretty much looked like any other chicken. Then he took me in to henhouse and showed me something amazing! He reached in to where one of the new hens had been laying and he pulled out a pale blue egg. It looked just like an Easter egg! I immediately thought the Easter Bunny had paid an unexpected visit to my uncle until he told me about the Araucana chickens.

This breed of chicken was known for its uncanny ability to lay colored eggs in pastel colors! Of course, when Uncle Charlie came across any new and exciting breed of anything he could raise on the ranch, he had to have it. When I saw these special chickens, I wanted some of my very own. Uncle Charlie promised me he would see to it I got a pair — a hen and rooster — and he would send them to me as soon as he could arrange it. Shortly after the school year got underway, I received my baby chicks!

It took until springtime for my hen to lay her eggs. I was anxious to share my new pets and their colored eggs with my classmates for show and tell. When the time came, I took two of the blue eggs to school and anxiously awaited my turn. My teacher then called my name. I stood up and took my place in front of the class and presented the two blue eggs, saying, "I have a chicken that lays colored eggs!" The class started laughing; this was not the response I expected. I then lifted the two blue eggs up and rephrased the statement. "My chicken Bertha laid these blue eggs, one yesterday morning and one this morning." Once again there was laughter from the kids! Then it happened; the worst thing that had ever happened to me! My teacher stood up and shouted out to me, "Karen, you're a liar!" I stood there silently. "How dare you come into this classroom and tell such a lie!" she continued. The class laughed even more and before I knew it, I was running out of the classroom, then out of the school, all the way home. By the time I got there, I was hysterical. My mother tried to calm me down so she could understand me. I was sobbing hard but was soon able to tell her what had happened at school.

My mother hardly ever got angry. As usual, she was calm this time until she heard what had just taken place at my school. I have to say, I never saw my mother that angry again! She went straight outside, picked up a wire cage we had in the backyard, chased down my hen Bertha, put her in the cage, grabbed my hand, and off we went! She marched me back to the school with chicken and cage, went straight into the principal's office, past his secretary, told him he had better follow her, and then marched straight into my classroom! She set the cage down on the floor, and then with my startled teacher standing there looking at her, my mother let her have it with both barrels!

"How dare you call my daughter a liar! I'll have your job for this, lady!" There was silence in the entire class. My mother then turned around and addressed the principal.

"Those chickens are staying put until the hen lays an egg!"

She then grabbed my hand again and pulled me out of the classroom while stating, "And Karen is going home with me now!" Then off we went!

1-31-2007   **207.5lbs.**

In my second year in the fourth grade, I had some problems with my legs. My knees were turning inward causing me to be knock-kneed. My parents were concerned about this condition and took me to the doctor, who recommended orthopedic shoes. These shoes were to help my legs straighten out before I got older. All was good until the shoes were ready and my mom and I went to get them fitted. When the doctor brought the shoes out and showed them to me, I was mortified! Those shoes were just plain ugly. They were Oxford style in blue leather with composition red soles. They laced up with brown shoelaces. Those shoes had to be the ugliest shoes I had ever seen! You can imagine how I felt. Here I was, a nine-year-old girl who was already struggling to fit in with her peers. I was sure they would laugh me out of school. It was too easy for the kids to make fun of me to begin with. Now I was giving them a loaded gun with the okay to go ahead and shoot! I cried all the way home from the doctor's. My mom told me it would be fine but I was not buying it at all. She even told me how pretty my legs would be after wearing the shoes for a year. Not caring about "pretty legs" at the age of nine, I was not the least bit impressed.

When I went to school the next day wearing those ugly shoes, it was just as I expected. The kids in my class made fun of me, the kids on the playground made fun of me, and in the hallways and cafeteria they made fun of me. I was called "retard", "crooked-legs", "ugly shoes", "weirdo" and "white trash." Again, I was an outcast. If I didn't have the support I had at home, there's no telling what would have happened to me; I was so alone at school. There was one change for the better at school, however. The teacher who had made life so impossible for me the previous year, was gone, and I had a new teacher who was more compassionate. She made sure that when she caught the kids teasing me she called them down on it. Thank God for small favors!

Surviving the fourth grade for the second time was a triumph! I passed into the fifth grade with average grades, and this was sort of a turning point for me. I met my best friend, Robin, my fifth grade year. We became "The Bobbsey Twins!" We were together from the fifth grade through high school, lived together as roommates in an apartment in our late teens, and remained friends throughout the years until Robin's death in 2004. When we became friends in the fifth grade, the kids were not quite so mean to me because I finally had a friend of my own; you know what they say: there *is* strength in numbers! Robin and I also made friends with a few other "outcasts" in our school. We had our own little group of nice kids, and together we developed tougher skins to resist the torment of others. I also discovered I had a talent for running when we started track that year in P.E. I had never felt the least bit athletic the years before, but suddenly I found something I was really good at and it helped build up my terribly shattered self-esteem. Entering my first track meet in the fall of that year, I won the 50-yard dash, taking home a blue ribbon! You would have thought I won the New York Marathon! It was indeed one of my greatest moments, especially when seeing the look on some of my tormentors' faces when I won, making it a victory in more than one way. I was floating on cloud nine!

Running track through the year gave me something to work at. It no longer mattered that I was not good at softball, basketball, or even pull-ups on the monkey bars; I could not climb the big rope in the gym either. My upper body strength has never been good, but during this time, I also found out I was very good at tetherball.

Robin and I played it all the time; we played at school, at church and at home. We became hard to beat at school and at home but several of our friends would challenge us. One other friend of mine who lived directly across the street from me, Maggie, was the best tetherball player amongst us all! She and I would play for hours, and she was always ahead of me. Maggie was one of the best athletes in our school. She and I also ran against each other in meets but when it came to the 50-yard dash and later, the running long jump, I usually took the ribbon!

2-1-2007   **206lbs.**

Starting in about the fifth grade, I discovered in choir that I had a special singing voice. I had taken orchestra the previous year playing the cello but it was so large, it was hard for me to handle. Loving music, I was always eager to sing whenever I got the chance. Before long, I was entering talent shows at school and the principal invited me to sing solos during holiday programs. Many kids resented my talent. Nevertheless, I also had some fans! Music and singing became a huge part of my life from that point onwards. My mom enrolled me in private voice lessons and I was beginning to learn how to play the guitar. At the age of ten, my parents bought me a beautiful piano for Christmas and I started taking lessons. I could play almost anything by ear so the piano lessons were very slow for me. Playing "Mary Had A Little Lamb" became boring when I was already composing my own music! Eventually, I gave up the piano lessons but continued with the guitar. To this day, I regret giving up playing the piano; it would have helped me years later. By the sixth grade, I was beginning to come out of some of my shyness and my circle of friends was growing. I was still running track, singing in choir and was beginning to feel more comfortable in school. By the end of that year, my best friend and I decided to try out for cheerleading. We worked hard every day after school mastering our cheers; we were required to make up our own cheer for the tryout. Each of us learned our routine and we went to buy special outfits for the event; Robin and I had to match, of course! The tryouts approached and the girls who considered themselves the best at everything started giving me a hard time once again. They taunted me as much as they could, trying to get me to back out of the tryout. Looking back, I now know how much of a threat I must have been to them because they would not have bothered me otherwise. I kept my cool and made up my mind that I really wanted this and their nastiness was not going to stop me this time.

When the day finally came, we all gathered in the gym and the tryouts got underway. This was the first year our school would have a cheerleading squad. We were the first squad the school would have, so the pressure was on! Three teachers acted as the judges. There were probably thirty girls trying out for six spots. It became my turn and I took my place, nervous as heck, and did my cheer without any mistakes! I was so proud of myself. My best friend followed me and she did great also.

The tryouts ended and we all sat there anxiously, awaiting the announcement. Who made it, who did not? The head judge stood up and started calling out the six names. Of course, five of the "social butterflies", the "special ones" made the squad, but so did I! Those girls booed me (they should have been kicked off at that moment!) My best friend made alternate but she should have made it instead of *those* girls. I was sad for Robin when she was named alternate and even felt guilty about it, but I was also excited at the same time. For once, possibly, I would be popular!

When you hear the phrase "popularity is not everything" you think to yourself, *at least let me try it for a while!* Well, this is kind of the way the seventh grade, my first year of junior high, went. To begin with, we did not change schools from elementary to junior high. We stayed at the same school so all was familiar. There were no big adjustments to go through, but it was the first year we had a football team. The cheerleaders spent the summer getting ready for the season; not the best of times for me because of who I had to cheer with, but I tried to keep an open mind. My mother was the one who made all the girls' outfits, which meant *those* girls had to spend lots of time at my house. They acted so sweet and innocent around my mother and their own mothers, it made me want to puke. Of course, my mom saw right through them! She did, however, encourage me to hold my own and not let them ruin what I wanted so badly. With this in mind, I tried to keep the peace no matter how snide they could be. We practiced and practiced, learning new cheers and getting ready for the football season. After the beginning of the school year, they called us into assembly where the football coach introduced the cheerleaders for the first time. Excitement was mounting and I felt good!

2-2-2007   **206lbs.**

The football games were played on Saturday afternoons. During the year, we practiced after school while the football team was practicing, working out our cheers during the week for the up-coming Saturday game. I was not getting along with the other cheerleaders, but I continued working hard. The harder I worked, the more they tried to get me to quit; it really started to bother me. It was becoming more of heartache than it was worth but I was not a quitter! My mom knew something was bothering me but I did not tell her what was going on. Then one Saturday, at the beginning of a game, we were to do the routines we had practiced during the week. When we got up for the first cheer, I took the po-sition I had during practice, but the others took *different* positions than we had planned. Before I could say anything, they all moved out in front of me and started a cheer I did not know. We had never practiced it before and they totally left me out! I stood there like a total outcast, not knowing what to do. When they stopped, they all turned around and gave me smug and dirty looks. I was really ticked off. Evidently, they had all gotten together without me and planned this. When I confronted them, they started calling me names and I in turn shouted back at them! After this con-frontation, I had my fill of the backstabbing little witches so I left the game and went home. By the time I got home, I was so an-gry and upset I had tears running down my face. My mom came home about 10 minutes later from shopping and she asked me if the game had been canceled. I had to tell her what happened at the school and she became furious! She wanted to know where our coach was during the episode and I told her he was not paying any attention to what the girls were doing; if I *had* told him, I knew I would have hell to pay at school the following Monday.

Regardless, she was not going to put up with their nasty behavior. We went back up to the school, she gathered up the coach and the girls, then read them the riot act; she was fed up. My mom bawled out the girls, the coach and any parents of those girls standing by! She would not put up with their petty rudeness, taunting, threats or appalling behavior anymore. She told the adults she would go before the school board with her complaint if changes were not made immediately. She requested all the girls be kicked off the team for misconduct and she gave a time frame in which she expected the changes to be made. When she finished what she had to say, we went home.

There were some changes made at school. Two of the girls involved were kicked off the team; they were considered the ringleaders of the whole incident. They were all equally involved and nothing was going to be any different because the remaining girls were the puppets of the two who were kicked off. I decided I did not want any part of their group so I immersed myself in choir and left cheerleading. It was a social club for "wannabe" gang members and I had better things to do.

During the last two years of junior high, I came in contact with two more teachers who had no business teaching. These two men did nothing but harass the female students. One of them spent his lunch hour at a bar down the street from the school. We would see him drive off campus and go straight to this bar. Then, when he came back, my best friend and I unfortunately had to endure his class and his constant harassment. He would pick on us for any reasons, then make us stand up in front of the classroom and make us bend over for swats with a ping-pong paddle! It was only the girls who ever got into trouble, never the boys. He was a pervert, and the only reason he made us bend over was to take a peek! We despised him and it reached a point where we would only wear pants to school. His buddy, the other male teacher we despised, had the classroom adjacent to his. They had a signal between them. The students were not allowed to be in the hallways without a hall pass. If one of the girls got in trouble, for some reason they would send her out into the hallway without a pass and then knock on the wall to alert the other. Then, the other teacher would rush into the hallway with his paddle and make the girl endure his swats. It was just plain sick! Soon, some of the boys started to realize what was going on and they started sticking up for the girls. They became very vocal but we had a principal who was about to retire and had absolutely no interest in ruling the school. The students were in control, not him. He simply did not care! I remember being kicked out of class and running to the principal's office and demanding he call my mother immediately. Sometimes I think my mom spent more time at that school than I did! Finally, graduation from junior high came and we could not wait to get out of that hellhole! High school had to be better by far; a new place, new people and new hope for better memories were a summer away. I was excited and scared all at the same time, but when September 1972 came, I was a freshman and proud of it!

2-2-2007   **206 lbs.**

When I begin my first year of high school, I was excited. It was a chance to make new friends and learn new things. Ysleta High School had an enrollment of about 3,000 students, and my freshman class had about 1,200. We were the largest freshman class the school ever had. My old friends remained the same but I made many more friends during my two-and-a-half years there. I had good teachers most of the time and my grades improved immensely. There was one woman, a Home Economics teacher, who was very prejudiced towards the Anglo students and would go out of her way to speak Spanish in class so we would not understand her. There were three of us in the class who were not Hispanic, but we all worked together very hard and passed the teacher's class in spite of her. I think we all made C's in the class when we should have made A's. I think that C was the only average grade I got the rest of my high school years. Involving myself in everything, I kept very busy. Socially, I was much happier than I'd ever been. I got involved in the massive pep rallies we had every Friday in support of our football team. The school spirit at Ysleta was a major fever caught by everyone who was part of the school. I loved it! To see so many people coming together to show school spirit was amazing. I started dating a little during the first year of high school; of course, my parents only allowed me to go out with a group of kids and they made sure a chaperone was present. I attended games, dances and concerts. In addition, I found my first love during my freshman year. Meeting Brian was a happy time in my life and I truly loved him with all my heart. He was handsome and strong. He played football on the freshman team and he was smart, clean-cut, and any parents' dream. His politeness and good manners impressed my parents. I loved him but he ended up breaking my heart.

Unfortunately, along with the good things at Ysleta High School came some bad things. During the 1970s, drugs were used heavily among high school students. My friends and I were totally against any type of drug activity and we made it very well known to others. I can remember during pep-rallies the "druggies", as we called them, would sit up at the top of the bleachers smoking it up with marijuana; we could smell the offensive odor drifting down. It was hard for the faculty to keep those students under control because of the size of the student body and by the time they realized the drug activity going on in the bleachers, the evidence would be gone and those students who were in violation would spread out into the crowd. Nobody wanted to "narc" on them but friends and I would have if we knew who was doing it. It was huge a problem on campus.

While I was dating Brian, my best friend Robin was dating his best friend Jim, an undercover cop posing as a high school student. He was put there to break up a drug ring that had infiltrated our school. Jim was believable; we had no idea of who or what he was. He and Brian were inseparable and the four of us spent a lot of time together. One evening I was at home and the doorbell rang. I answered the door and there stood Jim by himself. I asked him where Robin was and he told me he needed to speak with my parents. I invited him in but was not prepared for what he had to say to my parents and myself. In disbelief, we sat there while Jim started to explain himself; he explained why he was posing as a student in my school. He proceeded to tell us about the sting operation that had been going on at the school and how he was involved. Then, without warning, Jim told us that my boyfriend, the boy I had fallen in love with, his best friend, was the ringleader of the drug ring at our school! He had been busted. I was horrified! Never in a million years would I have ever suspected him of being involved with drugs. Jim told us Brian was not a user, just a pusher. He made money off drug users. It made me sick; it tore my heart out! I was totally betrayed; not to mention all the other people who bought into his act. The saddest thing of all was the fact that such a promising young man threw his life away at the young age of fifteen.

I saw Brian a few years later, about four days before I got married. He came to my door and my fiancé and both happened to be there as we were on our way out. Standing there, I could tell he was stoned. He had finally sunk into the despair he had given to others. Standing there, he told me he had seen our wedding announcement in the newspaper and he only wanted to wish me good luck. He then turned to my fiancé and told him he had better take good care of me because I deserved all the happiness in the world. That was the last time I saw Brian, but the memories linger on.

1-5-2007   **200 lbs.**

During high school, gang activity became heavy. One day, while sitting in class, a huge noise roared through the hallway; it sounded like thunder. Suddenly, there was a bang on the classroom door. More than half of the class stood up and ran out of the room! Those of us left sitting there, including our teacher, were unaware of what was taking place. What occurred next made history in the city of El Paso. A Mexican gang, the Chicano Unidos, had planned a citywide walkout involving all of the high schools. At precisely 10 that particular morning, all involved students were to walk out of the schools and stage a riot. This was one of the most frightening things I have ever been through. Hundreds of students trashed the hallways, classrooms, and injured teachers and other students on their way out to the front lawn of the school. It was total mayhem! I literally snuck out of the school and when I got outside, there were police cars everywhere. Seeing others and myself who managed to escape the school building, a police officer shouted for us to run. I ran all the way home! The two miles to my house took me about three minutes. I never looked back; I just kept running. This incident kept the Anglo and Hispanic students not involved in the gang home from school for two full weeks. I never wanted to return; it was frightening. These people were protesting absolutely nothing. It was uncalled for! Our library was trashed and the elderly librarian was badly injured because of stupidity and hate. The only thing accomplished was destruction, fear and many bad memories for those who were innocent during the whole fiasco.

After the riot, my heart was no longer in school. It was hard for me to keep my mind on studies when I feared being there. During my sophomore year, I suffered a knee injury playing tennis. That spring, I underwent surgery to repair my knee resulting in me missing the last two months of the school year. My studies continued at home and I advanced to the eleventh grade. Those two months at home were joyous to me; I did not have to live in fear.

When I entered my junior year, I decided to take a vocational study at a different campus. It was still the same high school, but the vocational campus was about five miles away. This decision was great for me; I felt safe at that campus and I made a great deal of new friends. My study was Horticulture. I loved working in the greenhouse and the teacher was great! One day, I was absent from school, and the next day when I returned my whole class informed me I had been nominated Future Farmers of America Princess! It was a total surprise for me and I was indeed honored. Competing in a pageant against other girls, I took the runner-up title. I lost to the girl at our main campus, but even though I was disappointed, I was a lady and many commented on how graceful and how beautiful I looked. These comments stayed with me for a long time.

I was able to leave school during the last half of my junior year. My assigned counselor called me into her office and informed me I had enough credits to graduate at the end of 1975 instead of 1976. I was able to leave before the spring semester got underway. This suited me just fine. The quicker I got out of high school, the quicker I could start college. As it turned out, I did have to attend one more class that spring due to a mistake in my records; my transcripts were transferred to another school and my diploma came from a school I actually never attended! Their graduation requirements called for one less credit, so I was set!

As you can tell, my experiences with school were overshadowed by a lot of turmoil. Getting out of the requirements of school was a lifesaver for me. There were some good times, but overall I despised school and when I was finally free from it, I was more than happy. College was different; my freedom and safety was more in my hands and I felt more in control. I would never want to go back to any of those school years from the first to eleventh grades. In fact, to this day I still have nightmares of those times.

One dream frequently repeats itself. I am getting ready to graduate and someone informs me I still have more classes to attend before I can graduate. I wake up in a frantic state; this is a major nightmare to me! It always takes me a few seconds to regroup and realize it is only a dream and I am far, far past that time in my life. Thank God once again.

CHAPTER FIVE

A LETTER TO MY MOTHER
(THE THINGS I NEVER GOT TO SAY)

2-6-2007   **200lbs.**

Dear Mother,

I find this time in my life the perfect time to tell you some things that I never got to say while you were still with us. Eighteen years have come and gone but it still seems like yesterday when I think of how early you were taken away, and now I find myself back at that time experiencing those feelings all over again. I am sad that you had to leave this earth but I know in my heart it was your time and you had suffered enough in your 64 years of life. You gave up the fight when you were told it was cancer. This was so apparent to me that very moment when the doctor called you at home and broke the news. To this day, I believe the doctor should have handled that differently and I only wish he gained more compassion in the following years. Life-altering news should never be delivered so impersonally, especially over the telephone. I was angry over this but I have now put it to rest and I have had to forgive. When the phone call came from the doctor telling you about the cancer and the fact you most likely had four to six weeks left, I saw the life fade from your face and then I saw you take to your bed. It was so final. Your fight was gone. I knew you were very ill but all along, we thought it was your heart condition because of your past problems.

I was in Kentucky to visit you for the Fourth of July, my annual trip, but I was not prepared to learn you were fading so quickly. The guilt I felt when I had to leave you, to return to California and

Jeff and the kids and to my job, was heavy. I had just started the job and they allowed me to keep my vacation plans, but I knew it would be difficult to ask for more time off. I had only been there a month. This guilt has haunted me for all these years because I missed out on being there to take care of you in your final days. I know Father probably needed me to help, but at the time I did not have my priorities straight. Possibly this is only an excuse because deep down, did I really want to see you slip away from us, one day at a time? I think I justified my fear with the fact that I needed to go home. I regret that decision now. I robbed myself of precious time with you. This became very apparent when I had the honor of taking care of Sheri, your first born — my sister — when she was leaving this earth. Those precious moments will never be forgotten.

When I went back to California, I waited every day for a phone call telling me it was getting close and that I needed to fly back to Kentucky. That phone call came sixteen days later. I caught a flight and was met by Sheri and Father at the airport. We went directly to the hospital and when I saw you lying there, I did not even recognize you. That was not my beautiful mother laying there. You were so distorted and twisted up because of the unbearable pain; there was hardly any resemblance to you, lying there all hooked up to tubes and lines. I almost had to leave the room. From that point on, I went into some kind of a daze and I do not think I was functioning in complete awareness. I went through all of the motions, but it was as if my soul was somewhere else.

When you passed away, I remained strong, at least so I thought. Up until about four years ago, I did not remember Sheri giving the eulogy at your funeral. Someone had to bring it to my attention. I guess I had blocked out most of that day. I remember saying "How did she do it? I could have never got through it." I now know she had *you* guiding her and pouring out your love to her, to see her through such a difficult time. What a precious gift she gave.

Looking back, I now know that you watched over us during those days after your passing. I know you were instrumental in giving me the backbone to stand up to Jeff when, the day after your funeral, he demanded I return with him to California immediately. I kept firm my plans of staying with Father and Sheri for the following week to help them go through some of your things and to just be together as a family. It was so important for us to have that time together. Standing up to my husband was very hard because of the guilt trip he tried to put on me but for once, it did not work. My father and my sister were more important at that time. Jeff has since apologized for his behavior and I accepted his apology.

When I returned home, I felt such emptiness in my heart. The rest of 1989 was difficult for me and I went through some life altering experiences. There was another career change, more marital turmoil, and the first holiday season without you. It was hard. Then came 1990 and with it, more emotional distress. I decided on divorce and then we reconciled, renewed our wedding vows and tried again. I was still very unhappy and I backed myself into a corner; I was feeling so helpless. Father also moved on with his life and I was unsure of how I felt about that whole situation. On one hand, I wanted him to be happy, but on the other hand, I was still sticking up for you and I felt it was too soon. You knew how and what I felt.

My first Mother's Day without you was also very emotional. I remember being at Sheri's and we spent Mother's Day together. Did you know that I wrote you a letter, took it out to Sheri's rose garden, and placed it with the roses, hoping you somehow knew what it said? Knowing you loved roses so much, I couldn't think of any place more appropriate than the rose garden to be close to you at that time. That letter stayed there withering away from the desert heat and weather. Sheri never removed it.

Your passing had such an emotional effect on me. I guess I never realized how attached at the hip you and I really were. I know you never get over the passing of a loved one and that time passes by and heals, but I miss you more today that yesterday, if that is even possible. Not a day goes by that I do not think of you and how wonderful it would be to hear your voice once again. Sometimes I struggle in my mind to hear your voice, to remember how you sounded when you spoke. Even more, I long to hear your laughter and the way it filled my heart with happiness. Most of all, I miss the friend you became after I grew up and started to look at you in a different way. The *woman* that you were, not just the *mother* you were, was a pleasure to get to know as an adult. You had the feelings of a woman and you became comfortable enough to share some of your most intimate feelings with me, your baby. I learned so many things about you and your life when I became your confidant and I looked at you in a very different light. You were not just my mother; you were a woman with some of the same dreams, the same fears and the same questions of life as I. What an honor for me to know you trusted me with some of your deepest feelings and even asked me for advice at times. How beautiful it is for mothers and daughters to appreciate each other as women — as equals — sharing the same feelings and issues. What a gift from God.

Mother, when I grew up and became a mother myself, I realized what big shoes I had to fill to become half the mother you were to me. What sacrifices you made for your family; how could I even come close? The truth is, I never did. I never gave up my hopes and dreams to raise my family. I thought I could do both successfully, but I could not. Something had to suffer along the way. I fear that "something" was Sandra and Jeffrey. You know I loved my kids, but I was selfish in the way I justified my career as being more important to being a full-time mom. I really wanted to stay home and not work outside of the home but my selfishness did not want to give up that lifestyle two incomes afforded. Also, the pressure Jeff put on me to work did not help. I had no backbone when it came to what he expected, but all in all, I have only myself to blame because financially, I always seemed to put myself in a situation where I had to work to dig myself out of a hole. That hole always got bigger and bigger. As you know, this has not changed much. I have never learned that lesson but I am still working on it. Anyway, the sacrifices you made for us went unrecognized for many years; I have to wonder, did I ever really thank you for giving up your dreams so I could have mine? I honestly do not think I did and even if I did thank you, it could have never been enough. How can you truly thank someone who gave up their life's ambitions just to give *you* life and then pour their heart and soul into you? You can't, but I at least want to try. Mother, thank you, with all my heart.

2-8-2007   **200 lbs.**

Being a mother myself, I know children do and say things to their parents they do not really mean. I know this is a natural part of growing up. We as parents always forgive these actions because we know this. Mother, there are things I did and said to you, however, as a child and as an adult that I am not proud of and I owe you many apologies. For the times I told you I hated you when I was a child because you were telling me to do something I did not want to do, I apologize. For the times I smarted off to you when you would not let me go or do something I wanted to do because you obviously had a reason, I apologize. For the times I would play you against Father trying to go past you to get my way, I apologize. For the times I lied to you because I did not want to get into trouble for something I had done wrong, I apologize. For when I got a little older and would talk about you to my friends, telling them how unreasonable you were, once again, because I did not get my way, I apologize. For the times you tried to give me your advice and I would think you were interfering in my life, I apologize. For when you tried to tell me about mistakes you had made so *I* could learn not to make the same ones and I would say to you, or think to myself, "I'd never be that stupid," I apologize. For the many sleepless hours you spent worrying if I would ever make it through school, I apologize. For the many hours you spent making my clothes for which I never showed you proper gratitude because I felt my clothes needed to be store bought like all the other kids' clothes, I apologize. Then there are all the times you worried about me when I faked being sick so I did not have to go to school, and you thought I really was ill. For this, I apologize. For all the times I rolled my eyes at you because you were telling me something I did not want to hear, I apologize. For when I snuck around with my friends and you thought I was at one place and I was actually at another without you knowing it, I apologize. For all of the times I was actually embarrassed of your weight and made fun of you because of it, never to your face, but behind your back, you have my deepest apologies. I know how much this issue hurt you. I have now lived in your shoes and I know how much your weight affected your life. I always thought if you really wanted to lose the weight, you could do it. I considered you lazy, not realizing how difficult it actually was to lose weight and keep it off. For the times you asked me if I was anorexic or bulimic and I lied to you, telling you I wasn't, I am so sorry. There was the time you and I had a confrontation about something I was allowing Sandra to do as a toddler and you thought I was wrong, telling me so, and I yelled "I am a grown woman with a child of my own and I don't need you telling me how to raise her!" For this I owe you my deepest apology. You set me straight when you slapped me for talking to you that way, but it opened my eyes and I realized I had totally disrespected you.

Mother, I am sure there are so many things I have not mentioned. Never in a million years could I apologize to you enough. I only wish I had said these things to you when I could look you eye to eye but I did not and now I have to live with this fact. As I get older, I understand how important it is to say things to the people you love and not wait until it is too late. I did wait, and now I live with this regret. The only thing that eases my guilt is the fact I know you are watching over me and you know how truly sorry I am.

Mother, as I think about all of the apologies that I owe you, there is something else on my mind. I owe you many thanks as well. You gave me so much in my life. You were always there for me and I never lacked for your love. I know you gave up so much in your life to raise us girls, and the sacrifices you made for us should never go unnoticed. A mother's love is such a gift from God; there is nothing that can compare to this love. You gave the ultimate Mother's love. You always gave of yourself. You never held back when it came to giving us the support and caring we needed as children.

I know you had plenty of dreams of your own. Who doesn't? Your beauty and grace were incomparable. Your love for dance and art was also very apparent; you were very gifted. When I look back at pictures of you as an older teen, I see such incredible beauty but I also see self-doubt in your eyes. Mother, I do not think you ever really knew just how stunning you were. I've always said you should have been in pictures. Your flair for drama and your beauty should have graced every movie screen across the world. There is one thing for sure, however: Sheri and I were so fortunate to have you as our mother because the beauty and grace you possessed, you poured into us and taught us that grace goes along with beauty. A pretty face can get you somewhere, but the grace that lets you handle the prettiness is what carries you far. You never let us forget this.

When you decided to become a mother, I realize your priorities had to change. You chose to be a full-time mom and I now know you lived your life through your children. I know we were everything to you but I wonder if somewhere along the way you lost your self-identity. Deep down inside you had to wonder, what if? What if you had finished your college education? What if you had continued in flamenco dance? What if you had the chance to become a famous artist? I think as adults we all wonder "what if" once we have given up our dreams and chosen another path; this is only natural. Because you chose to be a full-time mom, I have to say how precious this was for you to give me life and then be content to nurture and watch me grow. I know how you must have struggled when I disappointed you from time to time, yet I also know how very proud you were of me. You were always on my side even when I was wrong, and you continued to stay by my side through thick and thin. How honored I was to know you were always in my corner.

When I got older, I pushed you to get your driver's license and open up a bank account of your own. I know how frightening it must have been for you to get behind the wheel of a car after being afraid for so many years. This was one time I had the chance to teach *you* something. It felt good to be able to watch you learn and conquer your fear. It was like taking your shackles off and watching you walk for the first time. I wanted you to be the independent woman you really were underneath your self doubt. I have always said you were born way ahead of your time! Your intelligence and intellect made you stand out. I learned so much from you and I now know what a gift you gave me. You taught me to look under the surface of things and not just take things for face value. I know I got my inquisitive nature from you.

Always studying, you were never satisfied with simplicity. You dug deeper and deeper until you uncovered something that made you question what everyone else accepted. This made you most interesting to those who had the honor of knowing you. Making people look deep inside themselves was a good thing for those who wanted to learn more. Those who were afraid to take a deep look were sometimes put off by your honest approach; I think the reason for this was because they thought you could possibly be looking straight into their soul. Sometimes I think you were. There were others who liked to challenge your intelligence and it was quite funny to see them squirm when they knew they had a tiger by the tail! I have to say, to this day, you were probably the smartest person I have ever known. When it came time for you to battle wits with someone, my money was always on you. Not only did you possess remarkable intellect, you backed it up with plain, old common sense, which made you a lethal weapon in the battle of intelligence. I don't know if I could name one person who ever got one up on you. Many tried, many failed, and many were just plain afraid of your "tell it like it was" approach because I think they recognized early on that they were not, nor ever could be, a match for you.

2-12-2007   **199 lbs.**

When I think about your quest for learning, I realize how much of your knowledge actually rubbed off on Sheri and me. I myself have never wanted to settle for the easy road. I have always had to question what is normally accepted to find out what might actually be hidden underneath the surface. Sometimes not settling on the standard answers has helped me understand myself so much more. You and Sheri were complex people and I see myself with the same complexities, especially as I get older. Nonconformity has become a part of my life. Questioning standard beliefs has helped me, but then again, this can lead to other people's disapproval. As I age, I am not so inclined to be consumed with what others think of me. When I was younger though, I only cared what others thought; this made for many upsets in my life. Now I know that the only truly important thing is how I view myself. If I am happy with myself, others will either like me or not like me. It just does not matter to me anymore what they think. As I look back, I recall you gained that tough exterior as you aged. Even though you were a very sensitive woman, you always held strongly to your convictions and for this, I was, and am, so proud of you. Who could ask for a better role model? Even though I probably never told you how much I appreciated your honesty, I truly did, with all my heart.

Mother, I wish I could still pick up the telephone and share my everyday life with you. I know you are always with me regardless, but how precious it would be to see you, or hear you again. Almost every night, you come to me in my dreams, so I know you are watching over me. There is something strange about my dreams though and it is always the same premise. You have been gone for many years when suddenly, you come back to us and tell us you never really passed away. You actually had your death staged so you could go away and seek unconventional treatment for your cancer. You knew you would face your family's disapproval by what you wanted to do, so you felt it would be easier this way. I know this dream does not make a lot of sense but I guess it is wishful thinking from my subconscious. I also know you are with me because sometimes when I dream about you, we deal with current issues in my life. Then again, sometimes you are not an active part of my dream but you are always there. You are always my mother, looking out for me, making sure I can always count on you to tell me the truth, sharing good times as well as bad, making me accountable for my actions, and always loving me, unconditionally. I can honestly say I had the best mother I could have possibly had. God definitely gave me to you to nurture and love. They say you cannot pick your parents, but if I could have, I would have picked you because you were the best choice for me. The Lord knew what he was doing in his infinite wisdom. I only wish I shared with you more of how very important you were to me and how much I loved you. You gave me everything of yourself and asked for nothing but love in return.

I love you Mother. I miss you. I know you are here with me and you always will be; this is how I know you go on.

GLORIA CLARK DYE
MAY 26, 1925 - JULY 29, 1989

A Mother's love is always soft spoken
A Mother's love is never unnoticed
A Mothers Love is unconditional
A Mothers love... the most traditional.

CHAPTER SIX

MY SISTER, MY FRIEND

2-13-2007   **198 lbs.**

Sheri Elaine Dye, my sister, was born January 6, 1947 in El Paso, and was a "one of a kind" girl. She was the first child of our parents, Gloria and Richard. Sheri was born 10 years before me and she was the ultimate big sister. My parents always told me what a difficult child Sheri really was. It was always hard for me to believe because she was such an incredible sister; she was always well behaved in my eyes; well, almost! There were times when I was growing up that she imposed some aggravation upon me. As any big sister should, she did her share of teasing and setting me up for trouble. But in all fairness, Sheri always looked out after me, even until her death.

My sister Sheri was one of the most beautiful women ever to walk the face of this earth. She possessed the beauty and grace of the most magnificent creature you could ever imagine. Her stunning statuesque build on her 5'11" frame, her beautiful long blond hair and her peaches and cream complexion, made her a truly beautiful dancer and model when she was in her teens.

Sheri was a ballerina and started dancing when she was only three years old. By the time she was in her teens, she was accepted into the prestigious Harkness Ballet in Texas where she danced on a scholarship for two years. Sheri ended up injuring her ankles, breaking them down so severely she had to give up dancing altogether. After Sheri was no longer able to dance, she took up modeling, and she was highly sought after for runway and print work in El Paso. Sheri had attended a modeling and finishing school when she was sixteen, so she had the foundations mastered. She was such a natural; her body was definitely the body of a high-fashion model. I think if she had gone to New York, she would have made a million dollars the first year there!

Before being a dancer and before being a model, Sheri was my big sister. As I have been told many times, she begged my parents to give her a baby sister! She told them she would cook and clean, feed me and change my diapers; anything she needed to get them to agree to give her me! My parents always told me that after having her, they had to wait the full 10 years to get up the nerve to try again! She was supposedly a real little "stinker" as a little girl. Our parents always said they could never take her out in public because she would always cause a scene. When they would travel to see my grandparents in central Texas, it would take them twelve hours to get there. Then, after being on the road that long, Dad would have to put her back into the car and drive her around until she fell asleep. Sometimes this took over an hour! Our dad *still* talks about it.

2-14-2007   **198 lbs.**

It is hard to believe Sheri was such a difficult child, but her reputation proves it. I know it would always make her sneer when someone would mention how terrible she was as a little girl, and how well behaved I was. Of course, this is not exactly the way it has been told but I always liked to hold it over her head! I know she would roll her eyes at me or stick out her tongue at me when someone mentioned anything about her misadventures of childhood. It was a funny part of our history together!

When I was a little girl, I was my big sister's shadow. Everywhere she went and everything she did, I felt I had to be a part of it. Most of the time, she was more than happy to keep me with her. There were a few times though, once she became a teenager, I became a major thorn in her side! I would want to be everywhere she was and there were times when she would let me know just how much of a nuisance I really was. Our mother would usually intervene and set her straight. I remember one time in particular when Sheri and her best friend Roberta were aggravating the heck out of me, I had to take a stand! We were arguing about something and they both told me I was wrong. Sheri's exact words were "Karen, you are mistaken!" to which I immediately responded with "I don't make mis-snakes!" As you can imagine, I never lived that one down.

When Sheri was in the eighth grade, she danced a flamenco dance in the school talent show. I remember being there with our mother and when I saw my sister on stage, I jumped up and ran up on the stage with her. She immediately scooped me up in her arms and continued her dance, with me in tow! What a great memory this is. My big sister did not let my interruption of her act detour her in any way. You know what they say, "The show must go on."

Sheri looked out for me all of my life. Because of our great age difference, it was almost as if I had a second mother to care for me. I know she loved me so very much and I loved and idolized her in every way possible. She was the epitome of everything I wanted to be. Her intelligence, good looks and kindness were the most difficult act to follow. I know I have never been as smart as my sister; school seemed to be so easy for her and as I have said before, it was difficult for me.

Sheri's gracefulness came so naturally to her; I have never been the least bit graceful. In fact, I have been a klutz all of my life. I always wanted to dance like my big sister, but rhythm was something I was not graced with. Yes, I tried, but I think I got our dad's sense of rhythm instead of our mother's! I would try to dance but could never get the hang of it. To this day, I would give anything to be able to sweep across a dance floor with the grace and ease my beautiful sister possessed. I remember when I was small and I was able to go to her dance performances, I would sit in total awe watching her. She would mesmerize me and I would almost fall into a kind of trance as I watched her glide across the stage with the ease of a cloud passing effortlessly in the sky. She was so natural and she was very at home on stage. I envied her so much.

For as far back as I can remember, ballet and every other type of dance consumed Sheri. Up until about three years ago, she still took dance classes to stay in shape. She did so until her health failed and it became too strenuous for her to continue.

Sheri always wanted to work with kids and dance. She always had a dream to incorporate dance while working with hearing impaired children, as a type of therapy. Unfortunately she never got the chance to do this. She had intentions of someday opening a special school to teach dance to those who would otherwise never get a chance to experience the beauty of movement with the body. Sheri considered dancing to be a spiritual journey of such magnitude that it was *sacred* to her. I think she felt children could be reached on a different level by allowing them to feel the vibrations of the dance and lose themselves in the whole experience, releasing their inhibitions. She would have been so good at this; I am so sorry for all the children she could have reached with her theories. She could have done great things with her love and dedication.

2-15-2007   198 lbs.

As I have mentioned, my sister was extremely intelligent. She made honor role all through high school and when in college she made the Dean's List several times. Sheri graduated with a Bachelor of Arts degree from Texas Tech University, majoring in Fashion Merchandising. She was always very talented in the field of fashion, design and art. She held two or three jobs working in the fashion industry and eventually taught Fashion Merchandising at a private college in New Mexico. This experience led to her discovering that she really liked teaching and it paved the road for her long-term career.

Sheri ended up in Phoenix in the 1980s. She started working for the City of Phoenix in the Streets and Traffic Department and, after being there for about two years, she transferred to the Phoenix Fire Department. There she became a trainer for the department. She loved it! As a civilian, she trained firefighters in several different areas, including critical stress management, work place ethics, motivation, etc. My sister fit right in with this group of people and she loved every minute of her teaching experience. After about 12 years with the fire department, she chose to make a transfer to another city department due to some management issues. Sheri ended up as a Training Coordinator for the City of Phoenix. Her teaching abilities coupled with her outgoing personality made her well loved by those who worked with her. Sheri had many friends at the workplace and she touched everyone who had the honor of taking her classes. She made everyone feel at ease and she went out of her way to make friends with everyone who crossed her path. I had the honor of meeting her coworkers, and they were like one big happy family! She spoke so highly about each and of them, and after having the pleasure of meeting these folks, I know why. What a great group!

The one thing my sister wanted more than anything else in the world was that "special someone" to love her. Sheri's luck with relationships was not great. She was married twice and was once in a long-term relationship with a man who strung her along for over 12 years. Both marriages took their toll on her heart, but I have to say the most difficulty I saw her go through was because of the person who could not make a commitment to her. She basically gave up 12 years of her life to someone who, I feel, had not intended to ever make a permanent commitment. Instead, he lied, cheated and deceived her. I cannot tell you how many times I saw her shed tears over this person who was not worthy of her love. It would anger me to see him hurt her, and I wish she could have just told him where to go, long before he got in his final stab to her heart. She never deserved what he did to her and he never deserved her love. There is one thing I know though: I am almost positive this man is very unhappy in life and unhappy with some choices he made. Because of this, I guess, there is some consolation for the way he treated my sister. What goes around comes around, I've always heard.

I think a lot of men misunderstood Sheri. She was a force to be reckoned with and tough as nails when she needed to be. She could make it in any man's world. Then again, she was all woman and loved the attention she got being beautiful. Sheri loved to play up her femininity and always did it quite well. She loved beautiful clothes and accessories; she always looked like a million dollars. My sister was a very strong woman but she had some insecurity as well. I don't think deep down inside, she ever felt worthy of her gifts. By this I mean she was never quite sure she deserved what she was blessed with: being intelligent as well as beautiful. Because of this, she seemed to attach herself to men who were not capable of handling her combination of brains and looks. I guess it was a matter of them feeling threatened. It is such a shame, because she had so much love to give and offer. Any man would have been lucky to have her in their corner, and Sheri needed love and acceptance *desperately*, like many of us. Sometimes, however, I think she needed more because of who she was at heart.

2-16-2007   **198 lbs.**

In the middle of October 1997, my telephone rang. I answered the phone and was totally unprepared for the conversation that followed. It was my sister; Sheri proceeded to give me some news that changed our lives forever. She had found a lump in her left breast the week before. She went to the doctor and they immediately put her in the hospital to do a biopsy. They ended up doing a lumpectomy. She awoke from the procedure and they gave her the bad news. It was cancer. The doctor had scheduled a mastectomy for the following Monday.

As I listened to my sister on the other end of the phone, I was in total shock: in shock from the news, in shock from the fact she had been through all of this, alone. She had never called me; she had not told anyone. I couldn't believe what she was telling me. As I struggled to take in the news, I was faltering. What could I say? How could I react and not put more fear into her? What did I need to do immediately? My mind was going in many different directions. Finally, I heard myself tell her I was on the next flight out of Nashville to be with her and we would figure it out together. I would be in Phoenix as quick as I could get there. We hung up the phone and I fell apart!

That night was a sleepless one. I had to wait until the following afternoon to leave for Arizona. I tried to rationalize everything in my mind. She was only 47 years old. They had either already gotten all the cancer, or *would* get it all when they did the mastectomy. She had on her side the fact that she had always been physically fit; she was always the picture of health. She ate the right foods. She exercised each and every day. She took care of herself and always had. There would be one more surgery, she would recover quickly while I took care of her, she would be back to her old self, and our lives would go on as usual. I had it all worked out in my head before I got to Phoenix and she met me at the airport.

We hugged each other with more strength than ever before; she started trembling in the embrace. When we broke apart, I could see fear in my sister's eyes for the first time. We both teared up; I told her I loved her, she told me she loved me and was glad I was there. Then we both quickly strengthened ourselves and proceeded to the baggage claim. In the car, on the way to her house, I told her not to worry about the surgery. I would be there with her to take care of her afterwards and all she had to do was focus on getting well. She listened to me without saying a word. I finished what I had to say and awaited a response. There was a brief period of silence then she spoke. I was not prepared for what she had to say. "I don't think I'm going to have the surgery," Sheri said. "You know how I feel about conventional medicine and I don't think it's for me." She continued while I listened. "That doctor scared the hell out of me. He immediately told me I had to have the mastectomy, then radiation and chemo. He didn't even give me a chance to catch my breath. He was so cold and matter of fact it totally turned me off and I shut down!" Sheri spoke with complete fear in her voice. I understood her fear because she had always been afraid of doctors and medical intervention. Since her experience as a small child when the family doctor broke off a needle in her behind, she had never trusted doctors. For many, many years, she feared needles and shots. I even experienced her passing out and then going into a seizure after taking her to have a simple mole removed from her back. I told the doctor not to let her see the needle but she did, and that was the end of that! It scared the hell out of the old doctor and needless to say, the mole stayed on her back. The fact that she was now balking at the idea of surgery did not really surprise me. It did, however, concern me.

2-17-2007   **197.5 lbs.**

I listened to my sister tell me what she had been through at the hospital and with the doctor. I knew she was backing down from their offer. She told me she had been in contact with a friend who had at one time worked with the fire department. He was a medical doctor who no longer practiced conventional medicine and was now involved in naturopathic medicine. He only confirmed her fear by telling her cancer was big business and that the medical profession made lots of money from cancer patients. He said all of the treatments and medications were chemical poisons; they would only make a person sicker by being exposed to them. Sheri listened to this friend; he made more sense to her than the doctor who treated her. In the frame of mind she was in, his words made perfect sense, because she had *already* been influenced by naturopathic studies. Sheri always tried to do things that steered clear of conventional medicine. A so-called "faith healer" had seen her for years. This man became a close friend of her and her second husband. I did not buy anything he had to say, or sell, for that matter, but this was her business and I tried to stay out of it. He did take them for thousands and thousands of dollars by selling them his vitamins and treatments. I even went to see him under false pretenses just to confirm in my heart he was a fraud, which he proved to me when he supposedly "operated" on my kidney to relieve me of kidney stones! I went in there not believing and I came out of there knowing for sure it was a scam. Knowing I would never convince my sister, all I could do was remain silent. After all, they were adults.

After Sheri talked to me about her feelings, she did say she had not made up her mind completely. She wanted the next few days to think about it. She did ask me if I would support whatever decision she did make and I told her I would. Even though deep down I knew which direction she was leaning, I hoped whichever decision she made was the right one. I wanted her cured of this monster. I asked God to see her through it and to see to it she made the right decision. Of course, I felt the right decision was what the medical doctor wanted to do, but was I sure? At that particular time, I could not say yes with 100% certainty.

2-19-2007   **197 lbs.**

Sheri and I spent the next few days together, just enjoying the closeness that sisters share. We decided to take a trip to New Mexico to see family and then go to Mayhill to see the old farm our family had owned. It was a bittersweet trip. As I discussed in chapter three, we found Mayhill run down and not as we had left it, yet we also found serenity at the little farm in the mountains. It was a time of self-reflection for both of us; it allowed us to find inner peace, so needed at that particular time of our lives. We shared laughter, tears and joy. We shared fears, goals and love but most of all we just enjoyed our time together.

When we returned to Phoenix, it was Halloween and Sheri and I dressed up like sugarplum fairies and handed out candy to the children. Sheri always had a flair for costuming and I myself love dressing up, so we went all out! We were the talk of the neighborhood! Several children came back two or three times just to see us and let us sprinkle "fairy dust" (glitter) on them. We had the time of our lives. It was good to see my sister take her mind off the cancer and enjoy herself.

The next day, Sheri told me she had made the decision not to go through with surgery. I had already guessed this was what she would decide, so I was not shocked at her news. She explained she wanted to treat the cancer her own way, naturally, and she needed me to respect her decision. Even though she knew I probably wanted her to take the more traditional road, she also knew whatever her decision was I would stand by her. And I did. I am not saying it was easy because it was not by any means, but I knew Sheri well enough to know when she sets her mind to something, that was it. She was dedicated in making this work for her. If anyone could succeed with this course of action, it would be Sheri.

From that moment on, Sheri studied and learned all she could on natural cancer treatments. Her life became consumed with diet. Everything she ate was scrutinized to make sure it would not work against her goal. She removed all chemicals from her home and her life. She started consuming large amounts of vitamins and minerals and she started growing wheat grass in her kitchen. She also juiced fresh vegetables each day. I remember after I left her in November, it was a little over a month before I saw her again when she came to Kentucky for Christmas and stayed with me. My house became a center for vitamins, tonics, soy-based products, potions and books on how to use all of these ingredients to make her healthy. It was quite overwhelming; I don't know how she gained so much knowledge in such a short period of time! You have to understand that she was also working an extremely hard job, which sometimes took her away from home twelve to fourteen hours a day. How she found the time to do all of the research and learn all of the things she had learned up to that point, I'll never know. It was as if she had been through two years of Naturopathic school in a little over a month!

After that Christmas, we tried to see each other at least twice a year. With 1,800 miles separating us, we spent a lot of time on the telephone. We talked, sometimes three times a week, especially in the beginning. Sheri would always have some new and exciting diet or natural treatment she was trying. She always said she was feeling great and had never felt better. She always sounded so positive on the telephone. When I did get to see her, she always seemed to be doing well and was always totally committed to whatever diet she was on at the time. She appeared to have it all worked out. Who was I to question her choices? It looked like she had everything under control.

Over the next three years, Sheri continued doing her thing and I continued to support her in every way I could. Then, in September 2000, we met up in Virginia. My daughter Sandra was expecting her first baby, my first grandchild, and I was there to help Sandra out. Sheri flew to Kentucky, and then she and our dad drove to Virginia to be there for the birth. When I saw Sheri, she looked very tired and her color was not good. After about two days of us being together, she told me she had a hole in her left breast and it was draining. I immediately wanted to look at it; she would not let me. She told me she did not want me to overreact. I told her that was totally ridiculous and that I had just been in training to become an emergency medical technician. I explained it would not gross me out. She would not give in so I backed off, but not without telling her I thought she needed to see a medical professional. She told me she would handle it her own way, which she did. Her way was to try different things like castor oil packs to draw out poisons from her breast. She spent hour upon hour enduring this treatment.

2-20-2007   **196 lbs.**
When Sheri refused to let anyone look at her breast, I knew in my heart that something was terribly wrong. We continued talking on a regular basis but each time I talked with her, she would tell me she was fine and that she was still on the right path. Then the time would come when I visited her and she would still be treating her breast with the castor oil packs. In October 2003, I went for a visit and once again tried to get her to let me look at it. She was really upset with me and told me not to push her. She told me she knew what she was doing and this was her choice, and hers only! She wanted me to back off. Once again, I did as she asked, even though I felt very uneasy about the whole situation.

About one month after I returned home, while talking to Sheri on the telephone, she had to stop the conversation because she had a coughing spell; she said she had allergies. Two days later, I called her and again, she had a hard time talking because of the cough. She told me about the treatments she was doing to get over it. I started getting a bad feeling in the pit of my stomach; I asked her to go see a doctor. She refused and tried to pass the cough off as smog, heavy allergens or the dry desert air. She told me not to worry; she was doing fine. But of course, I worried. I worried night and day. Our whole family worried about her.

This went on for months. I even talked to one of her friends who agreed with me she needed to see a doctor. Whenever this friend tried to bring the doctor issue up to Sheri, she would get angry and before long she started to completely ignore her friend. My sister was hiding; she did not want anybody interfering with her plan.

Worrying about Sheri became my life. I wanted her to seek a different approach to her health. She continued doing things her way but I continued making subtle comments to her and when I did, I could feel her backing away from me. I did not want to alienate her so I watched what I said. She had already distanced herself from our father and most of her close friends. She was still talking with me, however, and I knew I had to keep the lines of communication open between us. It was hard being so far away and I kept telling her I wanted to go for a visit but she would always have an excuse as to why it was not a good time. She would say she could not take time off work because she had such a full teaching schedule, for example. It *never* seemed to be a good time. There were times I wanted to just jump on a plane and go see her but knowing her well, I knew she would have just resented me for interfering and intruding; she was a very private person in many ways. So, I had to sit back and have faith in her, respect her wishes and wait for her to call and tell me she needed me. It was a very long wait.

In early 2005, I could tell in Sheri's voice she was weak. She continued working but took time off to rest. I asked her to go to a naturopathic clinic and at least see *someone* and she did. She told me they ran all kinds of tests and actually sent her to a medical doctor who worked in conjunction with the naturopath. They started her on I.V. therapy for nutrition and vitamins. They were testing her for "Valley Fever." This was all she told me. Her cough was getting worse by the day and in the pit of my stomach, I knew what the cough meant.

At the beginning of April 2005, my son planned a business trip to Phoenix and called me to see if I thought Sheri would like to see him while he was in town. I called and asked her; she immediately started making excuses as to why she could not see him. This was not like her at all; she loved Jeffrey. I insisted she needed to make time to see him and at least let him take her out for dinner. Reluctantly, she agreed. They had a great time together that weekend and she called me afterwards to tell me all about it. Jeffrey called me also; he told me I needed to go there immediately and see her. She was going downhill fast and he was very upset at how she looked. He told me she was very thin and she was hardly eating. I called her back and once again told her I was coming. Again, she reassured me and told me to wait and to trust her. What could I do? I made her promise she would call me to come when she needed me and she did make me that promise. I went to our dad and together we decided to fly her to Kentucky for a "vacation." I made all of the arrangements and then called her and told her she was coming to see us! She balked at first but then started to give in. The trip was planned for June.

May 8, 2005 was Mother's Day. I had gone to church and when I returned home, my phone rang. "Happy Mother's Day!" Sheri sang out to me I started laughing!

"Why are you calling me to wish me a happy Mother's Day?" I asked. "I'm not your mother!"

"You're a mother, aren't you?" she replied.

Well, I guess she had me there! We laughed and joked and she sounded better than I had heard her sound in months. Her voice danced, she was jolly and she was not coughing. It was Sheri; she was back!

We had a great talk. I told her how great she sounded. She told me she had been to see someone who was really helping her, an acupuncturist. She was drinking large amounts of pomegranate juice to detoxify her system. We then talked about her impending visit. She told me she was supermodel thin and told me not be surprised. I did not tell her what Jeffrey told me about her weight, but

I was feeling a little more at ease because she sounded great. We ended the call by me telling her once again to make the promise to me she would call me if I needed to go to her, and once again, she promised. We said we loved each other and then we hung up. Her call made my day. I was very happy!

%

REFLECTION 2

2-21-2007   **195 lbs.**

In the last three chapters, I have touched on some very personal and painful memories; there have been precious memories as well. It has benefited me greatly to be able to actually write these things down. I have been able to touch some deep feelings that I thought were lost or did not even exist. This has indeed been a journey for me. I have learned so much, as well as dealt with some things that have bothered me for years. I recommend to *anyone* who needs to move on and not dwell on issues, to take the time to write down those feelings; it gets them out in the open so you can deal with them face to face, so to speak. Writing the letter to my mother gave me the opportunity to say the things to her I did not say in her life. It also gave me such pleasure to remember the beautiful woman my mother was; those memories will last a lifetime.

Writing about my sister also gave me the chance to remember her grace and spirit. As I left off, she was going through a difficult time in her life. I experienced this difficulty along with her. Her courage and strength gave me life when my own seemed out of balance. I always looked up to my big sister, even at times when I thought she possibly needed to make different decisions for herself. I'm sure she felt the same way. I know she always loved me unconditionally even if she did not agree with some of the choices I made. Is this not the way it is with unconditional love? We shared such a special closeness. She was the best sister I could have ever asked for.

This month has been a whirlwind of busyness! I have been on my diet religiously and to date have lost 31 pounds since January 1! I feel great and it has not at all been hard this time around. As I stated before, one's frame of mind has so much to do with how we accomplish goals. My mindset entering this endeavor was to go all the way, and I have not faltered from this in the least. I even traveled two weekends ago, with great restaurants all around me, but I stuck to my diet! I still got to eat great things and it wasn't hard at all. I'll see my medical doctor tomorrow for my monthly check up and I know she will be happy about my progress. I've lost 15 pounds since last month's visit!

I have also been very busy with my church getting ready for Easter! It is so great to be with people I love, doing the Lord's work. He is always with us, seeing us through each day. Those I worship with arc all close to my heart and I know the Lord brought us together as a team so we can do what He calls us to do, enjoying fellowship along the way.

As I go into the next chapter, I know I will have some difficulty writing it. Everything is so fresh in my mind and I have not had the chance to deal with all of it yet. My hope for this chapter is to once again give me the insight and strength I need to deal with my loss. God has seen me through to this point and I know He will help me express myself with honesty and love. It will not be an easy chapter to write but it will be written from my heart. I ask forgiveness in advance for any anger I might express to certain individuals who I feel exploited my sister. I feel they deserve my anger but it only hurts me now. I know I have to let this go in order to do God's will. It is a very hard process; I ask for strength during these next few days.

I hope you as the reader are able to identify with something as I continue my writings. I know we have all traveled different paths in life but sometimes these paths are side by side. It is nice to be able to look over and see someone beside yourself who has gone through tough times and is willing to share it with you. Sometimes, it gives us the opportunity to realize we are never alone in our journeys. I think knowing this helps put our problems into perspective at times when we are foggy and unable to see the forest for the trees. I know it does for me and I hope it does for you. As you continue with this book, I wish you happy reading and may God bless you!

As we journey through life's highways and byways,
we are never alone. Call upon your Faith when in need, for it
will always see you through those dark tunnels and
there will be a light awaiting you at the other end, guiding you to
peace and acceptance.

CHAPTER SEVEN

"BOWS AND FLOWS OF ANGEL HAIR"

2-22-2007 **195 lbs.**

May 9, 2005. Monday morning, 8:00, the day after Mother's Day. My telephone rings again. On the other end of the phone was my sister Sheri. She sounded weak and she started to cry.

"I hate to bother you, but can you come? I need you to take care of me for awhile." She sobbed. "I am really weak and I need someone to cook for me and help me."

I listened to her and as I did, a sinking feeling hit me. How could she sound this way when just yesterday she was doing so well? What had happened overnight? As I thought this, I knew I had to say something quickly to her.

"Of course I will come. I'll be on the next flight out!"

Sheri broke down completely on the other end of the phone. I consoled her the best way I knew how and reassured her I was on my way. She, being the person she was, worried that she was putting me out in some way. Sheri never wanted to be a bother to anyone. She was concerned about my schedule and how hard it would be for me to pick up and leave home on such short notice. I told her to not be silly. I had told her all she had to do was ask for my help and I would be there as quickly as I could get a flight from Nashville to Phoenix, and this was exactly what I was going to do. Sheri relaxed some after we talked, and the relief in her voice was very apparent. She then told me she had to go to work because she had a class to teach and had not arranged for someone else to do it for her. By the sound of her voice, I knew there was no way she could even drive to work, let alone stand up all day to teach a class!

I told her to call work and stay home. She tried to humor me by saying she would be fine, that she would take it easy, etc. I knew she was going to do what she wanted and all I could do was get there as quickly as possible and take care of her. We hung up the phone and I immediately started making plans to go to Arizona. It took me one day to make all of the arrangements: find a flight that was not fully booked and tie up loose ends at home. I did not have any idea how long I would be away.

The following morning, May 10, I was on my way to Phoenix. The seven hours it took for me to get from my home in Kentucky to Phoenix Sky Harbor Airport were seven of the most unsettling hours I have ever spent. I did not know what faced me when I got there; I had not seen my sister in over a year. I knew in my heart how ill she was, but until I could see for myself, it was hard to visualize my sister as anything but the beautiful and strong woman I had always known. Remember, my son had warned me from his visit the previous month just how frail she was. I wondered what had changed, if anything, since he was there. Then, when I talked with her on Mother's Day and she sounded like her old self, it gave me false hope. What was in store for me? Was she as bad off as she sounded on the phone the day before when she called me crying? After about seven hours, I learned the answers to my questions.

A neighbor of Sheri met me at the airport to take me to Sheri. I had never met this person before. When we were driving to Sheri's house, this neighbor asked me how long it had been since I had seen my sister. She asked me if Jeffrey had told me anything about his visit. How did he think his aunt looked? I told her what Jeffrey told me. The neighbor was trying to prepare me for what I would find when I saw my sister, telling me Sheri had been very sick and was going downhill quickly. I was numb. I did not know this person and she was telling me things about my sister that I really did not need to hear from a total stranger! She even seemed somewhat pushy to me. She was giving me her thoughts on how she thought I should approach Sheri and how I should react when I saw her. This "help" was building a wall between the neighbor and myself.

I appreciated her picking me up from the airport but I was not receptive to her unwanted opinions about my sister. After all, she had only known my sister for a few months! This was *my* family! Who was she to tell me about how I needed to act with Sheri?

2-23-2007   **195 lbs.**

I arrived at Sheri's house and rang the doorbell. Her dogs started barking and it took her about one minute to open the door. When she did, she stood there, yelling at the dogs to "get back!" I stood there for a second or two, unable to move or speak. There was this gaunt, skeleton of a woman staring back at me. I was in shock! Who was this woman? It could not possibly be my beautiful sister.

I thought I was prepared for what I would find when I saw her, but I was not. She was balancing herself up against the door and the wall to keep from falling down. I stepped inside and gave her a hug. In the embrace, I felt every bone in her torso. I could not hide the expression on my face. I tried but I knew she felt my disbelief. This person who was there before me, so weak she could hardly stand, was not my sister; at least she was not the sister I had known all my life. As we got inside the hallway, she immediately told me she had to go lay down. I started to follow behind her offering help, but she refused. Then, as I absorbed the house around me, I realized I did not recognize anything. Where was I? There were things lying everywhere. There is no way for me to possibly explain what I found inside her home. Clutter, trash, pet hair, you name it, these things were totally taking over! Sheri made her way through a barely passable hallway to her back bedroom and I followed her. When she got to the bedroom, there was a very small pathway leading to one side of her bed. It was so small you had to turn sideways to fit through it. *What on earth was going on?* I thought as I remained in shock. Sheri eased herself onto the bed and when she was still, you could see all over her face she was exhausted. She started coughing uncontrollably and could not catch her breath. I tried to offer assistance but she put her hand out to me as if to say, "stop!" Finally, she wheezed in a few breaths and started to relax. Her face was a combination of blue and red. I knew this was critical and I was panicking inside. Me, a professional trained to deal with patients who were in trouble, trembled in fear! I had to keep this reaction on the inside because I could not let Sheri see.

After she settled down, we talked for a short time. She told me she was so glad I was there and I told her I loved her and I would take care of everything. For myself, I needed to assess the situation, which took me about two minutes. I told her I felt she needed to go to hospital immediately, but she promptly refused. I knew not to expect a different reaction but at least I was hoping, for her sake.

We discussed what was going on with her, me trying to pry out information as we went along. She still had her naturopathic ideas in full force and, according to her, she was just suffering a minor setback. I listened, disbelieving, that she actually thought her condition was a "minor setback" but the more we talked, the more I think she truly believed this to be the fact. I felt I was between a rock and a hard place and my sister's innocence sometimes overpowered her judgment. It was hard to get past her beliefs, harder still to get past her fears. When dealing with medicine, modern treatments, doctors, etc., she feared for her life! In her mind, these things would kill her long before the cancer would. She was not going to give in and I knew this because of past experiences. I had to accept this, no matter how hard and unreasonable I thought it was.

So this is what we were faced with; I did not know if I could do it. I prayed constantly to God for strength and help. I anguished over her suffering and wanted to take it away. She pretended not to, be but I knew in my heart she was hiding behind her strong façade. My sister was *still* looking out for me, her little sister. She put on this act to keep me from falling apart. Her needs were not as important to her as keeping me from hurting and worrying. In her mind, she still felt it was her job to protect me from the bad things that can happen in life. Her unconditional love was still in full force.

2-24-2007   **195 lbs.**

Sheri's coughing was uncontrollable and she hardly ate anything because every time she swallowed, it set off a coughing attack. She also had herself on a ridiculously strict diet. The person she had been seeing, whom she called her "Chinese Herb Lady," put her on some crazy diet to rid the toxins from her body. Sheri would try anything anyone told her about, as long as it was not coming from the medical profession. I don't know where she found this "quack" (no other term is appropriate) and the anger I have felt for this woman still engulfs me. My sister spent hundreds and hundreds of dollars at this woman's business, and I have to wonder, for what? This person strung my very ill sister along and continued selling her a bunch of (excuse the expression) bull crap! Being as vulnerable as Sheri was, she bought into this type of fraud, truly believing she was going to be cured as long as she did as this woman said. This meant buying the woman's herbs, vitamins and taking her "treatments." Sheri believed the woman was helping her and I could not change that fact, but what I saw was my sister literally starving herself to death. Her illness was bad enough, but topped off with some crazy eating plan, her system did not have a chance.

That first evening I was with my sister, I tried to get food into her, but it was difficult. She was very uncomfortable and having extreme difficulty breathing. Once again I suggested we go to the hospital and once again, she refused. I tried to comfort her and tell her I would be with her all of the time at the hospital, and I would not let them do anything to hurt her, but she still wanted to stay home, so we did. As I worked to try to get her to relax so she could sleep, I told her I would rub her back. This pleased her and she agreed. When she positioned herself on her stomach, I lifted up the t-shirt she was wearing so I could use massage oil on her back. I was not prepared for what I saw; I had a huge shock. There were tumors completely covering her entire back. They were protrusions, some of which were one to two inches in size. I tried not to overreact, but it was difficult. Sheri sensed my astonishment and immediately told me the Chinese Herb Lady said those tumors were the toxins leaving her body. I had to bite my tongue to keep from screaming in disbelief. I cried silently to myself; I could not believe what was, and had been, going on. It saddened me deeply to think my intelligent sister could believe all of the stuff she was being fed. How could she actually think she was getting better? I did not understand.

By the end of that first evening there, I did not think Sheri would live until the next morning. I was scared, but I had to hide my fear. I prayed a lot and asked the Lord to not let her suffer more than she already had. Even though she said she was not suffering, I didn't believe her. I could tell that when she moved, her body hurt. She was skin and bones; there was nothing to cushion her movements. I could also see the pain in her face even though she tried to cover it up. It was really bad.

2-26-2007   **194.5lbs.**

Sheri's will was amazing! She made it through that first night and seemed to be a little better the next morning. I was able to get a smile out of her and we spent quality time together, just talking. My main focus was to try to get nourishment into her. I made smoothies with fresh fruits, and I made broths with fresh vegetables hoping this would work. Some she could keep down, some she could not. I made numerous trips to the health food store and the organic market for supplements and organic foods. The first few days were trial and error when it came to her diet. She could not digest solid food at all so the focus was keeping her hydrated while trying to get proper nutrients into her. When she had her coughing spells, this would set her gag reflex into overdrive, which would sometimes make her throw-up. It was a difficult situation. She made it perfectly clear she would not go to a doctor, let alone the hospital, so I knew I was on my own in taking care of her. She trusted me, but I could not force her to do anything she was not willing to do. Her mind was strong and clear but she hated medical intervention so I had to respect her wishes, no matter how hard it was.

Anything I could do to make my sister comfortable, I did. She loved massages, so I rubbed her back and worked on her feet; this would relax her. At one time, Sheri had studied massage and she had purchased many different massage oils to use; I tried them all. Sometimes I would work on her for two hours at a time, especially at night before she tried to go to sleep. It was difficult for her to lie down because she could not breathe while lying so she tried to sleep while sitting up. She would sit meditation-style with pillows piled up in her lap and then she would put her forehead on the pillows. This is how she tried to sleep but it became apparent after a few nights that she was not getting any rest. I tried to let her rest during the day as much as she could, but I also had to worry about her consuming sufficient liquids. Sometimes it took her over an hour to drink just eight ounces of liquid. We were losing ground.

Sheri was still holding strong in her faith that she was going to get better. I knew in my heart that we needed a miracle, so I kept asking God for one. I knew I had to make the most of the time we had left together. There were things I needed to discuss with her, but I did not know how to approach the discussion without upsetting her. Finally, I just jumped in and asked the questions to which I needed answers. Sheri had not prepared a will. This was a delicate topic but I knew we had to get it done. She was not in a hurry to call her attorney and inside, I was panicking! There were also work-related issues with things like retirement, where beneficiaries needed to be updated. She had no power of attorney assigned. I also needed medical power of attorney in the case she became incapable of making medical decisions for herself. This was the most difficult conversation to have with someone I loved so much. We made it through, though, and Sheri told me her wishes. She pretty much left things up to me but we still had to get the legal work done.

After about two weeks, I was getting very tired and was completely stressed out. We had a daily struggle in getting and keeping liquids down her. I ended up putting her on a pediatric electrolyte liquid to try and keep her functioning. She was losing ground quickly and I was exhausted. My family kept calling me from Kentucky and Texas wanting me to put her in the hospital, but I had made a promise to Sheri and I was not going to go back on my word as long as I could keep going. It was, however, getting harder and harder each passing hour.

2-27-2007   **194 lbs.**

I continued to try everything I could think of to comfort Sheri. She loved the time I spent pampering her. While watching TV, I would do her fingernails and give her a pedicure. I would brush her hair. We continued with the massages to relax her. The one thing that seemed to work the best was when I sang to her. She loved for me to sing so I did it whenever she wanted me to do so. She loved ballads and old folk songs. One evening while singing, I thought of an old song I loved when I was a child and I started singing it to her. "Both Sides Now" was the song. When I sang these first words, Sheri got a smile across her face; I continued and she got tears in her eyes. When I finished, she told me it was beautiful, and she had also always loved that song. I probably sang "Both Sides Now" to her more than any other song because it always seemed to calm her. This song became another special bond my sister and I shared.

As the third week came, I was functioning on very little sleep. My nerves were on end. I know I was becoming cranky and the last thing I wanted to do was to let Sheri see my frustration. In a way, I was distancing myself from her except for when I was taking care of her; I was not spending as much time just sitting with her. I think she sensed my exhaustion because she would make comments to me that she was worried about me, and she kept apologizing to me for being such a burden. I tried to tell her it was not her, that I was all right, but I think she read between the lines.

Actually, I was functioning on no sleep and a poor diet because I was not taking time to feed myself properly. The lupus I suffer from was also starting to flare. My legs had swollen so severely, it was painful for me to be on them. I couldn't stop though; Sheri was depending on me.

I was feeling anger as well. I was angry at the situation. I was angry with others who were doing their best to undermine how I was handling my sister, by making sure her wishes were met. I was angry from negative comments and actions from these individuals. I was angry with myself for being angry. Most sadly, I was angry with Sheri. Yes, I was mad as hell at her! How could she have let herself go through all of this without being honest with me about her condition? All this time had passed when she would tell me she was doing well and then I come to find out she was very, very sick. I felt like she was being an ostrich, burying her head in the sand and not looking around to see what was really going on. How could she have honestly thought she was beating this illness in the condition she was in? How could let people who were only concerned about making a buck off her, convince her to do some of the harmful things she was doing to herself? How could she give these people thousands and thousands of dollars to cure her and yet not see a doctor who possibly could have helped her earlier on in the illness? How could she pull away from her friends and family members who only wanted the best for her? She had totally shut out her old friends and then, when someone who did not know the *true* situation came along, she totally trusted them instead. This proved to be a really harmful. One person in particular, the neighbor I spoke about earlier, was doing a number on my sister's mind. She inserted herself right into my sister's life, actually taking over in some instances. My sister was totally in the dark about what was actually going on with this woman. Of course, I saw it immediately and took matters into my own hands. Boy, did this person try everything she could to do harm. She was a piece of work, to say the least! I put a stop to her unwanted intrusions. It still ticks me off to think of the ways she tried to undermine everything I was doing. What a despicable individual she proved to be.

My anger was very hard to hide. As time passed, I was getting more on edge about the fact that Sheri had not made any legal arrangements in getting her affairs in order. I knew that time was running out and with my exhaustion, I struggled to keep my composure. I had just about reached my wit's end. I did not know how much longer I could keep up what I was doing all by myself. Something had to give and I struggled with what to do. I prayed and prayed for the Lord's help. I did not want my sister to know my anger or frustration. *Lord, please help me!*

2-28-2007   **194 lbs.**

Thursday morning, June 2, 2005, was three weeks and two days after I arrived in Phoenix, I awoke early and went in to check on Sheri. I knew she had been up a big part of the night because I heard her coughing and at one point, I thought I heard her crying. I was so exhausted I could not drag myself out of bed to check on her when I thought she was crying. Every bone in my body ached. I knew if she needed me, she would call for me. I forced myself out of bed at about six. When I walked into her room, I found her sitting on her bed with papers all around her. She had a notebook she was writing on. She looked up at me and smiled, then she told me to get comfortable, that we had work to do. I asked her if she needed anything to drink and she said no, but told me to make myself some coffee and then come back so we could get going. I had no idea what she was doing but I made my coffee and then returned to her room. As I sat on the bed, she handed me the notebook she had been writing on and told me we needed to go over some things. In the notebook, I found an inventory of her belongings on the first page. As I was looking at it, she explained these were the things she wanted to keep with her if we decided to go back to Kentucky. We at one point had discussed me taking her back to my home so I could better take care of her and have some family help and support. I looked over the list and then turned the page to find she had written down all of her bills, what she owed, including her mortgage, credit cards, loans, etc. She had also written down a list of names and phone numbers. She told me we needed to make several phone calls in order to get her affairs in order.

We spent the next few hours on the telephone making the calls and getting information on the things she needed to do. There were papers she needed to sign from her place of employment so a friend and business associate of hers went and picked up the paperwork and brought it to Sheri during her lunch break. Sheri signed the papers, which updated her beneficiary information, and her friend left to go back to the office. After all of the phone calls had been made, Sheri told me she needed to call her attorney and after she talked with him, she was going to let me take her to the hospital. I sat there for a few seconds, not sure I fully understood what she had just said to me! After it sank in, I asked her if she was *sure* she wanted to go. She told me she thought they might be able to give her better nutrition in the hospital and even though she really did not want to be there, it was probably for the best, at least for a few days. As I listened to her, a sense of relief came flooding over me. I had prayed to God that she would decide to go to the hospital because I knew I could only do so much for her and I wanted her to get the best care possible. Also, with me being so tired, I felt I was wearing down to the point where I would not be able to keep up what I had been doing.

I know Sheri sensed my relief. She told me what she was willing to allow the doctors to do, which meant she wanted no invasive treatment. She also told me she was putting her care into my hands because she trusted me fully, and knew I would not let anyone do anything to hurt her. She asked me not to let them give her any type of chemotherapy and I agreed. She also told me that she did not want to know her condition. I was not sure I fully understood what she was saying so I had her explain it to me; she told me that as long as she did not hear the word "terminal," she still had hope. She did not want to know anything that dealt with the fact she may be dying. She was still hopeful in what she had been doing all along. She told me she felt she was setting an example for other cancer patients, to not let doctors tell them that the doctors' way was the only way. Sheri fully believed in natural cures and she was not going to stray from her beliefs.

My sister had put her faith in me. This was such a huge honor, but also a tremendous responsibility. I did not know if I could live up to her trust. I knew it was going to be hard dealing with the hospital and making sure her wishes were met, but I knew I had to do my best for her. She trusted me and I was not about to let anyone hurt her. My work was cut out for me.

3-1-2007   **194 lbs.**

Realizing there was no way I could take Sheri to the hospital in her car as she was not strong enough to walk outside and get in it, I knew I needed to call an ambulance for transport. I talked to Sheri about this and she said the only way she would ride in an ambulance was if they did nothing to scare her while she was in it. I reassured her that I would talk to the EMTs and make sure they understood they were to transport her only, and she agreed. After arranging the transport with a private ambulance company, we waited for them to arrive. Sheri had also contacted her attorney and he was going to get all of her legal paperwork ready and meet us at the hospital so she could sign everything.

At approximately three p.m., the ambulance arrived at the house. I knew Sheri was getting anxious while we waited;. I could see the fear written all over her face. I decided to meet the EMTs outside to make sure they fully understood Sheri's fears and did not go in the house like gangbusters with all types of equipment that would frighten her. I needed to make sure she did not back out of going.

The guys with the ambulance were terrific. They assured me they would handle her gently and not do anything to frighten her. We made it into the house and to the bedroom where she was. They instantly took over and started working with her, making sure they communicated to her everything they were going to do. They put her mind at ease, and we proceeded outside to the ambulance. She wanted me to ride with her, so I did. We started driving to the hospital we had decided on, which was only about two miles from her home. We no sooner turned the corner off her street when the radio in the ambulance went off with a dispatch informing the driver that the hospital we were heading towards was not accepting any more patients through the emergency room; they were completely full. The driver of the ambulance asked me where we wanted to go from there. I asked Sheri what she thought and she suggested another hospital she knew about. The driver then radioed ahead to the next hospital. We started traveling to it when the radio went off once again with dispatch informing us that the second hospital was *also* not accepting any emergency patients. I could not believe it! Again, we had to make another choice. The third destination was chosen and we started driving there. The driver called ahead to the third hospital and they informed him they were at full capacity and could not receive any more patients! This was outrageous; I could not believe what was happening! By this time, I was sure Sheri was in total panic in the back of the ambulance. I asked the driver what we were going to do and he suggested going to the county hospital. I heard this and immediately said no; I knew how most county hospitals operated and there was no way my sister was going to this type of facility. She had great insurance and I wanted the best of care for her.

Having worked in the medical industry in the past, my experience with county hospitals was not favorable and I expressed this to the personnel on the ambulance. The young man who was driving told me he understood my concerns but he felt this hospital was different. In fact, he told me if he had to choose for himself which hospital to go to in case of illness or emergency, he would choose Maricopa County over any of the others! It was a teaching hospital as well, so they were more into new and experimental treatments than some of the other, more conservative, facilities. Sheri listened and agreed to go so that is where we ended up. Remarkably enough, she was joking with the EMT taking care of her in the back. He had won her over and she seemed to be very relaxed. It was a miracle; she even let him give her oxygen, which she had said before she would not do. I think he put her mind at ease enough that she trusted him not to hurt her. When she realized how much better she could breathe with the oxygen, she was more willing to let them help.

We arrived at Maricopa County Hospital and it was apparent when we got there that they were also very busy. Evidently, there had been three or four serious accidents during the time we decided to go to a hospital and this had flooded all the area facilities. County was no different, but at least they accepted my sister. However, when we arrived, they had no room for her in emergency so we had to wait out in the hallway until they made room for her. We waited about one-and-a-half hours. I have to say though, there was not one person who worked there that happened to pass by us in the hallway that did not speak to Sheri. From the time we arrived, the staff was compassionate and professional in the way they approached her. The ambulance attendants had made extensive notes regarding Sheri and her fears. Everyone who approached tried his or her best to reassure her and make her comfortable. This was a Godsend!

3-2-2007   **192 lbs.**

When the emergency room had found a place for Sheri, they moved her into a cubical. I asked the nurse to let me speak to the doctor who was going to see Sheri before they examined her. The nurse went and spoke to the doctor and then the doctor came in, introduced herself to us, and stepped out of the cubical. The nurse motioned for me to follow the doctor and I did. I talked with her and told her about Sheri's fears and explained the difficulty I had getting her to the hospital in the first place. I told her no medical professional had seen Sheri for a long time. I filled her in on the whole situation. The doctor reassured me she would be gentle with Sheri and she would do nothing for Sheri without Sheri's consent. I also told the doctor about the tumors on Sheri's body and I told her she would most likely be in shock when she saw for herself my sister's condition. I told her to expect the worst thing she had ever seen when she examined Sheri; the doctor looked at me, a little puzzled. I told her that whatever she did, she was not to openly react when she actually saw Sheri's body. I talked about her left breast and the fact it had a huge area that was as hard as a rock. Even though there was no open wound, it was apparent there had been a huge open area at one point and scar tissue and the tumor had totally engulfed the breast. I wanted to make sure the doctor or doctors who were going to take care of Sheri fully understood the picture. My only agenda at this point was to see that my sister was made comfortable and that she had the resources to make this possible. The doctor agreed with my requests and we then went back to where Sheri was waiting.

The young doctor proceeded talking to Sheri and asked questions about how she was feeling and the difficulties she was experiencing. Of course, Sheri acted as if she was actually doing quite well! She told the doctor she thought she might only need some I.V. nutrition and possibly something to help her coughing, until she could regain a little bit of strength and return her home, or back home with me to Kentucky. My sister was the ultimate actress. The doctor listened to Sheri and then explained to her she was going to do a quick examination and then they would talk some more. Sheri nodded acknowledgement and then looked over to me for reassurance. I gave her a smile to let her know everything was going to be alright.

As the doctor started her examination of Sheri, she listened to her heart and lungs by placing the stethoscope on her chest. She then moved around to Sheri's back and started to open the hospital gown; I watched closely. When the doctor went to place the stethoscope on Sheri's back, she got a good look at the tumors covering her entire back. A look of total shock came over the young doctor's face. She looked over at me and it was apparent she could not believe what she was seeing. I in turn gave the doctor a warning look, making sure she did not outwardly react and alarm my sister. The doctor continued with the examination but, as she did, I could see tears welling up in her eyes. I could tell she was about to lose her composure. After speaking briefly to Sheri, she excused herself and said she would be back shortly. The nurse followed her out of the cubicle. Within a few minutes, the nurse returned and asked me to step outside; the doctor wanted to speak with me. I followed the nurse to where the doctor was waiting. She had a look of despair across her face. She told me she had never seen anything like what she saw when she examined Sheri. There was nothing that could have prepared her for the shape Sheri was in, even though I had tried. The doctor told me it was by far the worst case she had ever experienced and she had not thought when I told her how bad it was, it could possibly have been that severe. She asked me once again why Sheri refused to seek medical attention up until this point and she told me Sheri had to be suffering severely; she had to be in extreme pain. Her breathing alone was so labored; she was suffering with each breath she took. I agreed with the doctor, but told her my hands had been tied until this day when she finally decided to come to the hospital on her own terms. The doctor agreed that other than the fact Sheri did not want medical intervention, her mental status seemed to be completely intact. She also told me she did not know how I had handled the situation all by myself for as long as I had without completely falling apart. I told her it was only by the grace of the good Lord. She put her arm around my shoulders and reassured me I had done all I could have possibly done in the situation and she told me not to worry; they were going to treat Sheri with the utmost care and respect. They would not do *anything* without my prior approval. I appreciated the doctor's honesty and compassion and at that point, I knew we had been sent to the best possible place for Sheri to be.

I went back to where Sheri waited and the doctor followed me. She explained to Sheri that she wanted to run a CAT scan to check out her internal organs. Sheri started to panic. The doctor reassured her that the test was quick and would not hurt her in any way. Telling Sheri what to expect did not ease her mind. She started to become agitated. The doctor told her she would give her something to relax if she wanted and Sheri agreed to this. The doctor left the cubical to get the tests ordered.

While we waited, Sheri's attorney arrived. I spoke with him alone and then together we went in to talk with her. He had all of the papers prepared for Sheri to sign, including her will, power of attorney, and medical power of attorney. Sheri gave me full medical and regular powers of attorney so I could make decisions on her behalf. When everything was all signed and the attorney had left, Sheri turned to me and asked me if I was relieved; she got a slight smile on her face when she asked this. I answered, her telling her I was. Then it all hit me! My sister had gone through all of this for me! She realized how tired and worried I was, so she put her own feelings aside and agreed to go into the hospital. I could see a look of relief come over her when she heard me say I was relieved. Again, my big sister was looking out for my best interests.

Within about thirty minutes, the doctor came back in and told us they were ready to do the CAT scan. She gave Sheri medication in the IV they had started earlier. As we started to wheel down to the CAT scan, I could tell Sheri was fighting the medicine. She became agitated. I tried to reassure her and tried to get her to relax, so the medicine would take effect. When we got into the CAT scan room, she took one look at the machine she was going to be put into, and she started to panic. The x-ray technician and myself tried to talk her down, but they ended up having to call the doctor. The doctor came and together we tried to explain to Sheri that there was absolutely nothing that was going to hurt during this quick test but she did not buy it! Finally, I asked the doctor if I could stay in the room with Sheri while she went through the test. The doctor agreed, which they rarely do because of radiation exposure. But this time, they made an exception. I had to don the apron, taking all precautions so to not become overexposed to the harmful rays. We started the test and, after two tries, we were finally able to get Sheri through it. When they were finished, Sheri started to doze off. They wheeled her back to emergency and I waited for her doctor.

In about 30 minutes, a nurse came in and told me the doctor wanted to see me again. I followed the nurse into a small office and waited. I left Sheri sleeping. Two doctors came in as well as the head nurse of the Oncology Department. They proceeded to tell me that the cancer had spread all through Sheri's body and it was only a matter of a few days, if that. They all spoke with compassion and seemed to be concerned about me as well. They asked me what I wanted to do, and they gave me options to consider. The main thing was to see that Sheri did not suffer. After talking, we decided to go ahead and admit her there at the hospital and this would give me a couple of days to try to convince Sheri to go into a hospice facility. With her refusing any type of treatment, the hospital could only hold her for two days due to insurance requirements. I knew I could not possibly take her back to her house because it was so cluttered and unlivable and it would have been next to impossible to have hospice services visit her at home. I had to get Sheri to agree to go to a hospice facility. This was going to be an enormous task, seeing as how I had made a promise to my sister that I would not discuss her condition with her; she did not want to know anything. How do you convince someone to go to a hospice facility when he or she does not want to know they are at nearing the end of their life? This was a most difficult thing with which to deal. I owed Sheri the respect of letting her be a part of the plan, but then again, I knew it might come down to me having to do something that she was totally against. I did a lot of praying, over and over again, for strength and guidance. The Lord had seen us through this far, but I knew we still had a way to go. I knew He was by our side and giving us the strength, even though it was not an easy road ahead.

3-5-2007 **192 lbs.**

During the time they were admitting Sheri and getting her settled in her room, I met with the whole medical staff that would take care of her. Because Maricopa County Hospital is a teaching hospital, she had several doctors assigned to her. Every one of them was concerned and compassionate in their approach to her care. It was a group of fine young doctors. I had not experienced so many outwardly caring doctors at one place before. In my experience, most of the time I might have come across one or two who went beyond the call of duty, but to have all of the doctors involved, and genuinely feel your pain right along beside you, is rare. I have to say, this staff was the greatest possible group of people that could have been assembled to take over Sheri's care. They were the answer to many, many prayers.

Only one incident took place that should never have happened. When they got Sheri to her room in the telemetry unit, they placed a catheter in her bladder. Evidently, this was standard procedure for patients in this area. The catheter caused her extreme pain, and when I went into the room to see her, she was crying and told me how much pain she was in due to the procedure. I ordered the nurse to remove the catheter because they had placed it without my permission and Sheri was having no difficulty going to the bathroom on her own. The nurse got a little bit huffy with me but this did not matter to me one bit. They all knew I had medical power of attorney and nothing was to be done to my sister without my approval. Sheri trusted me not to let them hurt her and I was going to live up to this trust. This issue was resolved immediately and I apologized to Sheri and told her nothing like this would happen again. She relaxed, and the medicine they had given her for the earlier tests allowed her to go back to sleep.

By this time, it was about midnight. The doctor who was in charge of Sheri insisted I go home and get some rest. She assured me she would call me if there were any change; I made her promise, which she did. I caught a ride home with a friend and colleague of Sheri's who had come to the hospital as soon as she learned we were there. Manuela was one of Sheri's true friends and I appreciate everything she did for my sister. Manuela is one of the finest people I have ever had the pleasure of knowing. I thank her for all of her prayers and generous acts of love and kindness she showed to not only Sheri but also my whole family. We all love Manuela, and I know Sheri did also, with all of her heart.

After I returned to the house that morning, I could not sleep. I think I was so overly tired that my body had gone into overdrive and I had become completely hyped up. I spent the next few hours going through paperwork, such as insurance and unpaid bills that were due. I had many checks to write including for utilities to keep things from being turned off. Sheri had fallen behind in many payments so I had to spend time sorting through everything to make sure I did not miss something that would result in further problems. By about 4:30, I had finished and I made a call to the hospital to check on her. I asked for the doctor and the nurse at the nurse's station told me she would have the doctor call me back shortly; she was in with Sheri. I asked the nurse if everything was all right and she replied again with the statement she would have the doctor call me. This made me nervous. I wanted to jump in the car and drive back to the hospital but I did not want to miss the doctor's call. I was having trouble with my cell phone at the time; my battery was old and was not holding a complete charge so sometimes someone would try to call me and I would not get the call. I could not depend on it. So, I anxiously awaited the phone call to come. About 45 minutes later, the phone rang and it was one of the doctors. She told me Sheri had a bad spell with her breathing and there was some confusion with a D.N.R. order. D.N.R. stands for <u>Do Not Resuscitate!</u> I was confused when the doctor told me about what had taken place. Evidently, Sheri had quit breathing and because of the misplacing of the D.N.R. order in her chart, they did not know how to react. The doctors and I had discussed earlier that I really needed to convince Sheri to sign a D.N R. order because when the time came, they could sustain her life on life support, but there was no hope at this point that she could get better; it would only prolong the inevitable. When Sheri signed all of the other papers, she signed a D.N.R. order, but it seemed like she was confused about what she was signing. With the confusion, the doctor who answered the emergency call did not know the full situation. This doctor asked Sheri if she wanted them to do everything they could to save her life if it came down to this. Of course, Sheri nodded "yes" and they proceeded with the medications and actions to sustain her life. I was still unclear as to what had taken place. The doctor told me everything was okay at that point, but I could not stay at the house any longer. I got ready and went back to the hospital; I needed to get to the bottom of what had exactly happened.

3-6-2007   **190 lbs.**

When I arrived, the doctor met me outside of Sheri's room and told me they had talked her in to taking some pain medicine and that she was resting comfortably. After talking with the doctor, I stepped inside to see Sheri. She woke up and told me what had happened during the night. She told me she choked while she was taking a breathing treatment and the staff thought she had quit breathing. The way they reacted scared her. Then, when they asked her if she wanted them to do everything they could to keep her alive, she told them "yes"! This is what the confusion was regarding the D.N.R. order. Sheri knew she was only choking due to extreme phlegm. This had been happening quite frequently; they panicked, which in turn made her panic. We talked it over and she did agree with the original order she had signed.

That Friday was an extremely difficult day. I knew I had to try and talk Sheri into going to a hospice facility, but I knew I had to handle her carefully and to not get her upset. I scheduled a meeting with the medical staff and I asked some of Sheri's closest friends to join me so I had some moral support. Our father was scheduled to arrive in Phoenix on Sunday, so I was by myself with the exception of those close friends. I asked them to join me in the meeting because they had been with Sheri through the last few months and they knew how set she was against medical intervention. At one point, they tried to schedule an intervention with her because they all thought she needed to see a doctor. When they did this, she got wind of what they were doing and she got very upset with them. She basically told them to "butt out!" This hurt them deeply because they all cared for her and could see she was quickly going downhill. When they agreed to meet with me and her doctors, I was grateful. I knew they could shed some light on the situation and with their help, I felt we could together come up with some way to present the hospice idea to Sheri.

The meeting was very emotional for all of us. Sheri's boss also came to the meeting to express his insight and concern. As I had said before, she worked with a great group of people who showed her great compassion even though she had turned away from them at times, especially when she thought they were pushing her about her medical condition.

After the meeting, I had two days left to get her transferred. Her insurance was not going to allow her to stay at the hospital any longer, but they would pay for hospice. This was weighing heavily on my mind because I knew she was going to back away from the whole idea. She had made several statements to me telling me she could not wait to get back home. This only added to the problem.

As the day progressed, Sheri started getting sick to her stomach due to the drugs they were giving her for pain. She decided she did not want any more medication. Of course, we had to stop the drugs. Without the medication, her breathing became even more labored and I knew she was suffering. I tried to convince her to let them give her the pain medicine. She refused because it made her incoherent and she said she felt "spaced out." After having such a bad day, I told the doctors to give her a lesser dose of morphine. They agreed and I was able to talk Sheri into it by late that evening.

I stayed with her until about midnight. When she got the dose of morphine, she drifted right off to sleep. I was there in case she woke up and needed something. She was in a room that had three other patients and a nurse assigned to the room. The nurse stayed in the room at all times, monitoring the patients, but they allowed me to stay with her for as long as I wanted. When she was awake, I sang to her to help her relax. It always helped and soothed her. I also continued to give her relaxing back rubs.

When I left late that night, I went back to her house and hit the bed. Again, I could not sleep. When I was away from the hospital, I felt I needed to be there in case she needed me. I was torn, and this contributed to my not being able to sleep. After hours of tossing and turning, I got up and went back to the hospital and I remained there all day Saturday.

During the day, I tried to talk with Sheri about a hospice. I told her I knew she did not want to know anything about her condition but I had some things I needed to talk about; she told me she was not ready to talk about it. This just added to my stress because I knew I had to make a decision quickly. The doctors gathered hospice information for me so I could choose the place I wanted to move her. I decided on a place called Hospice of the Valley. This facility had many things to offer their patients such as music therapy, massage therapy, and aromatherapy. It sounded like the ideal place for Sheri because she loved all of those things. They also offered cello and harp music; musicians donated their time to travel to different hospice facilities and play for the patients. I thought this was a lovely act of love and kindness. I knew Sheri would thoroughly enjoy it. She loved the cello but most of all, she loved the harp. At one time, she had even taken harp lessons. She owned a beautiful harp of her own, which sat, regally, in her living room. She did not take lessons for long but she still wanted to learn to play. After reading all of the information on Hospice of the Valley, I made the final decision. Now all I had to do was present it to her and get her to agree, without me having to go ahead and make the decision without her approval. I only had one more day to get this accomplished.

Sheri had many friends who wanted to visit her in the hospital. She decided she did not want anyone to see her in the condition she was in, so she told me she wanted no visitors. This was difficult for me because so many of her friends came to the hospital to see her and give her their love and support. My sister was a very proud person; she thought she had to look like a million dollars at all times. I felt at this particular time in her life, Sheri needed all of the love and support she could get. Unfortunately, her vanity was prevailing over what I felt she really needed. I tried to explain that her friends wanted to show they loved her. She listened to me but she did not give in. Therefore, I had to make the call; no one could visit her. This hurt me deeply to have to tell her friends that she was not up to being seen. I smoothed it over by telling them she was weak and it was difficult to have people around her, draining her energy. In a way, I was telling the truth but in a way, it was not the complete truth. When I told her friends this, some of them had their feelings hurt. It was understandable, and it hurt me deeply to tell them this, but most of these people stayed at the hospital anyway to give me support even though they could not see Sheri.

Sheri did allow one friend from work to visit her. This friend had some of the same beliefs Sheri had. They were both into the New Age movement. This lady brought crystals to the hospital along with lavender oil and other items. She wanted to spend some time with Sheri so they could meditate together. I left them alone for about an hour. After the friend left, I could see an improvement in Sheri's mental state; she seemed to be much more relaxed. At this point, I welcomed whatever helped her frame of mind. Even though I did not have the same beliefs as Sheri, it mattered to me that she was at peace. It still bothered me, however, that Sheri would not see the friends who she had been so close to for many years. I could not understand what her reasons were. She let someone visit whom she had known for a short time, yet the people who she had known and loved for years, she turned away. I guess I will never understand this, but that is okay.

When I got back to the house, the phone rang. It was very late. When I answered, the woman on the other end of the line assumed I was Sheri. She started talking about an upcoming high school reunion. I had to tell her who I was, and when I did, she identified herself as one of Sheri's friends when she was growing up. I told her about Sheri's illness and gave her the news that it was only a matter of time. She was shocked! We talked for awhile and she told me she would let others know. About 10 minutes later, the phone rang again; it was Sheri's best friend from childhood, Roberta. She had just found out about Sheri's condition and she told me she was on her way to see her.

Roberta lived in El Paso. This was an eight-hour drive, but she was determined to come and I did not have the heart to tell her no. I just decided to surprise Sheri. I was afraid that Sheri would be gone by the time Roberta arrived; I told Roberta this and she accepted the news but she was coming, no matter what. We left it at that and she arrived at around ten in the morning. I did not get Sheri's approval to let Roberta see her; I just let her walk into the room. I warned Roberta about Sheri's appearance so she would not be so shocked when she saw her. When she got into the room, it took Sheri a couple of seconds to recognize Roberta. I know Roberta had to have been shocked because she had not seen Sheri in years. They both got tears in their eyes and talked for about 10 minutes. Sheri then told Roberta she could not visit anymore because she was so weak. Roberta took the signal and gave her a kiss and a hug, and then she left the room. She and I talked outside; she was very sad. She had come a long way to see her childhood friend and even though it was only for a few minutes, I at least hoped she got some closure. I felt bad she could not visit Sheri any longer but she fully understood. What a friend she truly was.

3-8-2007   **191 lbs.**

The same day Roberta came, our father arrived. A friend picked him up from the airport and brought him straight to the hospital. I told the friend to stop at the nurse's station and have them notify me before they walked into Sheri's room. I wanted to make sure our father was fully prepared before he saw Sheri. I knew it would be a blow for him. When they arrived, I spoke with him and then we went in together. When he saw Sheri, he was at a loss for words. He just hugged her and they both teared up, and then told each other they loved each other. We all sat there quietly for a few minutes and then she fell asleep. Dad and I stepped outside and talked. He was so taken aback by her appearance, he told me he would have never recognized her if he did not know it was her lying there. It was very sad for him to see his daughter in such distress and so ill. Even though this was most difficult for him, he ended up staying at the hospital most of the day.

The next morning came and I had to get Sheri moved to the hospice and still she had not approved it. I went in to see her by myself and told her we had to talk. I just opened up to her in the calmest way I knew, and told her about the place I had chosen. I tried to sell her on all of the things they offered there and she understood what I was saying. I asked her doctors to go ahead and plan the transfer.

Sheri's neighbor, who I was suspicious of when I very first arrived in Phoenix, showed up at the hospital and wanted to see Sheri. Sheri agreed to let her in as long as she did not talk; Sheri wanted complete quiet. I pulled the woman aside and told her to go in but not to talk to Sheri because she wanted complete silence around her. The woman stepped into to Sheri's room and I followed her in. Within a minute or two, one of the doctors came in and asked to speak with me. We stepped outside into the hallway to talk. Suddenly, I heard the woman in the room with my sister start talking to Sheri, asking her why she did not want to go back home to her own house where she would be more comfortable. When I heard this, I became furious! This woman knew it was impossible for us to take Sheri home due to the living conditions. How dare she interfere with plans that took me three days to get Sheri to agree to! This woman knew the difficulty I was faced with, and here she was trying to undo everything I had just accomplished. My blood was boiling and I walked into the room and told her to come outside with me because I needed to talk with her. When she did, I came unglued and basically told her to butt out, mind her own business and how dare she do what she did. I am still angry about that whole situation. This woman stepped in on my sister at a time when she was most vulnerable and tried to ramrod things into Sheri's life. I resented her then and truthfully, I am still working on this. I have to work it out internally, but what she did is almost unforgivable to me. During the course of Sheri's late illness and even after her death, this person tried time and time again to push her way into my business and she did some pretty rotten things to my family and me. It is so sad that there are people who think they can step all over somebody to further their own personal agenda. I think as far as the neighbor was concerned, she thought she was owed some part of Sheri, but this was the furthest thing from the truth. I still think she was worming her way into Sheri's business so Sheri would turn her finances over to the neighbor. I said it once and I will say it again; she tried her darnedest to take over my sister's life and not only was this apparent to me, but to others as well. Not one person trusted her and I feel that was for good reason!

3-9-2007   **190 lbs.**

The transfer of Sheri to the hospice was a traumatic experience for all concerned. I had built up the facility to her, telling her how great it was and explained all of the amenities it had to offer. I had not personally seen the facility but the representative told me it was a lovely place and I trusted this to be the fact.

When the time came to move Sheri, we had to take her by ambulance, even though the facility was only around the corner from the hospital. We made it there and when we got inside, they took us to a very small room with two beds crammed close together. This was not acceptable! Sheri was to have a big private room. I was furious. The look on my poor sister's face broke my heart as well as our father's. I assured Sheri we would see to it the situation was changed. I expressed my dissatisfaction to the staff immediately by telling them this is not what they promised me. They assured me Sheri would be moved into a private room later that evening. They had to transfer a patient in order to accommodate my sister. The move was done and all was well.

The next few days were touch and go. Sheri had made it longer than anyone expected. She was getting some rest because they were giving her drugs both orally and through her breathing treatments. She was not very aware of what they were doing but I gave them the go ahead because I knew she was trying to tough it out and I did not want her suffering. We spent as much time with her as we could but still allowed her to rest as much as possible, and the staff at the hospice was wonderful with her. They truly cared about their patients and their dignity, making sure they tried to accommodate their patients' requests, making them as comfortable as possible. I greatly appreciated this because when I was not there with Sheri, I knew she was in good hands.

On Thursday morning, June 9, 2005, four days after Sheri was transferred, we arrived at the hospice to see her. She was sitting up in bed smiling at us when we walked in. We were amazed to see her looking more like her old self. She proceeded to tell us how much better she was feeling and it definitely showed up on her face. We were able to spend quality time visiting with her for about two hours. She then told me she had had a brainstorm earlier that morning, and she wanted me to go out and buy a notebook and bring it back to her; we needed to make some notes. I had no idea what she had in mind but then she added, "You and I are going on *Oprah!*" I looked at her, and she had that little girl grin on her face. I started trying to pry more information from her but she would not go into it any further. My father and I left and went to eat and then I stopped and bought a notebook as per Sheri's request. We had some errands to run and she had told us to take our time coming back because she wanted to get some rest, so we took our time and did not return until later in the day.

When we returned, it was a different person lying there than earlier in the day. Sheri looked so weak and fragile. Her breathing was more labored and she was obviously in pain. I spent the next two hours massaging her shoulders and back trying to get her to relax so the medicine would help more. She would doze off and on. I literally climbed up in bed with her and cradled her in front of me so I could get a better angle with which to work on her. At this point, my own exhaustion was taking over and I could feel myself losing the battle with sleep deprivation. After a while, I am sure Sheri could feel my own exhaustion as I struggled to keep working on Sheri. Finally, I had to stop. She told me she knew I was tired but she asked us to stay just a little while longer because she could feel herself floating in and out of her body. She told me she needed me to keep her grounded. We stayed for about an hour more until she went to sleep and remained quiet. We left, but not before telling the nurses to call if she woke up and wanted me there. They agreed to do so.

We made it through the night without a phone call. Our father suggested we go get breakfast before going to see her but I told him I felt we needed to get straight to the hospice. There was a feeling hanging over me and I needed to see her as soon as possible. We arrived at about nine, and as we rounded the corner to her room, one of the nurses stopped us and told us they were in with her changing her bed. She also pulled me aside and told me she felt Sheri had already "let go." Sheri was not visibly conscious and the nurse, being a very religious woman, told me she felt Sheri's spirit had already left her body. I waited until they got the bed changed and then I went in. My sister was lying there completely still, with the exception of a labored breath every now and then. I went over to her and placed my hand on her head. I started stroking her hair and I talked to her very softly telling her it was okay for her to go to the light because I was there and she was not alone. I knew she was waiting until I got there. There was no doubt in my mind.

I spent the next thirty minutes or so singing gently and softly to her. I held her in my arms while her breaths became fewer and further between. She was gradually drifting away from us, with me by her side. After a while, our father stepped into the room and I gave him a look to let him know it was time. He sat down quietly as I sang the Lord's Prayer to her and within about a minute my beautiful big sister had taken her final breath of life. Slowly I got up and hugged my father and then I stepped out of the room and notified the nurses that Sheri was gone. One came in and listened to her chest and then they left us alone. We sat in silence for about thirty more minutes while I just stared at her, lying there so still. Then, I started glancing around the room and I spotted a hat that I had bought a few days earlier and gave to her to cheer her up. I stood up and retrieved the hat, which was sitting on the back of one of the chairs in the room, and I placed it on her head.

I tidied up around Sheri, kissed her goodbye, and then we left the room and found a private telephone so I could start making calls. Something kept running through my mind while I robotically made call after call. It was the words of a song that I sang to Sheri many times. I remember those beautiful and cherished words: "Bows and flows of angel hair and ice cream castles in the air...".

SHERI ELAINE DYE RYAN

JANUARY 6, 1947 - JUNE 10, 2005

Before I close out this chapter, and I know it has been a long one, I would like to touch on the funeral and memorial given to Sheri. Her wishes were very precise, and I wanted to stay true to these wishes. My family and I decided to bring her back with us to Kentucky and have the funeral there with her internment in our family plot, alongside our mother. My dad and I stayed in Phoenix for five days while I made all arrangements over the phone for her transfer and funeral. We wanted our own pastor to conduct the service; even though he had never met Sheri, he was very aware of her struggles and was a great moral support for all of us. Our church family also kept in constant contact with me the whole time I was in Arizona and they sent Sheri, as well as me, letters and cards letting us know they were praying for her and the family as a whole. She really appreciated hearing from my friends and she told me she thought it was so special that they cared for us the way they did. I told Sheri stories about my church family and how much I loved them and how much they accepted me and made me feel so at home in the church. Sheri knew what a big step it was for me to join a church and even though our beliefs were a little different, she respected my commitment and was genuinely happy for me that I had found a religious home.

Because Sheri had so many friends in Arizona who wanted to honor her life, we decided to also have a memorial for her there, about three weeks after the Kentucky funeral. I had to travel back to Phoenix to take care of her estate and I knew I would be there a majority of the summer, so we decided to do the memorial in July. Sheri had made it quite clear that she wanted a big party; she wanted a celebration with friends enjoying themselves and remembering the good times they had shared. Everyone who knew her well knew this was her wish and everyone wanted to pitch in to make sure it was the celebration she would have approved and been proud of.

Her funeral in Kentucky was small and lovely. I gave our pastor instructions on how I wanted it to proceed and he did everything he could to make sure my wishes were granted. I ended up giving the eulogy and it was a precious experience for me to do so. My sadness seemed to disappear and as I talked about her life, I touched on the beautiful, the humorous, and the precious times we shared as sisters. I had no script to follow but the words came to me without struggle and I felt her presence right alongside me the whole time I spoke. I picked a poem written by Robert Frost to recite and I had one of my best friends, Lucio, sing "How Great Thou Art." Lucio knew Sheri, and she loved him and his incredible musical talent, so this was very fitting. My daughter Sandra also chose a Faith Hill song and we both selected "My Heart Will Go On" from the movie *Titanic*, one of Sheri's favorite movies.

Everything turned out to be lovely. I ended up wearing a necklace that Sheri had made a few years earlier and on this necklace there was a little vile at the end of it filled with glitter. She called it "fairy dust" because she loved to dress up like a fairy at Halloween and entertain the neighborhood children by blowing the glitter, or "fairy dust", on them. I had no idea why I chose to wear that particular necklace of hers that day until the end of the eulogy. I opened up the tiny vile, poured out some of the "fairy dust" into my hand and walked over to her casket. As I said, "Dance, my beautiful sister, dance!" I blew the glitter into the air, showering it over the beautiful box in which my sister lay. This action just came over me and it seemed so fitting considering the "fairy princess angel" and beautiful "dancer" Sheri truly was.

Nothing more needed to be said after that moment.

My dad and I traveled back to Phoenix the first week in July. My daughter Sandra and my son Jeffrey joined us there. We decided to hold the memorial on July 14, 2005 at a cultural center in Phoenix close to where Sheri had worked for the city. Many of her co-workers and friends helped organize the memorial, which was a huge help to our family. Everyone pitched in by making most of the arrangements and they left little for us to do in the planning. The celebration took place that Thursday evening and what a celebration it turned out to be! We sang, we danced, we laughed, we cried, we ate, and most of all, we rejoiced in Sheri's life and celebrated her in a fashion she would have been most accepting of. Her friends put together a song and dance routine, which made us laugh! Sandra sang "Somewhere over the Rainbow" which made us cry. I sang "Both Sides Now" which had become Sheri's song, and a friend and neighbor of Sheri's conducted the service, paying tribute to Sheri's beliefs. This friend was an ordained minister and offered her services to us, which we greatly appreciated. I had never attended such a celebration of life and it was beautiful. Sheri was so well loved by everybody that knew her and this became even more apparent to our family as we listened to her friends tell stories about their special connections to her. My sadness upon losing my big sister eased as we celebrated her time with us and realized just how lucky we were to have had her in our lives. The light she brought to all who knew her will shine on and on for the rest of our lives. How special we are to have had such a beautiful person touch our lives and bless us with her grace and kindness. Her light will go on, as our memories of her will never fade.

CHAPTER EIGHT

THERE ARE ANGELS ALL AROUND US

3-12-2007   **190 lbs.**

Several times in my life, I know I have had angels watching out for me. Yet until the time just after my sister's passing, I was not aware of so many angels in my life being at one place and one time. This became apparent when I had to make plans to settle my sister's estate.

Before I returned to Arizona to spend the next two months finalizing the estate, I made two telephone calls, which put me in contact with my "angels" who saw me through a very difficult situation and became lifesavers to my family and me. When I left Phoenix to come back home for the funeral, I had thumbed through the telephone book's yellow pages and found a page of estate planners. I tore out this page and brought it back home with me. At this point, I really had no idea how I was going to approach the subject of taking care of all of my sister's belongings. It was completely overwhelming for me to think about. She had more possessions than anyone I had ever known and it was left up to me to decide exactly how to manage her estate and what to do with all of her stuff. Basically, she had left everything to me but there was no way I could keep all of her things. I would have had to build a five thousand square foot home to accommodate her things alone! The crazy thing though, was the fact that she had all of this stuff in her little eleven hundred square foot home along with her garage, a storage building and a storage locker she had rented.

In the last chapter, I talked about the condition of my sister's home and her living conditions. It became apparent that in the last two years of her life, she became obsessed with buying things and she basically cocooned herself into her home, surrounding herself with all of these possessions. She always had a lot of things, but I was in disbelief when I discovered how much stuff she had accumulated since I had seen her last. There was literally not one square inch of her house that was empty. You could not even walk in her home; you had to squeeze through furniture, clothes, books, magazines, suitcases, dolls and all kinds of stuffed animals, including a whole collection of designer teddy bears, ranging from twelve inches in height to life size! There were also boxes of fabric material, linens, china, glassware, etc. Her kitchen was completely nonfunctioning because there was no counter space that was not covered with something. The stove was completely covered up with stuff and even the inside of the oven was used for storage. The kitchen table was stacked up about to about two feet high in dishes, and the cupboards were completely full. The refrigerator and freezer were both crammed with old food. Then, to top it off, she had five cats living in the kitchen with two cat boxes, and all of their food bowls; she never allowed them out of the kitchen. They were all grown cats she had adopted from the neighborhood. Then there were her two dogs! One was a large three-legged shepherd mix and the other a little terrier mix; both lived in the house as well! The large bathroom in the house was not functioning. The toilet in this bathroom leaked terribly, so the water had to be turned off to it and the bathtub hardly drained. You could find no counter space to even place a toothbrush on, and you could not shut the door because of the clothes hanging on it! The other bathroom was very tiny, with a shower full of toolboxes and all kinds of household tools stacked three quarters of the way up the walls! Obviously, it could not be used. The tiny laundry room was full of bottled water, which was the only thing she and the animals drank. There were brooms, mops and vacuums in there as well. The dining room was completely stacked high with the large dining table being used as storage space for all kinds of things. The living room was a total disaster because she had hired someone to redo the electrical work, and this person started the job and then skipped out on her. It was all stripped with wires hanging down. There was plastic over all of her furniture, including three sofas, very large chairs, antique tables, tea carts, china cabinets, a baby crib full of bears, a large harp, rolled-up oriental rugs, a very large entertainment center and an oddly-shaped geometrical desk! The den was full of books, jewelry-making items, clothes hanging on three commercial clothes racks, all kinds of craft items, more stuffed animals, two large floor-to-ceiling doll cases and a very large therapeutic back massage bed that was about eight-feet long. There were Christmas, Halloween, Thanksgiving, Fourth of July, and Easter decorations everywhere! Even though I have tried to paint a picture, you cannot possibly imagine what this home looked like. As I write this and thinking back, I still cannot believe it; it was *totally* unbelievable. My sister had lost touch with reality and the more I got into it, the more I realized she had another illness along with the cancer that claimed her life.

3-13-2007   **189 lbs.**

With the situation as it was, I had to figure out the best way to clear the house so I could put it on the market to sell. The last thing I needed was a house in Arizona. Knowing I could only keep a fraction of my sister's things, I also had to decide what to do with the rest of her belongings. I knew there was a fortune tied up in these possessions. After giving it much thought, I pulled out the page I had torn out of the yellow pages and my eyes rested on one name and number; I placed the first call. A gentleman answered the phone and I started explaining my situation to him. He listened patiently, and after I finished explaining what I needed, he told me that his company would not be able to handle such a large job. He did, however know of two companies who could possibly help me. He gave me the name of both companies and their telephone numbers. I thanked him for his time and information then hung up the phone. I looked at the names he had given me and one name stood out: Sally Mae's. This was actually the second name the man had given me. I dialed the number. It was a cell phone number and I left a message. Within about twenty minutes, my phone rang and when I answered, there was a gentleman on the other end of the line stating he was returning my call. He introduced himself as Zack. We talked for about five minutes and I realized that the other person on the end of the line was genuinely concerned about my circumstances and he seemed helpful and kind. I explained to him that I would be back in Arizona in a few days and he told me to call him when I got in, and we would make an appointment to meet and talk about his company doing the estate sale for me. I tried to explain the extreme conditions we would be working with, the huge amount of stuff, and the limited space at the house, and I told him to expect the worst conditions he had ever experienced and multiply that by about one hundred! This could possibly give him an idea of how severe the situation was. He laughed and told me that their company had just done a next-to-impossible sale in a home with similar conditions. He said he was up for the job! We talked briefly about his charges and he gave me a quote so I'd know what to expect. I told him he ought to wait until he actually saw the house before he committed. He ended up giving me a high and low figure. In a few minutes we finished our conversation with the understanding I would call him when I got into Phoenix. He said he looked forward to meeting me and I felt hopeful after speaking with him.

Sometimes we come across people who just "click" with us. After talking with Zack on the phone, I never called the other company. I did not call anyone else, period. It felt like a done deal even though we had not met, Zack had not seen the house, and there were other options that I chose not to investigate. I felt secure that this was what I needed to do and it was going to work out just fine. My family was not as sure as I was but I told them this is what I felt needed to be done and I did not deviate from that position. When I talked to Zack on the telephone we seemed to hit it off so well that I knew we were matched up for a reason. His genuine sincerity and his sense of humor over the telephone impressed me and it felt like we were family, even though we had never met.

After arriving in Phoenix, I called Zack and arranged for him to meet me at the house. Within about an hour of me calling, he showed up. As I tried to walk him through the house, I could see on his face the amazement as he looked at all of the stuff scattered around. One thing he mentioned within just a few minutes was the fact that my sister had extremely expensive taste as well as good taste. She did not own junk even though the house looked junked out. All of her things were of the finest quality. As I had mentioned before, there was a whole lot of money tied up in her belongings. After Zack and I finished in the inside, I took him outside to the backyard where again, there were things everywhere. Sheri had prided herself in her yard and its furnishings and there was almost as much stuff in the yard as there was inside the house. After Zack looked over the yard, we moved on to the garage. When I opened it up, it was stacked completely to the ceiling with box upon box; you could not even get inside! All Zack could say was, "Oh wow!" It took only a few seconds to realize we would have no idea what was in there until we could take everything out and start going through it. At this point, I felt for sure that Zack would either tell me it was way too much for his company to handle or that the price would be at the high end of his quote.

After we walked back into the house, he told me he was positive they would do a good job for us. He said he thought it would take at least one week to go through stuff before the first sale. He explained that this would have to be a two-part sale because of the volume. There would be one week to prepare for the first weekend sale and then another week to plan for the second weekend sale. He said they were up for it if I was ready, and then he gave me his price. It was the lower price he had previously quoted. I could not believe it; I was jumping for joy inside! In addition, we hit it off in person as much as we did over the phone. He was kind, he had a great personality and he had a warm presence. I felt very good about the deal!

We discussed dates and settled on the day that we would get started. I wanted one week to go through things with my dad and kids before the company came in and started organizing. I knew we were going to have to rent a big truck to transport the things we chose to keep, and this would take a day or so to do. I wanted to get as much done as we could before Zack and his team started doing their magic.

We took the next week to go through some of my sister's things; this also was the week of the memorial service. Come Monday morning, July 18, Zack and about six of his employees converged on the place. It was unbelievable how, within half a day, they had set up in the living room some of the finest pieces of furniture and antiques I had ever seen. These people were like a whirlwind coming down, and it was incredible what they accomplished in just one day; I was truly amazed! Of course, the rest of the house looked like a tornado had hit it, but the living room had been turned into a show room!

This was the starting point. Later that evening, they invited some of their cherished customers to come and preview the sale. Zack gave these dealers first shot at the finery before it was opened up to the public. They sold quite a few items that first evening!

The rest of that first week was crazy. My kids had gone back home and my dad and I were still staying at the house trying to sort through stuff as the estate planners continued doing their thing. We knew we were going to have to move to a motel the following week because the company needed us out of their way so they could get into the bedrooms to set up displays. We still had plenty of work to do before the second week came.

The first weekend sale arrived, and it lasted two days. Zack advertised it as being the biggest estate sale in the state of Arizona! He later told me it was the biggest sale he or his company had ever done. My dad and I were not allowed to stay and watch; we had to leave the premises. This was their company policy and we abided by it. We left early, about six in the morning, and returned after six that evening to find they had done an amazing job! Even though it did not look like a lot of the things were gone, there actually was a great deal of stuff sold. We were all very pleased at the volume that first weekend sale brought.

3-15-2007   **188 lbs.**

The process of the estate company going through all of the things my sister had was a little painful to watch at times. They worked each day until late in the evening, trying to get everything organized. They actually had shifts working where there were at least five or six people working at all times; Zack even recruited help from his friends and associates. This turned out to be the greatest group of people I have had the pleasure of working with. Each person who worked at the house made sure I was comfortable. They all understood the emotional aspect of seeing a loved one's things being gone through by strangers. This was a difficult situation, even with the wonderful assistance we had received.

There were some things I had been looking for in the house that I knew existed but that I could not locate. I made sure the staff of the estate company knew what I was looking for so they could be on the lookout for the items. As they started going through closets that were packed to the ceiling, these things were located, with the exception of a set of silver that I knew Sheri had. We had found *other* sets of silver but not this particular set, which had meant a lot to me. It had been her first set of silver and the pattern was discontinued many years earlier. This set of silver matched my décor and I wanted to take it home with me. We looked and looked. I did not think she had sold it because with the condition of her home, it was obvious she never let anything go; she kept everything she had ever owned! In the second week of preparation for the second sale, one of the gentlemen with the company started working in the back room where she had all of her craft things. Underneath the table where she at one time made jewelry, amongst boxes and stacks and stacks of plastic containers, there lay a little blue cloth all wrapped up and tied. It was the missing set of silver. All of the dinnerware was rolled up inside of the cloth, hiding under that table. I started crying when he found it because up until that point, it did not look like the missing silver would ever be found.

I learned a lot of things while preparing for the sale. We had to rent a very large dumpster to accommodate all of the trash that was taken from the home. This dumpster took up the whole side of the road by the house. One evening while the estate planners were working, my dad and I went to dinner around 7:00. We finished around 8:30 and drove back to the house to check on the progress. As we rounded the corner, there were two women crawling out of the dumpster! They were not the estate planners; I recognized them as neighbors! Never in my life have I seen a dumpster parked anywhere and thought to myself, "Gee, I should go dumpster diving to see what treasures I might find!" This really has not been an issue for me, yet there they were and I could not believe my eyes! These two women looked very shocked when they realized I had come back and was there, staring at them in disbelief. They had thrown things out of the dumpster onto the ground so they could retrieve them and take them home. You have to understand, the stuff that was thrown in that dumpster was pure junk; the planners would not have thrown anything away they thought they could sell. Why on earth would someone jump into a dirty, filthy garbage container and pull things out of it? It was not a poor neighborhood; it was a very clean upscale area with nice, expensive homes! But you know what? Junk is still junk and trash is still trash, no matter where you are!

When I got out of the car, I approached these two women and asked them exactly what they were doing. I actually felt violated and I was very angry. It felt like they were vultures going in for the dead. I basically told them that if I wanted them to go through the trash, I would have invited them to do so. I was appalled! After me chewing them out, they left with their tails between their legs. I went inside and told one of the planners what I had seen. He told me he had run them out of there twice already! He basically told them the same thing I did. All I can say about this is "the nerve of some people!"

When it came close to the time of the second weekend sale, I had to turn over the master bedroom to the estate planners so they could get in there and set up the furniture for display. Up until then, I had used that room as my office. We were staying at a motel at night but were at the house during the day; I was conducting all of my business from that room. When I had to give up the room, it all became very final for me. That room was my last link to my sister's world, so this was a very difficult thing to do. The planners realized the frame of mind I was in, and they did everything they could to make me comfortable. It felt like I was giving up my security blanket and they knew it was a difficult time for me. Once I did move completely out of the house, however, it became a little easier for me to deal with the sale of Sheri's possessions.

The first day of the second weekend sale, we drove by and saw many cars parked along the street. It was a good crowd. At the end of that day, we went back to the house and at that time, we had the opportunity to take anything left over from the sale and keep it. The following day, everything was marked down half-price to help move it out; anything that did not sell that day became the property of the estate company. We had fully loaded a U-Haul truck with things to take home, and we chose very few leftovers to bring back. The next day was the final sale day. Again, we drove by, and again there was crowd of people going in and out of the house. We returned at about 4:30 and Zack gave me the good news of the total sale. They did an exceptional job and we appreciated their hard work. I think it was an eye opener for them because they did work very hard for two weeks for only 25% of total sales. It was a learning experience for all involved.

When the sale was finalized, the estate planners took what they wanted out of the house and then they turned the rest of the stuff over to an auction company. It took this company about three hours to clear the property. We stayed and talked with them and I discovered that the man in charge was actually the first person I had called from Kentucky! He was the one who recommended Zack's company to me. I thought to myself, *what a small world we live in.*

After the auction company got everything out of the house and everything out of the yard, they cleaned up the place. This was part of the deal. They did have to return the next day to finalize everything but they got it done in a timely manner. After they cleared out, I hired a cleaning service to come in and strip the place down from top to bottom. I was listing the property for sale at the end of the week and I wanted it completely free of any dirt so the real estate company could show it immediately. The realtor I chose told me it would sell within a couple of days because of the location. There was a lot of work to do on the inside, mostly cosmetic, but they told me not to bother with it because it would not affect the sale. We did as they said and chose not to repair anything.

After everything was finalized in Phoenix, my dad and I flew back to Kentucky, so we had to arrange for someone to drive the U-Haul truck back home for us. My son Jeffrey could not take time off work so he was not a candidate. I ended up calling my best friends in Nashville, and asked Lucio if I flew him and Rob, another friend, out to Phoenix, if they could drive the truck back for us. I would pay them to do so and pay all of their expenses. They agreed they would do this for me. I flew them out on Tuesday and they left Wednesday morning to drive home.

3-17-2007   **187 lbs.**

I have to tell the story about the U-Haul truck! Jeffrey and my dad went and rented the truck the first week we returned to Phoenix after the funeral in Kentucky. It all started out with a U-Haul trailer and a hitch installed on my sister's Toyota Camry so Jeffrey and Sandra could drive it back home. Well, it was soon apparent that the trailer was not going to be big enough to haul all of the stuff we were taking back. We came to this conclusion very quickly! Within about one hour of having the trailer, my dad and Jeffrey took it back to the dealer and exchanged it for a big truck. They came back with the truck and parked it on the street in front of the dumpster we rented. Jeffrey and Sandra left a few days later in the Toyota Camry and went back to Kentucky. Jeffrey then flew from Kentucky back to Texas. After they left, a few days passed and we started noticing something leaking from underneath the U-Haul. At this point, the truck was fully loaded down; we had already packed it full! I called the dealer where they rented it and they told me they would exchange it for another truck. There was no way; we had fully loaded that truck when the kids were there to help lift and stack things in it. Neither my eighty four year old father nor I could re-pack another truck. I told them this was not acceptable and they would have to come up with another plan. They ended up sending a mechanic out to work on the truck. He spent a full day on it and I'm still not quite sure what he did or what was wrong. He had it running for sometime, and I am sure he never paid any attention to the fuel gauge. Neither my dad nor Jeffrey had paid any attention to the fuel gauge when they brought it home, so why would the mechanic... right? Well, the gauge showed as empty! This was a diesel engine and you there was no service station anywhere close to us that had diesel fuel for sale. We were sweating it out, big time!

When Lucio and Rob got there to drive the truck back, we broke the news to them about the mechanic who had worked on the vehicle for a full day and the fact that it was out of fuel! I think if we had told them before they made the trip, they might have changed their minds about coming; I know I would have. Anyway, we located the closest service station that had diesel and we ended up following them as they drove there while all of us held our breath. We traveled about five miles and I think they coasted to the pump on fumes! They filled it up, and we all breathed a big sigh of relief. This was one obstacle down with still a major one to go; they now had to make it back home without breaking down somewhere. We said a lot of prayers before they left and many more for the next two days. We kept expecting them to call, telling us they had broken down out in the middle of nowhere, but they never did, thank the good Lord! They made it home in the two-day period without incident. I know and fully believe my beautiful sister Sheri was watching out for them. Yes indeed, there were angels all around.

The next thing I had to do was get the house listed. I had several realtors contact me about listing the property and I had pretty much made a decision. Then, Zack and I were talking one day and he asked me who I had spoken with about the house. I told him, and then he informed me that in the past he had dealings with these people and he would not recommend them to anyone. He then told me about a young man he recommended highly. This person had sold one of the homes Zack's company had done an estate sale for; he was professional and had been very quick to sell the home. I contacted the young man and we set up a meeting at the house amongst the confusion of the estate planning. We pretty much settled on an agreement but the papers would be finalized the Friday we were to leave town. I did not want the home listed until we were gone. We ended up meeting Friday, August 5, 2005 and I signed the listing papers. I told the realtor I expected the house to be sold that very weekend and I expected him to call me with at least three or four offers. I was joking, of course! He then told me this was quite possible! My dad was completely skeptical. I listed the house for $240,000. Dad felt it impossible for this house to sell for that much. We all tried to convince him it would, but he wasn't buying it! I ignored his skepticism and did what I thought needed to be done. Again, I did so with lots of prayers. After I finalized all of my business, we left late that afternoon to return to Kentucky. We actually were stuck at the airport for the whole night due to weather so we did not get home until the following morning, Saturday, August 6.

Sunday afternoon around 3:00, my phone rang. It was Brad, the realtor. He asked me if I was sitting down. I was not sure what to expect, but I was optimistic. He then presented me with five offers on the home! One offer came in at *over* what I was asking. I accepted the offer and we spent the next two hours faxing and signing papers. I called my family and told them the news, and they were elated of course. The house had sold in two days!

3-19-2007   **186 lbs.**

It was really hard to believe that the house had sold that fast because of my previous experiences with real estate. The properties in Phoenix, however, were turning over at light speed! People were selling their homes in California and turning around and relocating to Arizona, paying cash for property. The market was unbelievable; this was a fortunate condition for me. Being out of state and having a property to dispose of could have been a hardship if the situation had been different. Nonetheless, I felt certain the house would turn over immediately. There had been several inquiries about the property and it was located in a very fashionable area. This area had been deemed a historical district about two years earlier, which helped with the value of the property. It was also located close to downtown Phoenix. It was a desirable area to live due to the location, and this helped drive the price up as well as secure a sale. I have learned a valuable lesson. You know what they say: "location, location, location". Well, it proved to be the case, at least in this situation. I know if this same home were located where I live in Kentucky, in the exact same area where my home is located, it would have sold for about $60,000.00! What a big difference!

After I returned home, I still had many loose ends to tie up with the estate. It took me a few months to finalize everything and I remained busy during this whole time. It seemed like every time I turned around to finalize my sister's affairs there was something to do: paperwork to turn in, records to forward, etc. I kept very busy, methodically conducting my business on a daily basis, without allowing myself time to breath, or time to grieve. Everyone kept telling me I would reach a point where I would succumb to all of the emotion and finally break down. I thought I was actually handling things very well and I knew I had to be strong for my father who had just lost his first-born. I had to be the rock, at least so I thought.

3-20-2007   **185.5 lbs.**

In April and May of 2006, I started a physical fitness routine in which I worked out extensively each day. I joined a gym and went each morning to work out on the treadmill, the stationary bike, the elliptical machine and with weights; I was religious in my workouts. It was a good release for stress and I needed the physical activity. I poured myself into my workouts. Starting the month of May, the club where I was working out started a competition. They posted posters all over the health club explaining the contest and its rules; the person who did the most miles on any of their equipment during the month of May would win a free month's membership as well as a t-shirt. The minute I read about the contest, I was determined to go all of the way and win the competition. I started immediately; within about a week, I was doing up to six miles a day on their equipment. We were required to keep daily records of our accomplishments. I would look to see if anyone was getting close to me and then I would double my workout. Before the month was over, I racked up 160 miles at the club as well as about 20 miles on my own, over the weekends. The club was only open Monday through Friday so I did my own workouts on Saturday and Sunday. At the end of the month, I won the competition! I was indeed proud and felt I had done the impossible because of my physical disabilities. I have systemic lupus and had been told by many doctors I would never run again. As a matter of fact, my right knee was supposed to be replaced that very spring! In my condition I should not have been able to accomplish what I just accomplished; at least this is what I had been told. I decided to defy the odds and prove I could do it, and I did.

I cannot tell you this was not hard; I struggled every day. There were days when I felt like pulling the covers up over my head and staying in bed because I ached from head to toe and I could hardly stand it. But on these days, I forced myself up and made myself go and workout. I worked through the pain. Afterwards, I sometimes collapsed in my bed but I always made it up the next day to start all over again.

After the competition was over, there was a race during a local festival that had been posted at the club. I decided to enter it. It was a 3k race and I was doing up to 12 miles a day at that time. This should have been a piece of cake, at least so I thought, but was I ever wrong! I learned there is a big difference between running on pavement and running on a treadmill! Yep, I choked! There were about seventy-five runners in the race and I ended up finishing last, but at least I finished! I could not believe the difference between running at the club and running on the street!

After that experience, I thought I was through with running for the rest of my life. Then a friend told me there was a "Relay for Life" event taking place in our county on June 9 and 10. She asked me if I wanted to join up and do the walk, or run, whichever I preferred. I thought about it and decided at the last minute to go ahead and do it.

3-21-2007   **185 lbs.**

The race started at about six in the evening and went on through to six the next morning. I arrived at the stadium where it was being held at around nine. There was a big crowd; the running track was full of walkers and runners participating. There were all kinds of booths set up selling food, t-shirts and just about everything else you could imagine, and the place was buzzing with excitement. I immediately ran in to some folks I knew and we visited briefly. Then, about twenty minutes after I arrived, I took to the track and started walking. I walked briskly for about and hour and a half and then I stopped to take a break. My legs were starting to bother me; it had only been a short while since I ran the festival race and I had not fully recuperated. I got myself something to drink and made the rounds, taking time to visit with neighbors and friends. The more I rested, the more my legs started freezing up. I estimated

I had walked about seven miles up to that point. As I tried to get back onto the track, I realized just how tired I was, so I made the decision to leave and I went home. After arriving at my house, I took a long hot bath and then tried to lie down and fall asleep but it was impossible; I felt like I had not done my fair share in the relay. Unsettled, I got back up and got dressed again. I then went back to the track. It was about 12:45 a.m. When I got there, it had quieted down considerably, but there were still a few people on the track. They were having a "prettiest legs contest" involving men, at the center of the track. These guys had to dress up like women and then were judged, with the winner agreeing to shave his legs right there on the stage! Most of the people remaining were watching the contest. I took in a few minutes of the contest and then decided to start walking again. After about two miles, I got a sudden burst of energy and decided to start running. My legs felt weightless for about two miles. Then I started getting tired again, so I slowed back down to a brisk walk. I continued and did not pay much attention to what was going on around me; I was in my own little world. After awhile, my legs started cramping up and I had to start slowing myself down. I glanced down at my watch and it was three o'clock! I started calculating and realized I had done fifteen miles! When I realized how much I had done, I almost fell over! Even though I had taken a well-deserved break and decided to start back home, I realized this was the most I had ever done in that short amount of time. My legs were starting to feel like lead so I dragged myself out to my SUV and literally fell into the vehicle. I started the ten-mile drive home. My eyes were heavy, and I was so tired I had to turn the air conditioner on full power and drive with the windows down to get fresh air, so I could stay awake. The road from the track to my home is winding and I struggled to not nod off. As I was rounding a corner, something caught my eye and unsure of what it was, I struggled to get a better look. Suddenly, before my eyes and dead set in front of my vehicle, was a big black animal! Then it happened; something took the steering wheel out of my hands and somehow I made it past the animal without hitting it and then I came to a complete stop. Shaken, I glanced behind me to see a big black cow moseying across the highway, undaunted by my SUV. I was in a state of shock and had to take a minute to make sure I was still functioning! I thanked God out loud. Then, somewhat collected, I started to drive away. Within about 10 seconds of me starting home again, my sister's face flashed across my mind and then it hit me. It was June 10, 2006. My sister Sheri had been gone for exactly one year. In amazement, I realized that I had just done a "Relay for Life" race, an event to raise funds for breast cancer research, starting on June 9 and ended my participation on the first anniversary of my sister's passing! Not until that very moment, had I given any thought to the date. Totally blown away by all of this, and what happened to me with the cow, I started driving, but not back to my house. I went straight to the cemetery where Sheri was laid to rest.

3-22-2007   **184 lbs.**

Some people may think I was totally crazy to go to a cemetery in the middle of the night. Most people would never think to do such a thing, but I went there to be close to my sister and mother. At the cemetery, there is a bench close to our family's gravesites so you can sit and spend quiet time on it; this is what I did. Actually, I was so tired, I decided to lie down and I then looked up to the beautiful clear sky. There were a million stars sparkling above me as I took in all the beauty this early morning had to offer. I felt so close to my sister and mother. I talked to my Sheri and told her my feelings. I thanked her for always watching out for me. I said things to both of them I had not said up until that point. I poured my heart out in the peaceful surroundings and I was not bothered by anything or anyone. I never worried about being there all by myself; I was not scared in the least. It was so beautiful and peaceful and I relished all of it, in awe. I closed my eyes and prayed, silently as well as aloud. No one could hear me so I did not hold back any of my feelings; everything came out so naturally. I also rested. I sang my sister's song over and over again. I sang the

Lord's Prayer. I recited the 23rd Psalm. I sang "Amazing Grace", which was my mother's favorite and continued to sing all of these songs again and again. My heart was filled with complete peace and tranquility. I felt closer to both of them than I had in a very long time; it was as if they were right there with me, and I believe they were. There were no cars driving by and no lights were on anywhere around me. The rest of the world did not exist. It was only myself with my beautiful memories of my loved ones. My aunt and uncle are also buried there and it was as if a big part of my family was joining my peace. After awhile, my extreme fatigue disappeared and I started to feel rejuvenated; my heart was happy. Peace and stillness overcame me but at the same time, my energy started to replenish; I felt like I was given life again. As I lay still, I started to notice sounds around me. There was an owl making its presence known. I focused on its sound and started to realize the beauty of its call. As I concentrated more, I noticed many different kinds of bugs making their night music. Locusts were buzzing around me. It is funny that I did not notice them earlier when I had arrived. I could hear birds nesting in the massive pine trees above. Nature was wide-awake and I was there to take in all of the beauty it had to offer.

How often do we actually stop our world and take the time to appreciate the smallest things that can bring us such inner peace? I know up until that night in the cemetery, I had not. As I listened to the orchestra of various species making their special music in the night, I contemplated the wonder of it all. Nature is put on this world to make us stand up and realize that we as humans are but a tiny fraction of God's plan. Without nature to balance us out, we would have nothing. The tiniest insect on our planet has its purpose. In fact, *everything* has a purpose and it is a shame we never stop and take the time to realize this and gain from that purpose. That early morning, in a tiny graveyard, all by myself, I learned to have inner peace: peace with myself, peace with my surroundings, and peace with knowing that my loved ones who have left their physical body have not left me. They are around me all of the time, in every thing I do. I have always known I have the Lord with me at all times and I've never been alone, But on that tenth day of June, I realized my loved ones who have passed are still with me. They watch out for me and comfort me, even in ways I am not conscious of. Earlier that night, when I was driving, so tired I should have not been behind the wheel, my "angels" were right there with me, by my side. They kept a watch out for me when I could not take care of myself. What a wonderful gift! Sometimes we are protected, even though our actions could cause us serious harm. Where would we be without divine intervention? For me, I might have ended up on the side of a country road, injured or worse, if I was not being looked after from up above. I believe in God and His almighty vision. I also believe He has help from angels who keep watch over us when we need it. I do believe there are angels all around us. Fortunately, I know in my heart my beautiful sister was my angel this night and she got me safely through a situation that could have harmed me. How ironic it is that I saw her face, realized what day it was and now live to tell you about it. I will cherish that June night for the rest of my life; it ended up being the end of one of the most incredible days of my life. I searched my soul, made peace with death and loss and at the same time truly felt at one with nature. What a beautiful a life we have, and what a blessing the smallest things can sometimes bring. I love you Lord. I love you, Sheri and Mother.

2-23-2007   184 lbs.

Sometimes in our life, when we least expect it, people we come in contact with touch us and make an impact on our heart. You never know when you meet a stranger if that person is going to play a role in your life. In my life, I had many beautiful people come and go, but not without touching me in their own special way. I have cherished these experiences, and will do so, always. In one of my greatest times of need, I was fortunate to have several of these angels come into my life and help me through a very difficult time. Each one of my angels had their own way of touching me, and I hold each one of them close and dear to my heart. I truly believe that there are angels all around us, and when we least expect it they are there with open wings to wrap us up and cradle us safely.

Angels sing and do not cry
Voices ringing trough the sky
Folds of white and jewels of sight
Beacons glowing through the night,
Guiding hands and wings of gold
Gathering up within their folds
Those of us who have lost our way
Through clouded days and smoldering haze
There to catch us when we fall
And gently watch us through it all
Angels sing and do not cry
Joyful voices... through the sky.

CHAPTER NINE

SUGAR AND SPICE AND EVERYTHING NICE!

3-26-2007   **184 lbs.**

March 15, 1979, my mother-in-law phoned me. It was her birthday but she beat me to the telephone call. I answered the phone and on the other end, she was singing "Happy birthday to me, happy birthday to me, that baby's gonna be born today... happy birthday to me!" I listened, chuckled, and then cleared my throat to speak. "I certainly hope it's soon...I'm sooooo tired!" And tired I was! I was expecting my first child and was way past my due date. I wanted her to be born so bad, it was killing me to wait another hour, let alone another day.

My mother-in-law chatted enthusiastically and with hope on the other end of the line and I listened, awaiting the bomb to drop. Then it came. "You know," she said, "if the baby is born today, you all will have to call her Patricia. That is, if it's a girl!" There! She said it! I knew it was coming; my husband and I *both* knew it was coming! I sat still for a second and then I tried to make small talk to change the subject, so to speak, but she was not letting me off that easily! "You will, won't you?" she pried.

Let's see... this was not the subject I wanted to discuss with my mother-in-law over the phone. Actually, I did not want to discuss it with her at *any* time! As you might have guessed by now, *her* name was Patricia! Actually, that was not her real name, but it was the name she went by. At this time, we did not know it was not her real name; as far as we knew, she was Patricia Ann. Not until years later did we learn the real truth; that's another story though! Anyway, when I passed my due date, she was convinced

I would give birth on her birthday. We were hoping this not to be the case simply because we had chosen our names for the baby and "Patricia Ann" was not one of them. At first we liked the name and thought about it quite a bit, but to keep peace in the family and not name our child after one grandparent and not the other, we decided to go in a totally different direction. We knew there was no problem if the baby was a boy because he was going to have his father's name, but I knew the minute I got pregnant we were having a girl so the boy's name was not an issue for me.

While still on the telephone, I managed to pacify my mother-in-law and escaped without making a commitment. When we hung up, I prayed to the good Lord to let me make it through March 15 without giving birth. Any other time, I was praying for it to be over with, but not that day! As luck had it, I held on past midnight, past noon on the 16th., past 7:00 p. m., and then the phone rang again. "Guess who!" Yes, it was Pat once again. "Well, seeing as how that baby decided not to come on my birthday, it will be born tomorrow" she excitedly said. "Tomorrow is St. Patrick's Day!" *Here we go again*, I thought to myself. I had not thought about that date on my list of days I didn't want to have a baby. The thoughts started flooding through my head; my mother-in-law was telling me if the baby is a boy, the name would have to be "Patrick" and if it is a girl...well, you get the picture! Here I had escaped the "birthday" date, and here once again, I was faced with *another* date to not give birth on! I thought I was out of trouble after the 15th. passed without incident, but there I was, left to sweat out another twenty-four hours- feeling like I was going to burst at any given second!

3-27-2007   **184 lbs.**

At approximately five a.m., Saturday March 17, 1979, my water broke and awakened me; I immediately knew what was happening. I woke my husband up and told him it was time. We got up and got ready, made the phone call to my doctor, and started on our way to the hospital. While on our way, we made a stop by my parents' house to drop off our dog in their backyard. We did not want to wake them at that hour of the morning and we decided we would call our parents after we got to the hospital and got settled in. I was not having any labor pains. After arriving at the hospital, they got me checked in and settled into my room and they started monitoring me. We called our family at around 7:30. Around 8:30, I had my first labor pains. The contractions started out at about every eight minutes. It was not too bad in the beginning. My mother and father made it to the hospital around ten and my in-laws were to be there in the early afternoon. Everyone knew with this being my first child, I would be in labor for a while. As the morning progressed, so did my labor pains. We had gone through Lamaze classes so I practiced my breathing whenever necessary; I was bound and determined to give birth naturally, without any medication, so I worked through the pain with the techniques I had learned.

By about three, I was starting to get really uncomfortable. My blood pressure was climbing. I still refused medication. My contractions were about every four minutes. Things started progressing quickly and it soon became apparent that I was going to give birth on March 17, St. Patrick's Day! Of course, my mother-in-law was excited! She felt for sure her namesake was about to come into the world!

My mother's best friend, a registered nurse and the head of nursing at this hospital, was with me during my labor. She had actually helped deliver me when I was born at the very same hospital. I was honored that she made sure she was there for me when I was giving birth and I felt secure, knowing she was with me. My husband was also a great help to me. He kept me focused on my breathing so I could make it through the pain. We worked very well together as a team!

At about five they wheeled me into the delivery room. There is no way for me to describe what my body was doing at that point. It was as if this great force had taken over and I had absolutely no control over what was happening. The pain was enormous, but the force taking over my whole being was even *more* tremendous than the pain. My doctor was there, telling me when to push and when not to push, but I had no control over what my body was doing. At least I thought I had no control! I continued the breathing practices I had learned and my husband coached me through them. Even though it felt like I had no control, everyone in the delivery room told me I was doing a great job, and I guess I did a great job because at exactly 5:28 p.m., Sandra Leigh Walker made her debut in our world! Weighing 7 pounds, 13 ½ ounces and 21 ½ inches long, she was breathtakingly beautiful! She had blond hair and her skin was pretty and pink, not red and wrinkly like many newborns when they first come into the world. She looked like a three-month-old baby! Her blond hair was about one inch long in the back and curled up on her neck. She even had two little teeth breaking her gums! I knew I was overdue but it seemed I had been *very* overdue! Here was this beautiful little baby girl who looked like she should have been born at least two months earlier! Everyone in the hospital talked about her and how pretty and perfect she was. Of course, we agreed, and her grandparents were the proudest grandparents on the face of the earth. There had never been a more beautiful baby born. Sandra Leigh was already Miss America, the first woman President and Miss Universe, even though she was only a few minutes old.

3-28-2007   **184 lbs.**

The rest of the evening, we marveled at our newborn daughter and how perfect she was. The hospital served us a lovely steak dinner and everyone stayed with me until about nine p.m. After they left, I tried to settle in for the night. After about an hour, I started suffering extreme pain from an episiotomy my doctor had to perform during childbirth. I tried to tough it out but after about two hours of pain, I called for our nurse friend and told her I was hurting. She ended up giving me pain medicine, and afterwards I was able to go to sleep. I have to say, the episiotomy hurt much worse than all of the labor pains I had before. I was extremely uncomfortable for the next few days because to it.

The next morning, the pediatrician we had chosen for our baby came in to meet with us. He had already examined the baby and told us she was strong, healthy and beautiful. He asked us if we had any questions and was more than willing to answer our questions and concerns. I asked him about teething. What could I do to help her through it? His answer was comical, to say the least! He told me to get a bottle of whiskey and some cotton balls. When she was crying and obviously uncomfortable due to the teething, pour a shot of the whiskey into a glass, and then take the cotton ball and dip it into the whiskey. After doing this, he said to take the drenched cotton ball and rub it along her gums! "You take the glass with the whiskey in it and down it yourself! One of two things will happen: either the whiskey on her gums will numb her up...or you won't care, whichever comes first!" He had a twinkle in his eyes while speaking. Then we all laughed! It was a great ice breaker and from that moment on we felt sure we had found the right doctor to take care of our child.

Sandra and I ended up being the only patients on the maternity floor. We had the utmost care, and all the nurses were already spoiling her rotten. I had made the decision to breast feed so we attempted this during the three days we remained at the hospital. Sandra was really not taking to it, but the nurses encouraged me to stick with it and she would eventually get the hang of nursing. Everything seemed to be going well, and we were sent home Monday afternoon as I was very anxious to get home with my new baby. We had made the decision for me to go to my parents' house for a few days, just until I got back on my feet and I would at least have my mom there to help out.

On our way home from the hospital, we stopped by the flight school where my husband had finalized his flight training. He wanted to show off his beautiful baby daughter to all of his friends; he was so proud of her! Then, he took us to my parents' house. I was tired I decided to lie down and rest, but baby Sandra and her daddy went out to the private airport where he was starting his *own* flying school. He could not wait to take her up in an airplane, so he did! Sandra had her first "flying lesson" at three days old. Her daddy took her up and flew her around for about 10 minutes. She stayed awake through the flight and never fussed a bit. Her daddy was happy and proud; he had his own little co-pilot!

That night, our first night home, Sandra started crying at about ten p.m. and cried all night long! We had absolutely no idea what was wrong with her. She had not cried at all before then, and we were very perplexed. At about five a.m., my husband started rummaging through a big bag the hospital had sent home with us. It was full of all kinds of samples of baby items, including cans of formula. He went and got a bottle from the kitchen and put some formula in it. I did not want to give her a bottle because I was determined to breast feed, but at this point, if it got her to stop crying, I was all for it! I held Sandra close, gave her the bottle and she sucked as if she was starving to death! She downed the whole bottle and then happily fell off to sleep, content and full. Poor little baby girl; we did not know she was starving!

I ended up in the hospital later that same day with a major breast infection. Sandra was not getting any milk from me at all. I was so engorged that they had to give me extremely high doses of antibiotics, along with mechanically pumping my breasts to relieve the pressure. I ran a high fever — over 104 degrees — for about three days until the medicine finally started kicking in. I was a very sick new mommy! The baby however, was great after she finally got some decent nutrition. After that, I never tried to breast feed again. They gave me medicine to dry up my milk supply and our baby girl was happy with the bottle!

3-29-2007   **183 lbs.**

Having a baby girl was my dream. Actually, I knew exactly when I had become pregnant with Sandra. I had a dream one night about a beautiful little blond baby girl with a smile that lit up the world. She was fair, with light eyes and with laughter ringing out. She was my baby girl! I awoke that next morning knowing I was going to have a baby. I knew exactly what she looked like and she was going to be my little princess. I had always wanted two children, a boy and a girl, but I wanted the little girl first. I guess I still wanted to live out my baby doll years by being able to dress up a little girl in all of the frilly little outfits you can buy. Of course, I would have been just as happy with a beautiful little boy.

Sandra was quite a little girl. She quickly learned how to wrap her daddy around her little finger, not to mention her grandfather Dye. My dad has always had a soft spot for little girls and being his first granddaughter had its advantages! Sandra did not lack from attention, to say the least; she was the light in all of our eyes and she knew it from day one. All she had to do was ask for something, and if her daddy did not get it for her, her granddaddy would! Soon, she learned to go straight for the gusto by going directly to her grandpa. He could deny her nothing her little heart desired and he was really good at the spoiling game. He has continued on this path throughout the years!

When Sandra was about three years old, her daddy would take her out to the airport and she would assist him while he worked on airplanes. She was his right-hand girl. He would be busy rebuilding an airplane engine and she would be busy playing in the old oil and the gunk you use to remove the oil off your hands. Occasionally, she would hand him the right tool he asked her for, assuring her position as "little chief mechanic!" They would spend hours at the airport and when they came home, she would be covered from head to toe in grease. At this age, her blond hair was down past her middle back and that messy grease always found its way to her butter-colored head! Sometimes it would take me two or three washings to get her clean again. I did not mind it though. It made me happy that she and her daddy could spend this quality time together because I knew how important that was. I grew up shadowing my dad and I would not trade those times for anything else in the world.

From the time Sandra was a tiny girl, she was outspoken and at a very early age, she developed the vocabulary of an adult! She never really did the "baby talk" thing. She did, however, have a couple of words as a baby that were hilarious! For instance, her first word was not "mama" or "dada". No, her first word was her own version of airplane: "plairplane" to be exact. You have to understand, she was around "plairplanes" from the time she was three days old! She was an airport baby from the get-go. Remember, her first airplane ride was at three days old and we spent a lot of time at the airport due to the flight school being a new business. It took both my husband and me many countless hours of work to get everything off the ground, and Sandra was with me at all times, along for the ride. We lived a short distance from this private airport so it was easy to just pack up and go back and forth when needed. The fact was she was always a little trooper and was happy no matter where she was. This made my life much easier.

The next confusing word she spoke was "losh-lee" or, as we know it, lotion, and Sandra had an infatuation with liquid skin cream. She would try to eat it when given the opportunity so we really had to watch her! We would say "No Sandra, you can't eat that! You can't have the lotion!" and for some mysterious reason, she interpreted lotion as "losh-lee" and not until she was about four years old did we convince her otherwise! The crazy thing about it, though, was the fact she could say very difficult words like aluminum and spaghetti without effort; most kids have trouble with these words, but not her. By the age of two, Sandra could hold an adult conversation and would talk non-stop using *big* words. We always attributed it to the fact that she was mostly around adults in her infancy, and the fact that she talked non-stop, something that has not changed in the least. My daughter can spend hours talking, just like both of her parents. She came by it absolutely naturally!

Sandra was an easy child. As a baby, she never cried or fussed and we could take her with us anywhere, and she was almost never sick. She was, overall, a very happy and healthy baby and was also very well behaved. We enforced manners in our home and made sure our children knew how to act in public. We intended to raise our children in the right way. Regarding this subject, I remember an incident that took place when Sandra was about three years old. We were dining at a fast-food restaurant and we were the only ones there, with the exception of one other family. We were sitting quietly eating our meal and while doing so, the other family's children were running all around the restaurant without supervision from their parents. Suddenly, Sandra stood up and put her little hand on her hip then shouted out "Some people just don't know how to control their kids!" We sat there in total embarrassment, wanting to disappear, but at the same time, we had to agree with our pint-sized daughter! She was so disturbed by the other children's behavior that she had to comment about it to us. It actually was quite funny after the fact. She was never allowed to act this way and she knew it was wrong.

3-31-2007   **182 lbs.**

As Sandra started growing up, she became even more outspoken. She never tried to hide her feelings and you always knew exactly how she felt. She has always possessed the talent of speaking her mind, which can sometimes lead to trouble! We had to work with her from an early age, getting her to handle herself in a more reserved manner, especially in certain situations. Her outspokenness has been good in some instances, but sometimes, if she had used a little finesse, she possibly would have had different results!

Sandra and her dad started having conflicts when she was about six years old. Because she is so head strong and just like her dad in so many ways, they started locking horns! Neither of them was ever willing to just back away and simmer down, so I found myself constantly playing peacemaker between the two of them.

When Jeffrey was born, Sandra was three-and-a-half years old and was no longer the complete center of attention. I became very ill after the birth of her little brother and was away from her for long periods of time. Because I was in the hospital so much, she started suffering from anxiety separation. We had built up the baby's arrival and she was very excited about having a little brother, but after his birth, I was not around and she suffered because of it. Sandra was good with the baby but when she realized her daddy's attention was being divided, jealously started setting in. I felt so helpless for my little ones. When I was at home with them, Sandra would not let me out of her sight and she clung to me at all times. The whole situation was very difficult for her and I know she has emotional scars because of it. I elected to seek help and advice from a child psychologist. When the doctor evaluated our daughter, he told me it was the worst case of separation anxiety he had ever witnessed. He was very helpful in giving us ways to help her and I continued taking Sandra to see him for about two years. I thank God that my daughter was born with the strength and tenacity she has. If she had a weaker personality, she may have suffered irreversible emotional damage.

At a very early age, Sandra learned to speak fluent Spanish. We always had a Spanish-speaking housekeeper/babysitter so this made a second language easy for her to pick up, as well as the fact that we lived on the Mexican border, and we traveled many times into Mexico for shopping and eating. Because Sandra and her little brother had white-blond hair, they were always the center of attention whenever we were across the border. The fact that Sandra could speak the language gave her even more attention! She never knew a stranger and she would converse with the people of Mexico fluently. Of course, we had a hard time keeping up because neither her father nor I spoke the language. It was always entertaining to watch her!

4-2-2007   **182 lbs.**

Sandra is blessed with being a very gifted and talented girl. We discovered very early on that she had a beautiful singing voice. I entered her in her first talent contest when she was in the second grade. She did a rendition of "King of the Road" and brought the house down. We practiced and practiced, which came in helpful because she took first place! After that, I worked closely with her and when she was in the fifth grade she was honored by being asked to sing "God Bless the U.S.A." for Martin Luther King Day in her school district. She did an outstanding job and received a standing ovation! From that moment on, she was hooked and sang whenever given the opportunity.

When Sandra was in the eighth grade, I moved to Kentucky and brought her with me. Her dad and I went through a divorce and I wanted to take her to a place where she would have the opportunity to use her singing talent. My dad was living in Kentucky and he told me about a place where Sandra could sing and be close to Nashville. This place was Libby's, a family place where new singing artists were given the opportunity to sing for a huge live audience and have the chance to be "discovered!" It sounded like a great place to go, so we packed up and moved to Kentucky. Jeffrey was in private school in Texas so we made the decision for him stay with his dad. It was hard being separated from Jeffrey, but at the time it was the best decision we could make and he got to visit us any chance he could, when he was not in school.

After we were moved and settled, we made a trip out to Libby's and arranged for Sandra to audition for the *Live at Libby's Show*, a live radio broadcast airing every Saturday night on a local radio station. The *Live at Libby's Show* could be heard in a one hundred-mile radius. Many big stars got their start on Libby's stage and the show brought in music professionals from across the country to discover or be discovered by major record labels. It was an exciting atmosphere to say the least, and Sandra's first audition, at the age of thirteen, went well. However, she did not make the "live" show.

Somewhat disappointed, we decided to continue her auditions every Friday night, giving her the chance to hone up her talent and become comfortable performing with a live band. She sang and sang and sang! We became close friends with the owner of Libby's, Mr. Libby Knight, and he encouraged Sandra to keep going. He spotted talent in Sandra but wanted to hold her back until he felt she was ready to move forward. Sandra wowed the audiences and became very popular at the establishment. Her ease and grace on stage started coming through and you could see her blossoming right before your eyes.

When Sandra was fourteen, she was asked to sing in a Christmas show featuring several big-name artists. The show production lasted for two nights in December of 1994. She did an outstanding job! Shortly after that show, she was asked to compete in the Miss Kentucky Teen pageant. This pageant held a talent competition and we all felt sure she would take home first place. The pageant, held in Louisville, was a three-day affair. We arrived, and she went through the preliminary competition garnering great reviews! It looked as if there were no other contestants that could hold a candle to her voice and stage presence. All that time performing at Libby'" was paying off! When the final evening's competition took place and she got up and started singing, you could have heard a pin drop. The audience was held captive by her beautiful voice and rendition of "When You Say Nothing at All." When she finished, she received two standing ovations and it was very apparent she would win the Miss Kentucky Teen talent completion, and she did! She won a music scholarship as well as a modeling scholarship for her hard work. Needless to say, we could have not been more proud of her.

4-3-2007   **181 lbs.**

After Sandra won the talent competition for our state's pageant, we placed a call to Libby's. It was a Saturday night and many of our friends were there enjoying the show. They were all supportive of her and we could not wait to share the news! When the crowd received the great news, they all shouted and cheered for Sandra; they were all very proud of her. When we returned home, she was informed that she would be on the live radio broadcast the following week! This is what she had worked for and we were all excited. When the time came, she performed with the expertise of a seasoned professional. Even I was blown away by her performance.

Libby, the proprietor of the establishment, even commented on how far she had come since she first started singing there. He was not one to give out compliments lightly and this was a major deal for him praise her performance. I think he was a little hard on her because he knew she has a great talent but he wanted her to live up to her potential and not just settle for good singing; he wanted her to be the total package! I also think, because Libby and I became very close friends, he was prone to be harder on her and he did not want to show favoritism in any way. Even though it was difficult for Sandra to understand, I think this made her tougher in the long run. She kept trying to improve her performances in order to get his approval and recognition.

Several months later, I arranged for Sandra to make a demo tape in Libby's recording studio. Joe Silver, a great friend of ours, ran the studio and he was more than willing to help us get the project off the ground. Sandra recorded five songs, and even though it was her first attempt at recording, she did a great job! We gave most of the tapes to friends and relatives and did not intend to try to peddle them to record labels but this was a great learning experience for Sandra.

During the following months, Sandra kept busy singing and studying in high school. She did several festivals and personal appearances during this time; she tried to sing whenever given the chance. Sandra entered every talent competition she could find but sometimes they were more of a popularity contest than a talent contest. It hurt her if she lost because of this, but in the end, she developed more of a tough skin because of those losses.

When she came to her senior year in high school, she was given a great honor. She was asked to sing the national anthem for her own high school graduation! This was the ultimate honor she could have been given. Even though there were many of her peers that were jealous of her talent and accomplishments, they all rallied behind her and supported her in this. When the time came, her voice was crystal clear and she blew the audience away, once again. To this day, people still talk about her graduation performance!

After high school, Sandra decided to take some time off to get her thoughts straight about what she wanted to do with the rest of her life. She wanted to attend college but at his time in her life, she was very tired of school and needed some time to herself. She decided to go to Texas for a few months and spend some time with her dad. Jeffrey had moved to Kentucky to live with me and go to high school there and Sandra and her dad had not spent much of the last five years together and she hoped to get their relationship back on track. This move turned out to be a major disappointment for her because all she did was work and he was never around to spend time with her. Basically, Sandra was all by herself, in a strange place with no friends. Her dad was involved in a new relationship and unfortunately, he chose to spend time with his new love instead of spending time with his daughter. She came back home hurt and angry about the whole situation. This did not help their relationship at all and it ended up driving a bigger wedge between the two of them. Of course, as always, I was there to pick up the pieces. I never spoke badly of my ex-husband and I always tried to make peace between the two of them, but at this stage of the game, I was having a hard time getting her to accept her dad and his faults. We all have faults and I know he is a great person; I have never been able to explain why the two of them have such a personality conflict at times. The older Sandra got, the more this came into play. I just kept praying the two of them would find their way back to each other and have a good and healthy relationship at some point down the road.

4-4-2007   **181 lbs.**

Sandra started college in the spring of 1998 and she moved into the dorms at Murray State University. She also worked at a restaurant while in school. She was dating a boy she had met before she went to Texas and he attended the same university; they were both very young but before long, they decided to get married. He enlisted in the Navy after the spring semester and he was sent off to boot camp. They ended up getting married in September of that same year.

Sandra's husband was stationed in Florida while he trained in air traffic control school. Then they were sent to Norfolk, Virginia where he was immediately sent out on a ship for a six-month tour of duty. Sandra was left alone with no family or friends to support her. I do have to say though, she did make friends quickly. She also went to work in order to stay busy because she was not ready to start back at school. She missed singing because after the marriage, she had not sung as much as she had in the past. Being in a strange town, she really did not know where to go to perform other than in karaoke bars.

My family was not very happy about her marriage; we all felt she could do better for herself. Her husband had some serious issues and his family life was strange to us. He was a spoiled, rotten brat who could not sneeze without asking his parents when or how! His family constantly interfered in their relationship, which made her life a living hell. She considered leaving him until she found out she was pregnant.

Sandra was very happy about her impending motherhood and I was excited about having my first grandchild. I hoped that fatherhood would make her husband grow up and be more responsible. Don't get me wrong, he was brilliant at his job and he excelled in the Navy; he was even awarded a sailor of the year commendation in 1999. At home, though, he was verbally abusive and very difficult to live with. I also found out he had a major drinking problem, which made me concerned for her and the baby's safety.

The pregnancy was difficult, so I went to Virginia to stay with Sandra the last three months of her pregnancy. Her husband was away on and off during this time, which was a good thing as far as I was concerned because Sandra was much more at ease when he was not around. As the time neared for the birth, she became very ill and the doctors did not know what was wrong with her. We spent many hours, day after day, on the labor deck of the military hospital, thinking she was going into labor, when in reality she was not. They ran many tests on her and kept close track of the baby. Finally, one of the doctors who had never seen Sandra before thought about a very rare condition in pregnant women, which occurs once in every one hundred thousand births. Sandra fit the profile, and this doctor ordered the test to prove the condition. The test was sent to Florida so we waited three days for the results to come back. When the results came in, the doctor admitted Sandra directly into the hospital and induced labor. It was a very high-risk birth and Sandra and baby were both in danger. We said many prayers and put both of them in the Lord's hands.

4-5-2007   **180 lbs.**

On September 15, 2000, Clayton Andrew came into our lives! He was perfect at birth. Sandra, however, was still very ill. She had a rough labor and delivery and she had to keep taking special medication for the rare condition she contracted. This medicine made her feel very bad and baby Clay was not allowed to stay in the room with her until the next day. They both remained in the hospital for three days until she was feeling better and was out of danger. After they came home, I took care of baby Clay so Sandra could continue to get her strength back.

I remained in Virginia for the next month. Clay's father was getting ready to be sent off out to sea again so we made the decision to bring Sandra and Clay back to Kentucky. They moved in with my husband and me. I was overjoyed to have them both living with us and I was thrilled to have my first grandchild! Being able to help take care of him was so much fun; I spoiled him rotten the best way I knew how.

The baby's father came back home after about four months. When he was gone, he and Sandra continued to fight over the phone and by e-mail. It was apparent this marriage was not going to last. He was too immature to be a husband, let alone a father, so Sandra made the decision to file for divorce. Our family fully supported her decision; in fact, we were relieved. She and Clay ended up staying with us for about one year.

Sandra wanted to go back to school but she also had to work

to support herself and the baby. It took a long time before she got child support. Through a few people she had met, she became very interested in police work, so she started working with the county police in the area we lived. She trained and became certified in classes whenever she could. After a few months, she joined the sheriff's department and became a deputy, then she was assigned and stationed in the courts as a bailiff. Sandra loved the police work and she made many friends and connections with her job. This is how she met her second husband.

Sandra and Jimmy dated for four years before they got married. During that time, they lived together on and off. She did, however, live with me for one year after I divorced my fourth husband. I bought my house so she and Clay could stay with me because none of us were sure if she and Jimmy would actually make it down the aisle. They had their problems, but after breaking up with each other many times, they always found themselves back together.

Jimmy has been in Clay's life since he was eight months old and he is the only daddy Clay has known. Jimmy took Clay in immediately and called him his son. They have a wonderful relationship and love each other very much. Jimmy has been so good for Clay; Clay's own father has not seen him since he was eighteen months old. He has never attempted to have a relationship with his own son. This is sad, but true. The saying "any man can be a father but it takes a special man to be a daddy" defines the situation. I thank God everyday that Clay is finally blessed with a good daddy.

4-6-2007   180 lbs.

On February 25, 2006, Lily Glori-Ann came into our lives two months early. Clay finally got his wish to have a baby sister. Lily did not come into the world easily. Once again, Sandra had a high-risk pregnancy and was on complete bed rest two months before Lily was born. Because of complications, Sandra was taken to the hospital one week before she gave birth to my tiny granddaughter. The whole ordeal was hard on all of us, but especially to Sandra and Jimmy. Sandra's blood pressure was climbing and the doctors decided they would have to deliver the baby very prematurely. When it got to the point they had to induce the birth, we all said our prayers and hoped for the best. They induced labor early on the 25th. Sandra started to have strong labor pains so she asked for an epidural. The doctor did the procedure but it was not effective. About one hour later, he tried to do a second epidural. Again, it did not work. Even though Sandra was suffering from pain, it was a blessing from God the epidural did not take effect. At approximately 1:30 that afternoon, Sandra was complaining of extreme pressure; her blood pleasure had climbed to a very unsafe level and because of this, alarms monitoring her and the baby went off. Jimmy and I were the only ones in the room with Sandra; we kept expecting the nurses to come running in after hearing the alarm but they did not. Sandra screamed to me that the baby was coming! I quickly checked her and saw nothing. I tried to reassure her everything was all right while I waited for a nurse to come running in. Once again, I lifted up the sheet covering Sandra to look. About that time, she screamed out to me and without warning, Lily came shooting out onto the bed. Jimmy was on the other side of the bed in a state of shock. Sandra was crying out, "The baby! The baby!" Lily lay there, motionless and quiet. She was so tiny and lifeless. In what seemed to take a lifetime, one of the nurses came in and when she saw the baby delivered, and there on the bed, it seemed like she started moving in slow motion. It is hard to explain, but the next few minutes were like being suspended in animation. It seemed like nobody was in a big hurry. Jimmy was in a panic, and I was afraid he was going to pass out on me and Sandra's blood pressure was so high I feared she would have a stroke. The baby lay there, still with no signs of life. Soon, the neonatal team arrived and took over the care of our tiny baby girl. They worked on her for what seemed to be forever until they got her breathing, and then they hurriedly whisked her away to the neonatal intensive care unit.

Sandra's doctor arrived in the room while the baby was being treated and while Jimmy and I waited for the neonatal team to tell us the baby was okay. We remained frightened. Our minister then arrived, and he helped keep Jimmy as calm as possible. They gave Sandra drugs to calm her and bring her blood pressure down. After about thirty minutes, which felt like an eternity, the neonatal head nurse came and took us to see the baby. I, with Jimmy and our minister, went in to the neonatal intensive care unit to meet our baby girl.

It is hard to describe just how tiny Lily was. Weighing in at only 2 pounds, 15 ounces, she was lost in the large bassinet in which she was placed. There were tubes and lines going in and out of just about every inch of her tiny body. There were machines with alarms and buzzers helping her breath and bright lights shining down on her. Her eyes were taped shut. She was red and blue all over. She wasn't even half the size of a full-term newborn. Our minister said a prayer with us for her and then we had to leave the unit.

The next few hours were very scary. Sandra was still not out of danger with her blood pressure and she was frightened for her tiny daughter. Jimmy was a basket case, as you can imagine. I kept a strong outer appearance to keep them calm, but deep inside, I was petrified! Here, my daughter was in danger and my granddaughter had been born very, very early. I chose to stay overnight in the room with Sandra so I could be close to both of them. I never slept the whole night and I prayed over and over again for our baby girl's safety and for our big girl's safety as well. I bargained with God, that if he had to take someone, take me and please let our tiny baby live. Then I went down to the hospital chapel and knelt down to say my prayers, all over again. I went into the nursery to see Lily every time they let me and would sing to her, over and over again and tell her how much she was loved and wanted. Talking to her, I would tell her I was her "mamaw." Many times I shed silent tears, some out of fear and some out of joy, then I prayed some more.

4-7-2007   **180 lbs.**

Lily remained in the hospital for one month. Sandra started recovering soon after the birth and was allowed to go home after only four days. She and Jimmy went back and forth to the hospital to spend time with the baby, and I went to the hospital twice a day. Each day you could see a change in Lily. She was a strong and tough little girl.

My daughter has become an incredible mother! She loves her babies so very much, and I could never ask for a better role model and mother for my grandkids. Her children are her life, and they always come first. I am so proud of Sandra. She has matured into a fine woman in every sense of the word.

The relationship my daughter and I have is inseparable! Don't get me wrong, we have had our fair share of fights in the past years and I am sure we will have more in the future. There is one thing for certain: when we do fight, we always give it all we have! Both of us are stubborn and opinionated but one of us more so than the other! Of course, I won't say which one, but her name starts with an _S_! When Sandra and I do fight, we are passionate in whatever the topic! We each have very strong ideas and we tend to over-exaggerate at times. All and all, we always kiss and make up. We can never stay mad at each other for more than an hour or so (at least most of the time!).

Having a daughter is very special, especially when that daughter becomes an adult herself. You watch them grow up from being a tiny little girl into a beautiful and strong woman. All of the hopes and dreams any mother has for her little girl transpire right before her eyes in her daughter. The closeness you share with your adult child cannot be compared to anything else. They grow up with their own feelings and dreams but you know that your values and beliefs are there somewhere, deep inside your child. It is such a great feeling, knowing that you have had an influence in the development of such a beautiful creature; it is such a rush! You see yourself in your child and you see other relatives as well. This is particularly special when those relatives have passed on. Because of this, you relive times of your life where these individuals played their own important role in your development and who you are. When you look at your child, you see this person as an individual, full of the same hopes and dreams as anyone else, but your very own heritage. A woman having a daughter provides a chance for the mother to re-live their younger years, through their daughter. As a mother, you are able to give them advice because you have already been there. They learn from you the good things, as well as learning from your mistakes. As a mother, you are the ultimate teacher. When your adult daughter grows up and becomes a mother herself, she real-izes just how important *you* were to her development. I know for myself, I did not fully appreciate my own mother until I became a mother. Then, I realized just how much my mother had sacrificed for me. She did so with unselfishness and without hesitation.

4-9-2007   **180 lbs.**

Sandra is now grown up and despite my downfalls as a mother, she has turned out just fine. I have always wanted the best for my children but sometimes, while they were growing up, I made big mistakes just as all of us do. I have always tried to give them strength and encouragement. When I look at Sandra and how she is with her own kids, I know I must have done something right. She had me as an example, and even though I feel I fell short in some ways, I can see she learned good things from me as well. She values her family and her love for them is great.

I know Sandra has finally found her place in life. She was meant to be a mom. She was meant to be a wife. She was meant to be a sister. She was meant to be my daughter. Amongst all of this, she also found her career path. Up until about four years ago, she was not fully sure what she wanted to do with her life, as far as a ca-reer; she changed her mind many times. Then, while being laid up due to knee surgery, she found herself watching TV cooking shows. This sparked an interest from her and before we knew it, she found her calling. Sandra decided to take it all the way and just recently graduated with a culinary degree. She is a full-fledged chef! Sandra has such a great talent when it comes to cooking; she is an artist. As any artist does, she takes extreme pride in her work and you can be assured, her work will be perfection. She has had honors placed upon her very early in her career, including being just recently named as the president of the American Culinary Federation's chapter near where she lives. There are many more-seasoned chefs in the organization but Sandra's organizational skills are outstanding, and her pride in everything she does has become apparent to her peers. They all know she will get the job done, and do so, with professionalism. She makes me very proud.

As I close this chapter about my first-born child, I want to say it has been a pleasure to be the mother of such a special young woman. She has been a pleasure to know up to this point in our lives and I am looking forward to know her for the many more years. She has taught me *so* many things. She has taught me to have faith in myself. She has taught me to take a stand when I might have let things go or not stood up for myself. She has taught me to live my life for myself, and not for someone else. She held me accountable when I needed to be and she has always done so, with love. She has taught me not to be so hard on myself and to look at things with humor. She has taught me to never give up, especially when I felt I had no reason to live. She has been with me through thick and thin and has never judged me unfairly. She is my best friend. Not a day goes by without us talking to each other at least three times on the telephone. We have so many things in common like TV shows, movies, music, shopping, eating out, etc. She knows me better than I know myself. She has good instincts yet she still asks my advice on things of importance to her. She goes out of her way to make sure I know how important I am in her life. She tells me she loves me each time we see each other or talk to each other. The greatest thing is, I know she loves me with all her heart and wants only the best for me, as I want for her. We are in each other's corner, always. Yes, we are mother and daughter, but more than that, we are friends!

God created daughters so mothers have a second chance at youth.

CHAPTER TEN

IN HIS MOTHER'S EYES

4-10-2007   **180 lbs.**

I think every woman who has a son will agree with the statement "a mother's son can do no wrong!" Am I right, ladies? Looking at our sons when they are small, we see "little men" growing, exploring and learning how to be big, strong men when they grow up. With little boys, it's all about being the toughest, strongest "warrior" there is so they can protect their environment and especially protect their mommies! I know this instinct is natural in boys. They are programmed to protect the weaker sex from the time they were conceived. I think every mother out there who has a son can look back to when that son was an infant and recognize this protective trait. I even see it with my grandson; he is all about protecting his mommy! Now, after making these statements, I'll interject with some insight I have developed.

Women have always been perceived as being the weaker sex. It is in our make up to want to be protected. I think even the strongest, most independent woman will agree that she really likes it when a man looks out for her and acts as her protector. Am I right? This brings me to the point I am trying to make when it comes to mothers and sons.

When our sons are little boys, we can see their "big boy" development happening each day. They explore life with the intention of being the best there is at everything involving strength and courage. We, as mothers of sons, recognize this protective trait and it makes us feel a little more secure in our life. Our husbands, or men in our life, are our ultimate protectors, but we see our sons as mini versions of their fathers, and this gives us even more peace of mind. We know our little boys are growing up to be strong men, giving us another male in our life that loves us and wants to protect us. Being the mother of a son, I know *I* feel this sense of security; no matter what, my son will stand up for me and see to it I am safe and secure. This is comforting to know.

In other chapters, I have talked about my son, Jeffrey. He is the younger of my two children. Born August 12, 1982, he came into our lives after a long and difficult labor. My labor was induced and I suffered extreme labor pains from the beginning. We all thought after the easy birth I had with Sandra, this birth would be short... a piece of cake. Wrong! It was very different! I begged for drugs to knock out the pain, which they gave me, but it was hard because of my goal to not take any medication. With Sandra, it was natural childbirth all the way, but in this birth, I was suffering badly.

The nurse came in at one point to check me, and told my husband I would be in labor at least another six hours! When I heard the nurse say this, I started screaming, telling her she needed to check me again! The baby was coming! "I just checked you," she said, but I did not care, I was about to start pushing. She finally decided to take another look and when she did, all hell broke loose! She went flying out of the room, then came flying back in, threw a sterile gown at my husband and yelled at me not to push! "Your doctor is at another hospital delivering a baby!" My husband then excitedly said, "Who's going to deliver our baby?" The nurse glanced at him and said, "It may be you and me!" I then panicked; I did whatever it took not to push. Any woman who has given birth will tell you that you have no control after a certain point. What is happening is happening and you cannot stop it, no matter how hard you try! By the grace of God, I held tough until my doctor came flying into the delivery room, just in enough time, to catch Jeffrey David Lee Walker Jr. as he made his way into our world.

At 3:14 p.m., weighing in at a whopping 7 pounds, 4 ounces, and 18 inches long, Jeffrey was the boy we wanted! As had happened with my first pregnancy, I knew what gender I was carrying: a boy. When Jeffrey was delivered, my doctor held him up and said, "It's another girl," but he was holding the baby up facing me. What I was looking at was definitely *not* a little girl! Of course, my doctor was just messing with me; he knew we were expecting a boy but a little bit of the devil came over him, and he had to make me think twice. With the amount of medicine I was given for pain control, I might have *thought* I was looking at a boy but the baby could have been a girl! This was not the case at all; he was all boy!

With this pregnancy, we thought we had a good idea of the due date but Jeffrey was actually a little early; it was estimated by about three weeks because his lungs had not quite fully developed. Jeffrey had a little trouble after birth, but that soon passed and he did fine.

As I talked about in an earlier chapter, I decided to have my tubes tied if the baby was a boy. After the birth, my doctor asked me if we were on for the surgery the following morning and I told him we were. We wanted two children, we had our two children, and the surgery was on. The next morning at around seven, they came and fetched me for surgery. I was in for about an hour. I then went to recovery and then to my room. I felt fine; a little sore but it was manageable. After about four hours, they brought Jeffrey in so I could see him. My family came in and out most of the day. As the day progressed, I started feeling worse; pain started radiating throughout my abdomen. They gave me medicine to help with the pain and I rested as much as I could. I'll talk more about this in the next chapter because it warrants a whole chapter of its own, but right now, I want to continue with Jeffrey's story.

Jeffrey did not enter our lives very easily. Being a little bit early, and the fact that I took pain medicine while in labor, made his first few hours a little bit more difficult than his sister had when she was born. He was not quite as alert, but he was a beautiful baby boy and Sandra welcomed her baby brother; she was able to hold him after he was born and she was a proud big sister. She vowed to protect him forever. It was all so exciting for her. She now had a real living baby doll to play with!

Because of circumstances beyond my control, I was not able to take care of Jeffrey for the first few months of his short life. We did not get to bond the way mother and baby should because I became very ill shortly after his birth and my surgery. Jeffrey was passed around to both sets of grandparents because his daddy had to work and when he was not working, he spent as much time with me at the hospital as he could.

4-12-2007   **180 lbs.**
It was so difficult to be away from my new baby. By the time he was two days old, I could not hold him anymore; I was that ill. Jeffrey was allowed to stay at the hospital for four days, but then he had to go home. My in-laws and parents did everything they could to help take care of him and Sandra. It was hard on everybody, but poor little Jeffrey did not know what was going on. He needed me to hold him and love him but it was not possible. My heart ached for my baby; I wanted to hold him, comfort him, and share those first few days, weeks and months of his new life. He needed my touch and my voice to put him to sleep at night. He needed me to rock him and cuddle him. He needed his mommy, and I needed him just as much. It was such an empty feeling to know I had given birth to my baby, but he was being watched over by someone else. Don't get me wrong, I am so thankful for my family and friends who took over his care, but I still felt cheated in some way. I have to wonder, if I felt this way, how did my tiny baby feel? I know he missed me and he needed my love.

As months passed, and I was in and out of the hospital, it had to have been very confusing to Jeffrey. One day I would be home taking care of my son, then the next I would be gone and sometimes for weeks at a time. We never got to bond properly. At that time, I had no idea how all of that would affect my boy. Jeffrey was a very loving little baby, and later a very lovable boy, but he showed very early signs of a temper and anger. It was such a contradiction to his natural loving personality. He would be cuddly one minute, and then from out of nowhere, he would throw a temper fit and become uncontrollable. It drove us crazy because we did not know how to handle his outbursts. We tried everything; we tried showering him with love and attention; we tried discipline. You name it, we tried it. All we wanted was for our son to be a happy little boy who knew how much we loved and wanted him.

From an early age, we knew Jeffrey was very smart. He was an inquisitive little guy with a million questions. He wanted to know how every thing worked and why. He could take things apart when he was as young as four years old and then put them back together, perfectly. This was amazing! As a toddler, he became infatuated with vacuum cleaners. We could go into anyone's home, and within minutes, he would locate their vacuum cleaner and would want to vacuum for them. It was hilarious! For his second Christmas, Santa (my dad), brought Jeffrey his very own vacuum so he could clean whenever he wanted and not get fussed at for using mommy's! That vacuum was his favorite toy amongst many he received. I think he actually took it apart and then put it back together, just to see if he could!

Jeffrey was his daddy's little man, and they had a very special bond. In a way, I envied their closeness. Jeffrey always wanted his dad when he was hurt or upset; his daddy could always make it better. His daddy could also handle him better when he got into one of his tantrums. I could not handle him when he got out of control, but his dad could. If I tried to discipline him, he would always run to daddy, but his dad always backed me up. This fact still did not stop Jeffrey from trying!

Jeffrey has a huge heart. From the time he was a little kid, he had a sense of helping anyone or anything that needed help. He is also a very unselfish person. When he and Sandra were little, he would always offer to share with her anything that he had. She, on the other hand, wanted to keep her things to herself and was not too eager to let her little brother play with her stuff. We used to get on her constantly about this issue. She did, however, stick up for Jeffrey and protect him if needed. It was okay for her to beat up her little brother but no one else could even look cross-eyed at him because she would not stand for it! It was typical sibling rivalry behavior on her part.

4-13-2007   **179 lbs.**

My son was such a cute little guy. He has now grown up to be a great looking man. When Jeffrey was a baby, a close friend of ours, Don, nicknamed him Goober. He had a round face and was a chubby little person. Why, I do not know, but Jeffrey knew that as far as Don was concerned, his name was Goober! My dad nicknamed him Little Ed because Jeffrey, when four months old, had an uncanny resemblance to actor Ed Asner. Chubby and bald (sorry Ed), Jeffrey was Little Ed all over again; I have pictures to prove it!

When Jeffrey was a baby, we had a white German Shepherd named Chance. Chance was the ultimate protector when it came to Jeffrey. We would put Jeffrey in the crib in his room, and Chance would lie down in the hallway just past the bathroom. If anyone was visiting, they were allowed to go as far as the bathroom, but if they stepped past the bathroom door, Chance would give them a warning growl. He would never move unless someone decided to go past his comfort zone. Two steps past the bathroom door warranted a growl and then he would stand up and block the hallway. The person who was trying to get past Chance was soon to realize that they were not going past that point unless one of the family was with them to escort them further down the hallway.

Chance was Jeffrey's ultimate protector. He was good with the kids; they could pull him, drag him and do whatever they wanted to him, and he allowed them to do so. When he got tired of them tormenting him, he would get up and move away from their reach; never did he get mean with them. I would have felt sorry for anyone who tried to do harm to my kids when Chance was around. He would have never allowed it, period.

Jeffrey had no fear as a child. He tried anything and everything he could to show he was invincible. I think God gives mothers of little boys a special resilience, because if we did not have it, we would explode from fear. I cannot tell you how many times my son tried things that could have left him dead or seriously injured and these are only the things I knew about! God knows how many more things he did that I never knew. Still, today, I am learning about things he and his sister did as children that curl the hair on the back of my neck! I know they still have not fessed up to all of their antics. Each time they are together and I am around, I learn of another adventure they had at my expense. I am afraid that for years to come, they will uncover things, one by one, which, if I knew at the time, would have given me heart failure! They always get a big laugh out of it. Sometimes, they are even reluctant to tell me the truth, even though they are adults. I think their guilt is quite funny, even at their ages. I get a chuckle out of it, knowing they have lived with this guilt all of these years! I know with their own kids, they will be paid back a thousand times plus. There are just rewards in this old world.

Speaking of Jeffrey having no fear when he was little, I have to mention his episodes while riding his BMX bike. We were living in California at the time, and I was home from work early one day. The kids were outside playing with the neighborhood children, and I was busy doing something around the house. I happened to walk by one of our big picture windows and I glanced outside. There, across the street, my son was riding his bike at top speed down the sidewalk toward a big plywood structure I did not recognize. Before I could react, he was up on the plywood, then airborne! He had launched himself into the air from a ramp they had built without me knowing it. I stood there in fear as he sailed through the air, straight as an arrow, then landed about fifteen feet on the other side of the ramp, straight, and continued riding down the sidewalk. I was frozen! My six year old had just turned into a stunt man right before my eyes! It took me a minute to regain my composure and when I did, I ran outside and put a stop to Jeffrey's antics; at least I stopped it for the rest of that day.

4-16-2007   **179 lbs.**

Jeffrey had a problem with getting himself into trouble! When he was four years old, we were in the process of relocating to California. Jeffrey ended up going out there with his dad about two months before Sandra and I went. Sandra was in first grade and I wanted to wait until the end of the semester before pulling her out of school and moving her to a new school. Jeffrey joined his dad and they "batched it" for about two months. I have mentioned before that his dad could handle him better than I could, but that did not mean he had no problems with our son. They were staying in an apartment while we waited for our house to close. This apartment had a fake fireplace. I guess Jeffrey decided to make the fake fireplace into a real one, because somehow he set it on fire and ended up burning a hole in the carpet surrounding it before his dad realized what he was doing. Needless to say, Jeffrey was in big trouble and we had a ruined carpet to contend with! I know for a fact Jeffrey had a hard time sitting for the next week or two.

When Jeffrey was four years old, we took a trip from California to Kentucky to visit my parents. Big Jeff was not with us because he was on a business trip in Germany. We met my sister Sheri in Phoenix and then we all flew to Nashville together, Nashville airport being the closest one to where we were going in Kentucky. My family picked us up and we went to where they lived in Kentucky. Our family always had a family reunion over the Fourth of July holiday and we were there for the party. The Fourth of July was the next day and we were all busy getting things together for that evening. The kids were in and out of the house playing with cousins and friends. As the day progressed, I noticed Jeffrey coughing a little bit but I felt it was due to all of the cut grass and vegetation surrounding the area. The next day came and the picnic commenced with plenty of food and fun for everyone. Jeffrey's cough continued and we decided to call it a night and take him back to my parents' house. As we started driving the four miles back, Jeffrey started wheezing. When we got to the house, he was really having a hard time breathing. I was getting scared; I had my mom call my aunt and alert my cousin who was on the ambulance squad where they lived. My aunt made the call, and then called me back telling me the hospital in Clarksville, Tennessee was waiting for us. We started off, and because none of us knew where the hospital was, my aunt intercepted us on the highway and we followed her to the facility. My sister drove while I held little Jeffrey. He was struggling for each breath and I was scared for my little boy. We arrived at the hospital and they whisked us right in and started working on my son. There were tubes, lines, IVs, you name it. They worked on him and after about 45 minutes, he started coming out of his breathing problems and appeared to be all right. The doctor on duty told me he was having an allergic reaction to something he came into contact with but he was out of the woods and I could take him back home to my parent's house. After about one-and-a-half hours, they released him and we started back home. He was sleepy and dozed on and off during the ride. My cousin had alerted the ambulance service to be aware in case we needed them during the night. At that time, it was about 11:30 p.m. When we arrived at my parents' home, I carried Jeffrey inside. We had not been home five minutes when he started wheezing all over again.

4-17-2007   **179 lbs.**

Within seconds, my son was struggling for every breath; I had my family call 911. Literally within seconds, the ambulance was outside and the attendants rushed into the house to take over Jeffrey's care. He was crying and struggling to breath. I was in a panic because my little boy was turning blue and he was becoming lethargic. I knew this was a serious situation and I felt helpless as they whisked my tiny child off and I followed, riding with him on the fifteen-minute trip back to the hospital. Every once and a while, Jeffrey would get enough air to mumble out to me, "Mommy... I'm dying!" My heart sank each time he spoke. I was helpless and did not know what to do to help my child; I was crumbling inside. My son was struggling for every breath and there was nothing I could do to help him other than just reassure him and tell him I was there by his side. I have never been so frightened in my life. Each breath my little boy took seemed like it was his last as the EMTs worked diligently to sustain him. The trip to the hospital seemed like it took a lifetime. I thought my son would be gone before we pulled in to the emergency room.

As we arrived, they started working on Jeffrey, and they made me wait outside of his room. My family started arriving and they tried to keep me calm, but it was hard. I was falling apart inside but somehow, my outer strength took over and I maintained my composure. After about thirty minutes of me not knowing if Jeffrey was still alive, doctors came out and told me I could go in and see him. They had him stabilized. When I got into the cubical where Jeffrey was, there were once again tubes and lines running in and out of him. The doctor explained that Jeffrey was having extreme asthma attacks and it was very serious. They were going to admit him in pediatric ICU and I could stay with him because he was so young. Of course I was going to stay with him... this was my baby! Even if they had told me I could *not* stay with him, I would have put up a fuss. He was only four years old, in a strange place, with many strangers hovering over him. I know he was scared, the poor little guy.

After they got him admitted, he had a full week of treatments. I had to deal with little Jeffrey almost climbing the walls because the medications they gave him hyped him up. He could not sit still and I felt so sorry for him. He would try to sleep, but he was moving from head to toe unable to relax. They had him on many steroids, which caused his hyperactivity. I tried everything I could think of to get him to relax but nothing worked.

4-18-2007   **179 lbs.**

That time in the hospital was very difficult. Jeffrey was a very sick little guy and the fact that we had to keep him so confined did not help the situation. They put him in a big crib with steel bars and it looked like my baby was in a cage. They had to do this because it was the only way to keep him from running around. All of the steroids they pumped into his tiny body worked against any chance we had of getting him to rest. He was a wild man; he would grab the bars on the crib and shake them fiercely to try to escape. I felt horrible for my little boy. He was in a strange place, with lots of strangers coming in and doing all kinds of things to him. Jeffrey did not understand why he was feeling so hyperactive. Put any four year old in a confined situation and they are going to go crazy; add medications that are known to cause hyperactivity and you have a double dose of problems.

I stayed with my son during this whole ordeal, only leaving his bedside once to go out and get a bite to eat away from the hospital. When he was well enough to get on a plane and fly back home to California, they released him and we went home. After we arrived, I had to get him set up with our own pediatrician and start treatment immediately. Jeffrey had never had any asthma episodes before this trip, but he was highly allergic to many things. When he was an infant, we could not use disposable diapers because he was so highly allergic to them; we had to use cloth diapers and wash them five to seven times then rinse five times before we could use them again. We had to use special soap to bathe him because he was allergic to all commercial baby products, even lotions and oils. His formula was changed several times before we found one that he was able to keep down. He had problems as a baby, but as he started getting older, most of these allergies disappeared. We never noticed breathing problems when he was an infant despite his being so highly allergic to things that came into contact with his skin. He would break out with rashes, but that was about it. We were soon to realize we had to keep a close watch over our son and his breathing problems, always making sure he had the proper medications with him, inhalers, etc., and daily preventative medicines as well. It was tough on such a little guy.

If you are a parent of a child with extreme asthma, or you yourself suffer from this disability, you understand there is nothing scarier to witness or, I am sure, go through. As a parent of such a child, I can tell you I spent many sleepless nights worrying if he was going to have a severe attack, which would send us to the emergency room. I cannot tell you how many times we made that dreaded trip. It always seemed to happen when his dad was out of town on a business trip and I was left alone to go through the episodes with my son. Not until long after my marriage failed and Jeffrey was with his dad, did Jeff have to witness such an extreme attack, which sent them both to the hospital. He later called me and told me how scared he was during Jeffrey's attack and that he had no idea what I had been going through all those times when he was not there to give support. He actually apologized to me for leaving our son's care strictly up to me while he traveled. I was sorry my son had to go through yet another attack, but in a way, I was glad his dad was there to witness the episode, because it made it real for him. Only now did he fully understand just how critical it was when Jeffrey had the attacks. After this experience, Jeff became a much more involved parent with Jeffrey.

4-19-2007   **179 lbs.**

When we lived in California, we went to the beach quite a bit; the kids loved the ocean. We would take popcorn and feed the seagulls, which would bring them in by the dozens! The kids would laugh and squeal with delight. Neither of my children had a fear of the water; both of the kids were swimming by the time they were a year old. I made sure they knew how to swim early. When I was a teenager, I worked as a lifeguard and taught swimming for infants and toddlers. It was very important to me that my children knew how to swim and learned water safety. We had a swimming pool at home and we had a boat, so we spent a lot of time on surrounding lakes and waterways. The kids learned how to water-ski and how to play on a water boogie board at very young ages. They were water rats!

I have a funny story about my son and the ocean that I have to share. I had not yet relocated to California, but traveled there one weekend to see my husband and little boy. We made a trip to the beach, and Jeffrey and his dad were playing in the shallow water. Jeffrey was running out into the ocean and then running back as the waves came close to him. We had been there for about an hour and after eating a picnic lunch, they started playing in the water again. The waves were getting a little bit stronger. I was sitting on the beach with my camera. I do not know what Jeffrey's dad said to him, but suddenly, Jeffrey started running towards me and as he did so, I started snapping pictures. He was coming towards me but every once in a while he would glance back to a big wave that was gaining on him. I continued to snap pictures and Jeffrey's expression started changing as the big wave started getting closer and closer; he was getting very concerned. Before he knew it, the wave was on top of him! Of course, his dad was right there to rescue him. Jeffrey was one scared little boy. When I got the pictures developed, they proved to be priceless. You can see the wave gaining on him and his total expression change from fun to fear! I cherish these photos to this day.

Jeffrey has always been infatuated with speed and motors. When he was little, he wanted a go-kart. He started asking for one by the time he was five. We held out until he turned nine; his dad bought him one that Christmas. He lived out in a sandy hill area of El Paso and had plenty of room to ride. Sandra and I went to visit him in April during spring break; Jeffrey could not wait to take me out for a ride. Was I in for a surprise! My pint-sized son took me for the ride of my life! At three inches above the ground, we sailed across the sand dunes at lightning speed, me holding on to anything I could get my hands on. He was going for the thrill factor and I was holding on for dear life! When he finally took me back to the house, I wanted to get off the go-kart and immediately kiss the ground; I was never so glad to be standing still. Jeffrey was quite delighted with himself. "Oh Mom, that wasn't fast at all!" he chimed. "I could have gone much faster!" I was surely glad my son had taken mercy on me.

Jeffrey has never outgrown his need for speed! For as long as I can remember, he has wanted to race cars. When he was a boy, if you asked him what he wanted to be when he grew up, he would say "A race car driver!" He grew up with his dad owning a Corvette and having the same desire for speed. Anything Jeffrey has driven has been put to the test. His bikes, his go-kart and then later, his automobiles, have all been pushed to the limits, and I was concerned that when he became a teenager and started driving, he would get hurt because of his speeding. Jeffrey had his share of tickets, then, when he realized how much his insurance was going up due to those tickets, I think he started becoming a little more aware of his speed and now does his best to keep it under control. I have to say though, I always feel safe when he drives. Sometimes he does drive fast, but he is a cautious driver. My dad on the other hand hates to ride with my son. He says it scares him to death!

The Mustang was always Jeffrey's favorite car. He wanted one long before he could drive. I gave Jeffrey his first car; I had a Chevy Blazer that Sandra drove all through high school and I kept it for Jeffrey. By the time he was old enough to drive, he talked me into trading the Blazer for a Firebird that a relative owned. We made an even trade. The Firebird was not in the best of shape but it was fast! Jeffrey ended up going back to Texas to live with his dad after spending his first year of high school living with me. The school he went to where I lived was bad compared to what he was used to. He did not fit in, and we all felt it was in his best interest to go back to Texas to finish high school. Anyway, the Firebird ended up in Texas but this did not satisfy my son's desire for a Mustang. He finally bought one, and most of his friends had Mustangs as well. I think they formed a car club to show off their vehicles!

Within a year, the first Mustang was no longer quite good enough, so he bought another one. I think to date he has owned three different Ford Mustangs! He did drive the Firebird a little bit, but I ended up selling it for him here in Kentucky to a neighbor of my father's who has restored it back to its original condition. He is thrilled with it!

No one can ever say my son has cheap tastes! In fact, neither of my kids have cheap tastes. They both appreciate the finer things in life. This goes for cars as well, when talking about Jeffrey. There is no doubt in my mind that he will someday own a Lamborghini or whatever other car catches his fancy. If it is fast and looks good, he will own it! Right now he drives a sensible car but be assured it looks good and he has had it out on a wide-open road just to see exactly how fast it will go. I know he will never change when it comes to his need for speed. He just bought another new car and one of the first things he told me about it was the fact that "it ran good!" I know that means it goes fast!

4-21-2007   **177 lbs.**

As I have mentioned before, from the time Jeffrey was a tiny child, he demonstrated a temper. He was very difficult for me to handle because he would throw himself into tantrums and would even get physical. We never truly understood why he would get so worked up, but these situations would usually result in me trying to hold him down to keep him from hurting himself. He was in constant motion from the time he started walking. Back before hyperactivity was as understood as it is now, we knew he was a hyperactive child and we tried everything we could to get an expert to agree with us, so we could address the issue and know what to do to help him through it. I took Jeffrey to doctor upon doctor trying to get him tested because he had such a hard time concentrating in school and it was affecting him. No one would face the situation and make the diagnosis. It was a constant struggle; public schools were not equipped to handle him so we ended up putting him in private school where he got more one-on-one attention. This was a lifesaver as far as we were concerned! It was, however, difficult having him in private school and Sandra in public school. At one point, we moved her into private school as well but it was not as positive an experience for her. She needed more of the social activity that public school offered, so private school for her did not last long.

Jeffrey had an inferiority complex as a child, and it followed him into adulthood. I am still angry with a teacher he had in kindergarten because she actually told my son he was stupid, a word that cut our small child like a knife. He took it to heart and never got over it. She was an old woman who should have retired long before my son encountered her. She was actually getting senile and would lash out at the little kids one minute, then hug them the next. My daughter was tutoring in Jeffrey's class and actually witnessed this woman telling my five year old, he was stupid! When Sandra came home and told me what took place in that classroom, I was up at the school immediately requesting this woman be relieved of her duties as an educator. It finally resulted in us having to go before the school board to address this issue, among other incidents which took place in her classroom. She was relieved of her duties, but not before the damage was done to my child and, I am sure, many other children. What a shame it is that we have individuals like this in our educational systems who, with one word or action, can leave a dark mark on young impressionable minds.

My handsome son has fought self-esteem issues most of his life and it has been very hard for me to watch him doubt his abilities for so many years. Just now, at 24 years old, he is finally realizing how intelligent and gifted he is. This has taken lots of hard work on his part, and the help of many people he has been blessed to meet who have put value on his abilities and are teaching him how to love himself. He has surrounded himself with upbeat positive people who are movers and shakers. This has helped him tremendously. Now he has realized, as an adult, he may have a form of a learning disability, and when coupled with his ADHD, he now understands why he had to struggle so much through school. He is extremely intelligent but with these two things, he has had to fight hard for his achievements. Now, as an adult, he is more aware of the issues and realizes he is very smart.

Jeffrey has also been very shy most of his life. He is now in an occupation where shyness cannot exist and he has to reach outside of himself to find his comfort zone. I am very proud of how far he has come in the last few years. We have always known Jeffrey would do great things with his life and he is learning day by day how to accomplish his dreams.

4-23-2007   **177 lbs.**

Family members of mine, especially my mother and sister, always felt Jeffrey would get involved in the work of helping people. He has had a charismatic personality since he was a little boy, and has always had a big heart. Both my mother and sister used to say Jeffrey would probably end up being a minister or an evangelist. As a child, he would charm people with his honesty and grown-up attitudes toward peace and love. He has always been very loving and giving; even as a child, he would go out of his way to share and be fair. I remember when he was little, whenever he got a new toy, he would want to share it with his sister and friends. One Christmas, he got a remote control truck from Santa. He was outside, playing with the neighborhood children, and a new boy wandered into the neighborhood. Jeffrey offered to share his new toy with this boy and the boy took him up on it. Within minutes, the new kid disappeared out of the neighborhood with Jeffrey's truck, never to be seen again! We searched and searched for the boy but never located him. We had to explain to Jeffrey that he had to be a little careful about who he shared with because not everyone had his upbringing and his big heart. He was one crushed little person for a few days, but soon forgot about the toy and he continued to have a generous heart and giving nature.

I have talked about Jeffrey's temper and how he has related to me. As I've mentioned, I was very sick shortly after his birth and our bonding experience did not happen like most mothers and newborns. I know this affected my son, but not until he was 10 years old did I fully understand how it truly affected him. Shortly after Sandra and I moved to Kentucky, Jeffrey was on a long break from school before the Christmas season. We had been there about a month when he came to stay with us for two weeks. Sandra was in school, so Jeffrey and I had a lot of time to spend alone together. This was the first time I can remember him and I having time to just spend together and get to know each other. The days were full of us talking and doing mother and son things. It was great!

One day, we were sitting down drinking coffee. Both of my kids loved to drink coffee with me, but their coffee was with lots of cream, sugar and just a touch of coffee, to add flavor! Anyway, while Jeffrey and I sat there, something came up about me being sick after his birth. He broke down into tears and started telling me how sorry he was for making me sick when he was born. I sat there for a few seconds, stunned, as my ten-year-old son shed tears about how guilty he felt because he thought he had made me sick when he was born. My heart sank! He sobbed and sobbed while I tried to explain to him he had nothing to do with the fact I got sick. Then, it suddenly started to sink in; this little boy was holding this guilt for all of these years. He really thought he was the cause of my illness! What a heavy load for such a little person to bear. I wrapped my arms around my son and told him how very much I loved him, and reassured him he had absolutely nothing to do with it. Then, I explained to him what exactly happened 10 years before and why I almost died. He listened to me with adult-like attention. That talk we had ended up being our first true bonding experience. Not up until that point had my son and I shared so tenderly, and I truly believe his behavior toward me changed at that point. He was not only feeling guilty, but he was also angry with me because I was not around to mother him when he was a little baby. He missed this experience and I know he felt the closeness Sandra and I had and he resented it, even though he did not understand exactly what resentment was. He did not understand that I loved him just as much as I loved his sister. His anger towards me also made him feel guilty because I was his mommy and he did not understand why he was angry; it was a vicious cycle for my little guy. We cried together that day, and then we vowed to always talk with each other and express our feelings. A new bond formed between my son and me that December day and it changed our relationship forever.

4-25-2007   **176 lbs.**

Today, Jeffrey is approaching his twenty-fifth birthday, and not a day goes by that we do not talk at least once a day. With this book and the agreement we made to each other, he checks on my daily progress and we have become the best of friends. It is so nice to have a daughter who is a best friend and to have a son who is a best friend. We have made quantum leaps this year in our relationship. In past years, we have been close, but something has changed in our relationship the last few months that has brought us closeness that we had not achieved before. Sandra and I have been the best of friends because we have been together for so many years. Jeffrey and I were separated on and off since he was 10 and we have had to get to know each other over again. At this time in our lives, he is all grown up and I can ask his advice on things; I know he will always be honest with me and even though his answers many not be exactly what I want to hear, I know he has my best interests at heart. He is now more willing to let me know how he feels about a situation I may be going through, where as before, he might have held back and not told me how he saw it. He has always been respectful of me and treated me well.

At this point in our relationship, Jeffrey will tell me if he thinks I am missing the point or messing up. That takes a lot of courage on his part because he always wants to be diplomatic and never say or do anything to hurt either his dad or me. We raised both of our children to have respect for others, especially their elders. We not only count as their elders, but we are their parents as well! I know it is still hard for them to act as if we are friends and tell us exactly what they think. Jeffrey has just in the past few months reached this comfort level with me and it is great... we are on our way!

I can now, without reservation, tell my son exactly what is on my mind. It does not matter what the subject matter is; we talk about everything. We laugh a lot! Recently, something funny happened where someone Jeffrey knows thought his mother, me, was in her sixties! Why I am not exactly sure, because Jeff's only 24. In the future, I know I will meet this person. I was joking with Jeffrey and told him that we should *not* set the record straight and let this person go on thinking I am much older than I really am. Then, when they meet me, I told Jeffrey, "I will be the sexiest 'sixty-something' they have ever seen!" We both got a good laugh out of that one. With all of the weight I have lost and am still losing, I am looking pretty good and by that time, I'll be smoking hot! A year ago, I probably would have not talked to my son that way, but now it is comfortable and it's nothing for me to say things that I used to think would make him blush. I can tease him, make fun of myself, speak my mind, just be myself with my son, and not think anything of it. It is great fun to have another buddy, another friend.

The honesty we have shared and the things I have just spoken about bring up another issue. Never in the past have I remembered having a fight, or even a big disagreement, with Jeffrey. I can now say, with our newfound relationship, this is not the case now! We actually had a big disagreement about a month-and-a-half ago and we got downright mad with each other! I was upset about something involving my dad and I cried on Jeff's shoulder. Basically, I was having myself a good old fashion pity party. My son listened to me whine and then told me he thought I was in the wrong. Wow! That was not what I wanted to hear from him. I was expecting him to take up for his mommy and instead, he took up for his grandpa. I was infuriated! I sobbed, yelled, and moaned. He yelled back, and we even ended up hanging up our phones, angry at each other, me probably more so. We did not call each other back the rest of that evening and I know I was miserable because I expected him to call me back and make amends. Of course, I did not call him back either! I did not get a good night's sleep and by the following morning, I was feeling crummy! I had time to cool down and when I started thinking about it, I realized my son was right. I had simply been in a foul mood to begin with when all of this started. I picked up the phone and called Jeffrey. "I am sorry," I told him, and he followed me by telling me the same thing. "Mom, we should have just stopped and prayed," he said. "That would have put us both at ease and we would have probably worked it out, right then and there." He was right. It would have made me stop and think about what I was saying and doing. Boy, what a dose of reality Jeffrey had given me. His wise words in the renewed conversation made me realize just how small and insignificant my tantrum had been the day before and it I saw that my son meant his word. In the letter he wrote to me on the first of the year, he told me this was the year we were going to start holding each other accountable for our actions. He proved this by not backing down and telling me what I wanted to hear. This was a completely new ballgame and I was going to have to learn the rules! There will be no more stealing bases and sliding into home. I am going to have to learn to run the bases to get that winning run!

4-26-2007   **177 lbs.**

I think that at this stage of the game, my son is on his way to greatness! He is optimistic and dreams that nothing stands in his way of achieving this. He has the drive and desire to make a success of anything he chooses. With the combination of his hard work and honesty, I know his success is only a heartbeat away. If you measure success by honesty and scruples, Jeffrey has already achieved more than most people could ever wish for! I define success not by monetary value, but by how you are willing to reach your goals and remain true to yourself and above all, true to God. I can say without reservation that my son has always remained true to our Savior. He loves God and is not afraid to share this love and belief with those he meets. I know the Lord will see him through life and, in turn, Jeffrey will remain close to Him and never stray from his beliefs. What more can a parent ask for? To have children who care for others feelings and remain honest in everything they do is a parent's dream. I can say that both of my children possess these qualities and it makes me very proud to know that their father and I must have done something right along the way in order to raise such wonderful individuals. It was a great job to have when they were growing up and now we can see all of the hard work we put into our children has paid off a million-fold. They are great people to know and love. I am so very proud of Jeffrey and Sandra and it is hard to contain myself when I speak of them to others! I know my "proud mom" personality radiates around what I am doing, no matter what situation I am in. How can it not? I have a lot to be proud of!

I know if you are a parent reading this, you can look to your own children and see the fruits of your labor. We as parents all have bragging rights! What a great gift God has given us to be able to pour our hopes and dreams into our children, and then wait for their own personalities to emerge from this. We see a little bit of ourselves in them, but also have the chance to get to know a completely new person and make a new and exciting friend. Our relationship changes throughout the years and not only do we have our wonderful memories of yesterday, we have today, this year, and most importantly of all, the future

%%

REFLECTION 3

4-27-2007   176 lbs.

In writing the last four chapters, I have had the chance to once again touch on some very emotional issues dealing with the death of my beautiful sister. But I have to say, it has also been a wonderful experience to look back on our many years together and be able to cherish those memories again.

When I wrote the chapter about Sheri passing, it was bittersweet. How many times in our lives are we able to spend time with our loved ones when they really need us the most? Busy lives keep us focused on things that in the long run really do not matter. When you have the opportunity to spend time with someone you truly love, do not get sidetracked; you will never look back at a business venture and think to yourself, "That was the most incredible experience I've had!" If you do, I feel sorry for you. There is no greater gift than when you can look back and know you made a difference in someone's life, especially when it is someone who has given you so much throughout the years. No amount of wealth, possessions or status will bring the gift of sharing love with a loved one who is counting on you to see them through, no matter what their journey. When I had this chance, everything else in my world became insignificant. I was able to give back, if even only a little, to my big sister who had given me her unconditional love for 48 years. I know I could never come close to repaying her for all she did for me throughout the years, but I gave her my love, and hopefully my strength, so she could transition from this life on earth to a far better place. Those days that I spent with her, no matter how frustrated or tired I got, can never be replaced in my book of "what really matters most" in this earthly life. When it comes to those last cherished moments that I spent with my sister at the time she was ready to let go and go to God, there will never be anything that can compare to the feelings and emotions I had that June day. I can only tell you, even though it was a sad time for those she left behind, it was also her ultimate liberation; to be herself and to be free and to walk with her angels and dance in Heaven. What more could I ask for? Yes, the selfish side of me wants her here with us, but I have to know she is now where she is needed most, and that is my comfort, through it all.

The last two chapters about my children have been a hoot to write! I thought about things I had not thought of in years. It was great fun looking back at earlier years and actually see each of them develop into the people they are today. Yes, we had our trials and tribulations and we were by no means a perfect family but I think my kids survived, in spite of it all! There have been many times I have felt extreme guilt about situations I caused my family, but by the grace of God, He kept my children strong and close to Him, which I am so truly thankful for. They have persevered through tough times and have kept up their love of God in their lives. With this love, I can rest assured they are headed in the right direction. I cannot ask for more.

I have recently had a milestone happen in my life. As you can see in my daily writings and record of my weight loss, I have now lost 50 pounds! This just happened today and I cannot be happier. It is quite funny because I had a deal with my son-in-law that when I hit the fifty-pound mark, he owed me a piece of cheesecake from a well-known eatery in Nashville! Yesterday, my daughter and I were in Nashville for a doctor's appointment and shopping. She asked me if I had hit the "fifty-pound mark" yet. I weighed in yesterday morning and I was actually about a quarter of a pound from that exact mark. I told her I was shy of the mark a little bit and she said, "Good! We're going for cheesecake!" What the heck: 49 and three-quarter pounds are close enough, at least that was my reasoning.

We had an incredible meal and then we each had cheesecake and boy was it awesome! Do you know what the best part of it was? I weighed in today and I hit that elusive fifty-pound mark even after having all those calories! I cannot argue with success, but I have possibly been approaching this whole diet thing wrong. Do I need to develop a diet of cheesecake? I know if I wrote a book called *The Cheesecake Diet* it would be a best seller.

There have been exciting things that have happened to me in the past couple of months. I traveled to New Orleans this month and had a wonderful time! It is an incredible city despite Hurricane Katrina and the devastation it caused. Where else can you go to a city torn apart by a natural disaster, and still see so many smiling faces genuinely happy to see you and being so proud of their great city, no matter how bad times still are? Even though there is still more work to be done, more than you can possibly imagine, the people of New Orleans are proud of who they are, where they are, and their personal suffering does not show through in their smiling faces and kind words. I have to say that I feel such a closeness to this city and its people; never in my life have I felt such a connection. I have been many places, but the warmth and comfort I experienced in New Orleans cannot be compared, not even with my own hometown. If you have never traveled to this magical place, I encourage you to do so.

4-28-2007   **176 lbs.**

Church is still busy as usual. I am involved in many different activities and I enjoy every minute of it! We just had our first church directory made with our pictures in it and it came out this week. It really turned out great! At a prayer meeting this past Thursday night, we received the new directory. Everyone was excited to look through it for his or her family portrait! One of my close friends got to the end before I did and she turned around to me and said, "Boy, Karen, I'll bet you wished they would have burned this one before they put it in!" She was referring to my picture! A somewhat sensitive person might have taken that comment the wrong way, but not me; I had to agree 100% with her. They took the pictures only two days after I had had major dental surgery. I was swollen up like the Goodyear Blimp and I of course weighed 50 pounds more in this photo! I quickly turned the page and stared at myself and I excitedly announced, "That's not me, it's my *evil twin!*" Everyone got a big laugh out of it and I quickly turned the page, looking for more pleasant scenery. It's good to be able to laugh at yourself; if you don't believe me, try it sometime!

In closing this Reflection, I know ahead of time that the next chapter will bring up some further unpleasant memories. I will work my way through it, as I have done before, and I hope I will be able to further heal and possibly touch you if you have, or have known someone who has, gone through a similar ordeal. It was not easy to go through, but I have to say that who I am today was formed partially because I did go through it. It has made me a stronger person and has also allowed me to gain valuable insight into human nature. No one is perfect; we all make mistakes, even some that are life altering. However, we gain strength and redemption through how we choose to make these mistakes right, or at least *try* to make them right. The following chapter is a continuation of my story, and it was tough to write, will be possibly tough to read, but all of it the truth. I would like to say that I'm sorry it happened to me, and I'm sorry it happened to my family, but I know for myself, it brought me closer to God. With this, I know I have no reason to be sorry. It was painful at the time, and still is, but we made it through, I am here today, and what more could I ask for. I am alive!

CHAPTER ELEVEN

FRIDAY THE 13TH ???

4-30-2007   **176 lbs.**

I have never been a superstitious person. Occasionally, as a child, I played the childhood games such as avoiding the cracks on the sidewalk, not crossing the street if I saw a black cat ahead of me, thinking if I broke a mirror I would have bad luck, and many others. Of course, when I grew up, I also outgrew those childish superstitions. The logical part of my brain took over, and so did my religious beliefs; at least that was the case until Friday the 13th in August of 1982.

The day after I gave birth to my son Jeffrey proved to be the day that changed my life as I knew it, forever. The morning after Jeffrey's birth, I was scheduled for surgery. The day before I had made the decision to go ahead and have a tubal ligation performed, or having my tubes tied, for sterilization. This was a decision of which I was quite sure. We had our two perfect children, our girl and boy, and we chose to stop there. The next logical decision was for me to have the procedure done. I was absolutely certain and had been given all of my options. Because the birth control pill and I did not get along, I made up my mind that this would be the best thing for me.

Waking up early that morning in the hospital, I took a shower, and they came to wheel me down to surgery. I was feeling pretty good, a little sore from having a baby, but otherwise fine. I cannot say I was not a little bit nervous, but nonetheless I was ready. I made it into the operating room and from there onwards, I do not remember much until waking up in recovery. My doctor spoke with me, telling me everything went as planned, and then shortly afterwards I was taken back to my room on the obstetrics floor. In the next few minutes, my family came to see me and they brought Jeffrey in so I could see him. I was still groggy from the surgery so my family decided to let me rest and they left, promising me they would be back later. The rest of the day, I slept off and on. I remember that as the day progressed, when I was awake, I was in an increasingly considerable amount of pain, I asked for medication and they gave it to me every four hours. I was not expecting to be in as much pain as I was, but I attributed it to the fact I had a baby and then surgery the following day.

As the evening started, my parents, in-laws, husband and little Sandra came to see baby Jeffrey and me. I remember trying my best to visit with them, but I was drugged and still in a lot of pain. I tried my best to keep talking with my company but it was difficult. They were soon to realize I was not going to be the best of company, so they all excused themselves and went home except for my husband, Jeff. My parents took Sandra home with them so Jeff could stay with me for a while. He let me rest when I could and he spent time with our new baby. He ended up leaving around 9:30 that evening and left me in the care of the nurses.

5-1-2007   **176 lbs.**

Around two in the morning, I woke up in such pain that I could not stand it. I called for the nurse and she came in to check on me. She gave me more pain medicine but told me she could not understand why I was hurting so badly. "This is not known to be a difficult surgery," she said. That was exactly what I thought. I went back to sleep but awoke about two hours later in a sweat and again, extreme pain. I knew I could not get more medicine for another two hours, so I sweated it out, watching the clock until I could ring for the nurse once again.

The time passed slowly. I thought those couple of hours would not arrive before I started screaming. I did not want to be a bother but when the time finally came, I was in tears and begged the nurse to do something. Again, she medicated me and told me I needed to drink large quantities of fluids because I was probably dehydrated. I tried to drink as much as I could, because if dehydration was the cause of my pain, I was determined to drink fluids and alleviate it. Another two hours passed with me trying to doze on and off. Again, at about the two-hour mark, the pain became intolerable. I was starting to get chills and I knew I was running a fever. I waited until the shift change at seven in the morning; the new staff took over and they came to me to take my vital signs. I was spiking with a 102-degree temperature. They did not seem to be too concerned but *I* was, especially considering the amount of pain I was in and the fact the medication they were giving me did not seem to be helping that much. Again, they told me I needed to drink as much as I possibly could and that would help with the fever as well as my dehydration. I did as I was told.

My breakfast arrived shortly afterwards, but I did not feel like eating; I was hurting too much. One of my nurses came into my room and told me I really needed to eat if I wanted to feel better. I was feeling very nauseated and I struggled with the meal; I was not doing too well. I drank everything they had on the tray with the exception of the milk. Another nurse came in to check on me and when she saw I had not eaten much, she encouraged me to at least drink the milk. "Liquids, liquids, liquids," she expressed, so I drank it. I started to feel physically worse; the pain was increasing and my fever was going up. I was sick to my stomach and felt like I needed to throw-up. I couldn't, but I felt like I was going to. My body was aching from head to toe, despite the medication I was taking. The nurses came in intermittently to check on me but the doctor had not been there and it was approaching the afternoon. I asked about him and they told me they had not spoken with him yet. I was still being encouraged to drink, so I did.

My doctor, Dr. M.O. (I give his initials only), had performed my surgery the day before and then he left town on vacation. I knew he was leaving town and this is why I chose to have my labor induced with my son because I did not want a strange doctor performing the delivery. We had been doctor and patient for several years and I trusted him with my life. My surgery was expected to be simple and I felt confident he was putting me in safe hands. I did not know the doctor's name that was taking over his patients. I waited and waited for this other doctor to come see me, but he never made it in that day. I was getting worse and no one seemed to be too concerned, except for my family and myself. I did not want to be a constant complainer, but the sicker I got, the harder it was for me to stay calm.

5-2-2007   **176 lbs.**
There was something else going on with me; my body started to swell all over. As the day progressed, I was getting bigger and bigger, especially around my abdomen. I showed the nurses and again, they seemed not to be too alarmed. They got me up and told me I needed to walk; trying to walk was excruciatingly painful. I could hardly move. Feeling completely bloated, it was difficult to put one foot in front of the other, let alone walk. They continued to give me pain medication and continued telling me to drink as much as 12 ounces every 30 minutes. I was still getting my meals but it was difficult to eat anything because my nausea was out of control, yet I was not expelling anything. My family recognized something was extremely wrong, but when they questioned the nurses, they were told everything I was experiencing would pass in a day or so.

Again, I asked for the doctor who was supposed to be taking over my care. He still had not shown up. I requested the nurses call him and tell him what I was going through, and I was told because it was the weekend it was not unusual for doctors to run behind, sometimes not coming to the hospital until evening. In a couple of hours, it was evening, and still no doctor. My temperature was climbing. I was trying to do everything they told me to do but I was losing the battle.

Jeff stayed with me until late evening. Baby Jeffrey was brought in several times because I was too sick to walk to the nursery to see him. I was encouraged to hold my baby, which I desperately wanted to do but it was becoming increasingly difficult. Even *his* tiny body put pressure on my swelling abdomen. I wanted to hold him and feed him but it would always end up with his daddy taking over and me in tears because I really needed my baby but could not handle his care. I was starting to feel guilty because of this situation. If only I had waited to have the surgery, Jeffrey would not have suffered. My husband reassured me everything would be all right with the baby, and he took over the bonding and nurturing role. I only got sicker. The nurses told my husband there were calls to the doctor's answering service but he had not called back yet. My husband expressed his anger over the situation because he could tell I was in serious trouble and nobody seemed to be in the least bit concerned. In fact, they started acting as if my husband and I were making more of the situation than it was; you could tell they were getting aggravated with us for questioning my care and questioning what was going on with me. I felt this when they had to answer my calls because I was in so much pain I could not stand it, and would ask for anything to make me feel better. I knew something was wrong, my family knew something was wrong, but the nurses seemed indifferent. I was getting really scared, which made everything else worse.

The night turned into the next day. The nurses came in several times at night and made me walk. I was dizzy, lightheaded and in pain, but they insisted the dizziness and other symptoms were all due to the pain medications I had been given. They made me drink more and more liquid, even forcing milk down me because I was hardly eating. My throat was getting very sore, and the fever and chills were still there. The concept of time was getting difficult for me. When my family came in to see me, it was as if they had never left and the night had never come. Jeff asked me about the doctor coming and I did not think he had, but I was not sure. Then he questioned the nurses. They checked the night nurse's notes and looked for a doctor's orders, but there were none. Jeff hit the ceiling! He demanded the doctor's telephone number. They would not give it to him until he told them he was transferring me to another hospital. Then they reluctantly gave him the number. He made the call and even though I did not hear the conversation, I knew with my husband as upset as he was, it most likely was not pleasant. He came back into my room and told me he had to leave a message with the answering service and that he gave them a time frame to pass along to the doctor. He gave the doctor 30 minutes to return his call. The doctor did not call back. My husband placed another call to the service and told them not to bother, because he was moving me!

Within about 10 minutes of that last message, the doctor finally called Jeff back. He told my husband that until those two messages, he was not even aware of me being at the hospital! He had not received any messages regarding a patient of Dr. M.O. being at this particular hospital. He was attending some of his other patients at other hospitals, but had no knowledge of me. He expressed his sincere apologies and told my husband he would get there as soon as he could but until then, he would talk with the nurses about my condition and give orders for my care. After the conversation, my husband was feeling a bit better and he passed along the information to me and the rest of the family. This was at approximately 11 on Sunday morning. In a few minutes, a nurse came in and told me they were going to take me to have an x-ray as the doctor had called in the order. They wheeled me down to take a few x-rays of my abdomen then took me back up to my room. They brought me more food and many liquids and told me I needed to drink everything on the tray. I tried, but it was making me sicker to my stomach. After about an hour passed, a nurse came in and wanted to measure my waist. She had a tape measure and while I stood up, she placed the tape around me. When I saw the measurement, I was in complete shock! My waist measured *fifty-eight* inches! I wasn't even this big when pregnant! I started crying, not just because of the measurement, but also because I was in extreme pain and now even more scared. The nurse told me to calm down but I couldn't; I was petrified and afraid.

We waited for the doctor to come in but he did not show up until almost seven p.m. When he came in and introduced himself to my family and me, I burst into tears. I was in pain, I was scared, and I was very frustrated at everything that had taken place the past two days. I told the doctor how I was feeling and the pain I was experiencing. He listened to me and then did an examination. He told us he read the x-rays I had earlier and was able to make a diagnosis. He went on to explain that I had ileus paralyticus or "paralyzed gut." The x-rays confirmed this by showing trapped air throughout my abdomen. The doctor told us that all of the fluids I had been drinking were sitting in my stomach and causing the swelling of my abdomen. Now remember, the nurses insisted I drink everything they gave me. I did what I was told because, as they put it, this would make me better. They were wrong! Because of all the fluid accumulating in my stomach, the doctor had to place a nasal gastric tube down through my nose, into my gut, and pump out the liquids I had consumed. This was very unpleasant to say the least. The doctor also ordered stronger pain medication for me via injection and told me to stay down for the rest of the night and try to rest. He knew that with the medication he was giving me, I would probably sleep a majority of the night and then the next day I would be better. The doctor also explained the reason why I had this condition: due to the anesthesia I was given in surgery, this sometimes happens, and it take a few days to get everything working and back to normal. All of the liquids I had been consuming only made my condition worse. This explained the extreme pain because I was swelling more and more. It was apparent the nurses messed up by forcing me to drink. Of course, he did not come right out and say this, but the insinuation was there.

5-4-2007   **176 lbs.**

After the doctor left, I was able to go to sleep. I woke up about every three hours and waited until I could get another shot for pain. The medication was working better than what they had been giving me before, but it still did not hold me for the four full hours until I could have another dose. When morning came, the doctor came in and checked on me. He told me they would leave the tube down in my stomach for the next twenty-four hours. By this time, I should be well enough to remove it. He also said that after they removed the tube, I would need to get up and start walking as much as possible to get my system back in working order. Even though the pain medications were helping me with pain, they were also hindering my own body's ability to start working normally.

After the doctor's visit, they brought in a scale to weigh me. When I got on the scale, I was in complete disbelief once again. I weighed 215 pounds! When I arrived at the hospital, pregnant and ready to deliver, my weight was 160 pounds. I had gained a whopping 55 pounds in five days and was horrified! I called my husband in tears. He reassured me, but I could tell in his voice that he was worried. After we hung up, he placed a call to the doctor.

In mid afternoon, one of the nurses came in and told me Jeff was calling and calling to get information on my condition. I could tell that by her tone of voice, they were considering him a pest. I was too sick to respond much but I knew he was only concerned and very worried about me. I pretty much disregarded her comments and I waited for him to arrive. When he did, he was very upset because no one would tell him anything and the doctor had yet to call him back. He stayed with me until the doctor finally returned. Jeff had a thousand questions for him. Why had I gained all that weight? Why was my pain still so severe if the tube in my stomach was there to remove the pressure? Why was I running a fever? Jeff asked if I was getting any antibiotics. Didn't my fever mean I had an infection? As he asked the questions, the doctor reassured him with every answer. Everything he said made some sense. After all, he was the expert.

5-5-2007   **175 lbs.**

The next day arrived and the nurses came and removed the tube. I felt liberated... until I stood up and discovered there was not an inch of my body that was not rebelling against standing! It literally felt like my skin was ripping off my body, one excruciating inch at a time. There is no way for me to explain the pain I had. The nurses insisted that I walk, and because of what I had been told, I knew it was important, but I cried from the pain. I made myself walk; I had to tap into a strength I never knew I had. The pain of childbirth could not compare to this. As I tried to walk, I prayed to God to give me the strength to continue to put one foot in front of the other. I asked Him to give me strength and if He could not take the pain away, to at least help me do what I was told to do to make myself better. When I completed walking, I would literally collapse back into bed. I went through this repeatedly, each time feeling worse and hurting more than the time before. Nevertheless, I forced myself to keep walking, hoping I would reach a turning point where I actually started feeling better, but it did not happen.

My arms were turning black and blue because the IVs in me kept infiltrating, meaning my veins were not holding up. Each time, they would have to start a new one and each time it was getting harder and harder to find a vein. They would end up sticking me at least three times before they would finally get a sufficient vein. Each insertion left me black and blue. It looked like someone had taken a hammer to my arms and beat me severely; I cried each time they had to stick me again. I tried to maintain a strong mental attitude but it was becoming harder to do because I could see no improvement in the way I was feeling. I only knew I was getting worse, and the medical staff did not seem very concerned; they actually started treating me like I was being a big baby, and that it was not as bad as I made it seem. This was frustrating because I could not help the way I felt. I tried not to complain very much but it was becoming a bigger battle as time passed.

The next few days started to become a blur. I was forced to eat when I could not stand the smell of food, let alone the taste. My body was not working correctly. I was not passing anything; I could not go to the bathroom except to pee. They started giving me all kinds of laxatives but without results. The amount of walking I was doing was supposed to get my body back into functioning order, but it was not helping and the pain was getting even more intolerable. They decided to try enemas but again, no results. They took more x-rays and found nothing had changed for the good. In fact, there was *more* air trapped in my abdomen. The doctor told me to continue to walk, and he told me I had to eat solid food. This did not make sense to me. If I was not passing gas and not having elimination, where was all of this food going? My stomach was getting bigger and bigger and my skin was literally splitting open in areas on my abdomen and in my groin area. I had open sores where this was happening and I actually had stretch marks that broke open. I went through nine months of pregnancy without stretch marks but I had severe ones now.

5-7-2007   **175 lbs.**

After a few days, my baby boy ended up going home without me; I was crushed. This is not what we had planned. My baby did not have the chance to be with me so we did not bond properly; this upset me. My mental attitude was starting to fail. I was indeed very sick but it seemed like the only people who acknowledged that fact were my family. It got to the point where I was crying all of the time. The nurses and doctor decided to tell my family I was suffering from postpartum depression. Jeff hit the ceiling! "She's not depressed, she's sick," he told them. "Can't you see this?" They would not agree. He knew me very well and knew I would never have let my baby go home without me if something was not terribly wrong. He wanted more doctors called in on my case but they dragged their feet. Again, Jeff told them he was going to have me moved to another facility and again, they started to act more accommodating, but they always came up with a reason why I was experiencing the problems I had.

One evening, after about a week in hospital, I told my husband he needed to try to contact my first doctor, the one who did the surgery, and tell him what was going on with me. I knew he was still on vacation but I felt sure his office staff knew how to get in touch with him while he was out of town. I still trusted him and I knew he would find the underlying cause of what was happening to me. We placed the call. The next day, Dr. M.O. called me in my hospital room. When I heard his voice, I burst into tears and could hardly speak to him. My husband took over the call and explained to Dr. M.O. what had been happening. He sounded

shocked and then got very quiet. He told my husband he was cutting his vacation short and would be back in town the following day, and he would be up to see me as soon as he arrived in town. We both felt reassured after talking with my doctor.

It was one-and-a-half weeks since I came to the hospital to have my baby. I came to the hospital in perfect health and excited about the upcoming birth. I was now gravely ill and alone in the hospital while relatives were caring for my new baby. I guess you can say I had many things going on which could cause depression. This is not how we expected things to turn out; our happy little family had had a setback. I was lying alone in a hospital bed, very sick, and feeling like I had done something wrong to be in this condition. The thought kept going through my mind that if only I had not had the surgery, I would be home with my baby boy and my little girl, experiencing those precious moments of the first weeks of my baby's birth. Our daughter was so excited about the birth of her little baby brother. We had built up the birth and told her how great it would be for all of us. Now, she was at home, with relatives watching her, while her daddy worked and spent time with me at the hospital. She did not understand what was happening. She was sort of being pushed aside while everyone was focusing on the baby's care and me. She was only able to see me about every third day, which also made it worse on her. For me, I was feeling guilt because of all that was taking place.

The day Jeff talked with my doctor, Dr. M.O., he came in to see me. I could tell by the way he was acting he was concerned. He checked my incision from the surgery and seemed surprised that the stitches were still in place. He told the nurse to get him supplies so he could remove the stitches, which he did. He also called in a special surgeon to check on me. The surgeon made it in later that day. He reviewed my chart and then, after discussing it with my doctor, he ordered stronger antibiotics for me to start taking. He told me that after being on this new medication for one day, I would be able to go home. I was ecstatic! They told me it was obvious I had a wound infection, but the antibiotics should cure it and I would be on my way to recovery. I felt a sense of relief knowing my doctor was now in charge. I was still in intolerable pain but now it seemed like there was an explanation for what had been happening to me. It all made sense. The fever and the pain could be explained due to the infection. I could now see a light on the horizon, making my mental outlook much better.

5-8-2007   **175 lbs.**

The new medication was started and the next day came. I was not feeling any better physically, but I was excited about being able to go home and be with my family. My doctor came in and told me that because the new medication was of such a strong nature, the only way I would be released to go home was if I found a licensed nurse to administer the injections to me there. I immediately called a neighbor of ours who was a retired nurse from the very hospital I was in. I told her my circumstances and asked her if she would be willing to give me the injections. When she found out what the medication was, she seemed hesitant and told me the only way she would give me the medication was if my doctor issued a written order for her to do so. I did not think much of it at the time, but this request proved to be very wise. I told my doctor her wishes and he provided the written order. I was then sent home.

My husband got me to our house and then left to get my many prescriptions filled. He was gone for about two hours when he called me and told me he could not get anyone to fill the prescription for the antibiotic injection. I then placed a call to my doctor. When the doctor returned my call, he informed me that this particular medication could *only* be filled by a hospital pharmacy. No one told us this upon my release from the hospital. Jeff ended up having to go across the city to find a hospital that actually carried the drug. By the time he got home, it was around midnight and I had already missed one dose of the medication. My nurse neighbor had been waiting for him to return with the medicine so she could administer a dose to me before I went to bed. She gave me the injection but not before telling us how concerned she was in administering this drug outside a hospital setting. She explained to us that this particular drug had very adverse side effects and she was truly uneasy about giving it. I had, however, been given the medication at the hospital the day before and that morning as well, and no side effects. She gave me the injection and then stayed with me for about thirty minutes to make sure I was all right and then she told us she would be back at six in the morning to give me the next dose. She left and we went to bed.

I tried to sleep but did not rest comfortably. Baby Jeffrey was up and down all night and I felt I had to be the one to get up and take care of him because up until then, I had been robbed of those precious moments. Jeff would get up with me every time, always willing to take over because he knew how sick I was, but I knew he had to get up and be at work the next morning and he needed to get his rest. We would hurry to get Jeffrey settled down and then go back to bed. I remained in extreme pain and continued to take pain medication, but it was not as strong as what I had been taking at the hospital. At about the time I would get close to drifting off to sleep, the baby would wake up again. Six o'clock came very quickly, and my neighbor was back to give me another shot.

5-9-2007   **175 lbs.**

Before giving me the shot, she took my vitals; I had an extremely high temperature. She placed a call to my doctor whom she knew well and had worked with for years. They talked, and she told him how concerned she was for me and how she felt I had been released far too soon from the hospital. I only heard her side of the conversation but I could tell she was not very happy with the situation. She finished the phone call and went ahead and gave me the next dose, but not before telling us she felt very uncertain about the situation and she felt we needed to insist on placing me back in a medical facility. She encouraged us to go to a different hospital and not return to where I had been, the same place she has retired from, because she was very upset at what had happened to me there. She made it well known to us she felt they had totally screwed up my care. We listened to her, but I was so sick and tired of the hospital setting, I could not imagine going back and being away from my babies and husband again. We talked it over and she understood how terrified I was to go to the hospital again, so we agreed to give it the rest of that day to see if I made a turnaround. She stayed with me on an off throughout the day, and my mother came over early that morning to help with the kids. I rested as much as I could but I still wanted to be involved with the new baby's care. I was soon to find out this would become more difficult, not easier.

Day turned into night, and soon it was time to go to bed, but I had to be back up for my midnight shot. After again waiting up with me to ensure I had no reaction to the medication, my neighbor stayed until I finally drifted off to sleep on the living room sofa. Jeff came in to check on me and tried to encourage me to go get into bed, but I was hurting so badly I physically could not make the trip from the living room to the bedroom. I did not want to worry him more, so I smoothed things over by telling him I was actually more comfortable on the sofa because our water bed made me rock back and forth and caused me more discomfort. Actually, the warmth from the waterbed made me feel better, but there was no way I could get up and make it down the hallway to the bed. I lay there, sleepless, all night long, and suffered quietly by myself. When the baby woke up, I called out to his daddy and asked him to check on him. Jeff knew that because I was not getting up and going to baby Jeffrey, something serious was happening to me. He got up, took care of the baby, and then came in and sat with me. He told me he was going to call the doctor because he did not like the way I looked and he could tell I was burning up. It was in the middle of the night and I did not want him to disturb anyone at those hours, so I convinced him I was doing all right and told him we would call in at about six in the morning when I would receive my next injection. Thankfully, after he went back to bed on my request, the baby slept the rest of the night and I was able to drift off to sleep.

The doorbell rang at six and Jeff let in our neighbor. She checked my vitals; I still had a temperature but it was down a little bit. This was encouraging. My pain had also shifted, becoming more focused in my belly area. After taking my shot, I became very thirsty and drank everything I could get my hands on. I also wanted to get into the shower as this would be the first day I could since the day I had my surgery. I had been taking sponge baths that whole time, and frankly I was sick and tired of it! I wanted to feel the water run through my hair and over my body. I could not wait. My neighbor encouraged me to try to eat some breakfast first, while I waited for my mother to come and help for the day. I did eat a small amount, not wanting to force it much. In addition, my mental outlook had become a bit more hopeful. I had possibly reached a critical turning point and was now on my way to recovery. I knew I still needed to call the doctor but decided to wait until regular office hours to place the call.

5-10-2007   **175 lbs.**

The baby was sleeping and Sandra was off to preschool. I decided to get into the shower while I waited for my mother to come over. I had anticipated this shower for a very long time. I got the water running good and hot and I could not wait to get in let the water do its magic. I knew the hot water would help relieve the pain in my abdomen and the tension I was feeling. I disrobed and climbed in. The hot water felt like a miracle cure as it relieved the tension stored up throughout my body. I was totally enjoying the shower when, suddenly, I felt a sharp pain hit my stomach area. It almost doubled me over! Then, there was an awful smell that permeated throughout the enclosed bathroom. It smelled as if the sewer was backing up, so I immediately looked down to the shower drain but there was nothing there. The hot water was soothing me but the smell was getting worse. I turned off the water and opened the shower curtain to look at the commode. Surely it had to be running over because of the stench that had taken over the room. Again, there was nothing. I was somewhat confused until I happened to look down and see a yellow and red substance pouring out of my belly around my belly button! It was me that stank! My belly was oozing a foul substance! I immediately got scared, grabbed a towel, and wrapped myself up in it so I could get out of the shower. I stepped out and took one step toward the sink when my abdomen actually burst open, pouring out the foulest smelling substance you can ever imagine. I was horrified! The smell overpowered me and the fear was so intense that I trembled all over. I knew I was going to pass out. Here I was, home alone with my newborn, in serious trouble, and I knew I had to somehow keep it together and not lose consciousness. I had positioned myself where my belly was hanging over into the sink, and I tried to steady myself by hanging on to the sides of the vanity. The horrible smelling liquid literally poured from my belly into the sink, almost gushing at times. After what seemed like a lifetime, I heard my mother at the front door making her way into the house. I yelled out for help. By this time, the smell had taken over the entire home and she realized this as soon as she stepped inside. She came running to where I was and when she saw me hanging over the bathroom sink, she turned and ran out, screaming for someone to help us. My neighbor came running, along with others and soon... what followed is a blur. I remember a ride in the ambulance and all I could think of was apologizing to the ambulance crew for the horrible smell that was coming from my body. I was in grave condition, but all I cared about at that moment was the fact that those people were being subjected to that terrible stench; I was completely embarrassed.

The next few hours saw me in and out of consciousness. I remember being in the emergency room and again apologizing to anyone who came in to take care of me. I could not stand the smell; it was the smell of rotting and dead flesh, and it continued to pour out of my stomach. I remember the surgeon coming in and telling me they were taking me into surgery to clean out a massive infection but the rest of it was blurry. I remember my husband and parents coming in and telling me everything was going to be all right. I remember pain but it was less than before. I was in sort of a blurry, foggy state, possibly because of medication, possibly because of delirium. I do remember them telling me, after taking my temperature, it was over 104 degrees. I also remember them saying my blood pressure was dropping and then, the next thing I remember was waking up in a room, with my doctor, Doctor M.O., sitting there, holding my hand. There were tubes and wires everywhere giving me fluids and medication. I was very groggy and my belly was still hurting. I reached down and found bandaging clear across my stomach. My doctor realized I was awake and he looked at me with a worried look, and then spoke to me, saying he was very, very sorry. I tried to listen to him talk, but it was difficult because of the drugs. He proceeded to tell me I had been in surgery for a few hours and as he spoke, I could hear the apologetic tone in his voice. Soon, my family came into the room and they talked to him as I slept off and on.

The next day, I learned that I had a severe infection that had spread through parts of my abdomen; this is what was causing all of the pain and fever I had experienced for all the days before. When my stomach ruptured beneath my belly button, literally gallons of infected fluid poured out of me; this is what happened when I was in the shower. When they rushed me by ambulance to a different hospital than I had been in before, they took me into surgery immediately to clean out the large area where the infection was taking place. The doctors felt that after many strong antibiotics, I would start to get better.

I was very overwhelmed by everything I was told, but at least I knew I was not crazy. There actually had been something terribly wrong with me even though the medical staff that had taken care of me at the other hospital dismissed my continuing complaints. Remember, they kept telling my family it was "all in my head!" It still angers me to remember the attitudes of those who were supposed to have my best interests at heart when all they were concerned about was the fact that I was not the typical obstetrics patient they were used to. I had severe complications and it called for those people to step out of the ordinary and try to find the problem. Instead, they chose to "sweep it under the rug," so to speak, and hope it would go away. The result? I could have lost my life due to their total incompetence.

5-12-2007   **174 lbs.**

That first day after major surgery was rough, to say the least. They got me up to walk; it was terribly hard because the pain was still uncontrollable. Every time they took my vitals, I was still running a fever. I asked the doctor about the temperature and he assured me the medication would soon take effect and I was on the way to recovery. You couldn't tell it by the way I felt but at least I was given good news for a change and I was hopeful, regardless of how I felt physically. I tried to do everything the staff asked me to do to help with my recovery. Then the night came and I was restless. I drifted in and out of sleep until I finally awoke around three in the morning with such severe chills I could not control the shaking; I was freezing to death, or so I thought. I called for the nurses and they came in quickly. They took my temperature and again it had spiked to over 104! I wrapped myself in everything on my hospital bed, trying to get warm. The nurses immediately started to strip bedding off me and covered me with towels drenched in cold water. I was miserable! I cried and fought with them but they remained persistent telling me they had to get my temperature down or I could start having convulsions; this scared me even more. Soon they gave me medication that pretty much knocked me out, and when I did wake up, my room was filled with my family. I guess several hours had passed. I was too weak to move; I tried to talk but even opening my mouth to speak was difficult. Things were all blurring together; I was unsure what day it was. My husband came over to me and took my hand in his. I could see on his face he was even more worried than before. He tried telling me what was happening but I do not think I truly understood his words. All I wanted to do was go back to sleep because when I was sleeping, I was not in pain.

At some time late in the day, the surgeon, not my original doctor, came in and told my family they were going to take me down to do a CAT scan. They talked amongst themselves and I remember someone wheeling me away from my room. I then remember the surgeon coming up to me and talking to me in a place that was not my room. He told me the infection had spread through my abdomen even further, and he was going to have to take me back into surgery. By this time, I did not care. I was so sick that I did not fully understand what was being said to me. I only wanted to sleep.

5-14-2007   **174 lbs.**

At some point after that test, I was taken back upstairs. My room was filled with family and friends. The surgeon came in with my doctor. They explained what was found and what they needed to do. Someone came and hung blood for a transfusion. I overheard my doctor telling my family how sorry he was. The surgeon told them I was too weak to undergo the procedure until they could build me up with the new blood. It was all a haze to me. I again did not care. All I wanted to do was go to sleep and let all of the pain fade away. I was in and out of consciousness but I do remember a recognizable voice speaking by my bedside. I opened my eyes and looked up to find a very close friend of ours standing there looking down at me. He smiled and then cracked a joke, something to the fact that I better quit "goldbricking" and get back to work! Suddenly, the seriousness of the situation sank in.

Don, our friend, never went to a hospital! His own son had been in the hospital for surgery and Don refused to go and see him because he had a fear of stepping inside a hospital. Nevertheless, there he was, standing over me, making wisecracks. I don't know what changed inside my mind but at that instant, I knew it was bad; I was in trouble. It started sinking in to me just how bad I really was because all of these people were in my room with sad looks on their faces, and the one person who would have never been there unless it was grim news, was there. *This must be it*, I thought. *I am not coming through this.* I closed my eyes.

I drifted off to an unknown place. It was not somewhere I had been before, but it was peaceful and calming. Warmth surrounded me and every tension that was built up in my being was released. I felt like I was shedding my skin, but I was left with a fresh, new flesh, receptive to the warmth and peace that was surrounding me. I was drifting up, up and floating, gently being cradled by something that felt good. This was the greatest feeling. I cannot describe the inner peace I had; there was no more pain. I could move my arms and legs, as if I was swimming through space with no cares or worries. I could see light far out in front of me, begging me, calling me to its bosom. The light represented something more powerful than I had ever experienced. I was drawn to it, but it seemed to be so far away. I continued my journey, wanting nothing more than to reach the light and be engulfed by its apparent kindness. I was weightless. My body was no longer a part of me. I then became aware of sound, which was not apparent before. I felt myself hovering; suspended, almost, yet hovering over something below on which my eyes were focusing. The fogginess somehow lifted and I could see the hospital room where I had been. Everyone was still there. I felt peaceful. I could see my husband leaning over the hospital bed and I could see his lips moving. He was talking to someone laying there. As I tried to focus on who it was, the sound became louder and clearer to me. He was speaking quietly but his words were repetitive. He was holding someone's hand as I started focusing on his words. "Remember the children, remember the children... they need their mother, REMEMBER THE CHILDREN!" I was confused. To whom was he talking? It was almost smoky in the room at first, but then the smoke started to fade away and as I struggled to focus on the person in the bed; I soon realized I was looking at myself! There I was, lying there with tubes and wires running in and out of me. My skin was pale and gray and my lips were pursed tightly together. My eyes were frozen closed with dark circles around them. I was motionless. I could not see any breath raise my chest. Then there was another noise in the room, startling me. It was a beeping noise, which had started out strong but was slowing down and becoming harder for me to distinguish. I found a monitor and watched as it bleeped slower and slower, quieter and quieter. Then, those words rocked me! "REMEMBER THE CHILDREN!" They rang in and out of my head, crushing my brain, or so it seemed. Suddenly something snapped! I was jarred and the noise was deafening! I looked for the light. It was dissipating far into the distance. It was as if I was being torn in half! One part of me wanted the light, while the other part of me wanted my life! It was a tremendous struggle. The light was dimming and I was starting to feel pain again. Then a force came over me and I felt myself being literally being poured back into my body, which was laying there on the hospital bed. I was crashing into that motionless figure, lying there so still only seconds ago. Suddenly, voices throughout the room started ringing loudly in my ears. It was as if they were shouting! Every cell in my body felt excruciating pain. I felt like I was on fire, burning from the inside out. Taking a breath felt like a thousand bricks were crushing my chest, and I could feel my veins. They were screaming from all of the abuse they had withstood for many, many days. I tried to open my eyes but it felt like I had toothpicks pierced in them, holding them shut. I wanted to scream but my tongue was weighted down and my mouth was so dry it felt like everything inside was ripping apart! I couldn't take it! I wanted to go back! I wanted away from the pain and the noise! I wanted to go back to the light! I was suffocating! But then, I gasped and drew breath into my lungs. I fought for the tiniest bit of air. My chest rose up and it hurt like hell, but I could not get enough so I took breath after breath, rapidly. My head felt light but I noticed the loudness was diminishing away from my ears. Then I was able to open my eyes. It must have been startling to those who saw me. I tried to sit straight up but my husband and the nurses who had come into the room stopped me. Everything was quickly coming into focus. I was feeling everything, hearing everything, seeing everything; I was back in my body. I knew in that instant, I was alive!

5-15-2007   **174 lbs.**

It took several days to realize what exactly had happened to me. I know you have probably heard of near death experiences. Before this happened to me, I had also heard of these stories but I never really paid much attention to them. In addition, because of heavy medication, I was not clear of everything that had taken place for the previous few days. My husband told me later what I had gone through, being in and out of consciousness, but I vaguely remembered anything up until the point we had a conversation about how close I really was to death. He then told me that he kept repeating, repeatedly, "Remember the children!" This was the night my loved ones did not know if I would survive the third surgery. Then, everything I experienced that August night in 1982 started playing back in my mind. I told Jeff what happened to me and he sat quietly as I recalled everything I had seen and felt. I looked at him and he had tears in his eyes. I realized right then that I had actually been on the brink of crossing over to the other side and he was intuitive enough to know I was leaving him and the kids. He did the only thing he knew in order to snap me back into reality. He recognized that a mother's instincts can overcome almost anything, and he tapped into this. If I were not going to live for myself, I would live for my babies waiting for me at home! I thank God for giving me the choice that night. I truly believe our Heavenly Father did give me the choice to go ahead and live; live with whatever I had left to face, pain and all, or join Him in peace and no more suffering. I made the choice that was right for my children; I could not leave them motherless.

I have known for many years that life is a series of choices. We make choices that affect our daily lives. I guess what I never understood is that sometimes we are given the choice to go on and live, with unbearable pain, when we would rather have the pain gone, forever. I know many choices we make can cause us pain but we have to get through it and learn from it. However, in the circumstances that led up to my serious condition, I can honestly say I did nothing to cause the suffering I experienced. I had thought that maybe on some other level, or some other time, I did a wrong that warranted me to suffer the way I did, but now with the faith that has grown with me, I know that this is not the case. You see, I was not the only one to suffer. My family and friends suffered right alongside of me and I know they felt my pain. Did they deserve that pain? I do not think so. I think it was strictly the human errors of a group of people who did not set out to cause me harm but indirectly did. It was a series of many calamities that snowballed and got out of control. I believe that because of my children, God granted me the choice to live through the ordeal, not showing me the outcome, but giving me the strength to fight to get better so I could raise Sandra and Jeffrey, the two children I wanted and loved more than my life itself. Yes, it would have been easy for me to let go that night and go to the light. My life would not be easy, but look what I would have missed because of my own selfishness if I had chosen to not stay. I was given the chance to grow with my children and love them. There is no greater gift than this, at least not on this earth.

For you, the reader, I know that unless you have had an experience somewhat like mine, it is hard to understand, or possibly even believe, and this is fine. I do not expect you to understand. Because of this, I have told very few people about my experience. My mother knew, my sister knew, and a handful of others close enough to not want me committed know. I have always felt the experience to be very personal; something that need not be dis-

KAREN DYE-WALKER

cussed with the world. However, for me to tell my story completely, I had to include this in this book because it is a very big part of who I am! If it not had been for this experience, I would be a very different person; it made me open up my eyes and see what is really important in life, and it made me closer to God. Up until yesterday, when I actually wrote about it for the first time, I did not know if I could put the way it happened or how it felt into words. As I started writing, it just poured through me and appeared in print, on the computer. As I read it aloud, to my son last night, all those feelings were right here, at the surface. It happened almost 25 years ago and I was afraid I would forget things as I explained my journey, but it was as if it happened yesterday and I actually felt some of the same feelings I had when it happened. I hope some of you can identify with my story and know you are not the only one to have experienced such a profound passage. For those of you who cannot identify, I only want you to know that I speak from my heart and what I know was my reality. I went through it, I came through it, and I am who I am today because of it.

5-16-2007   **173 lbs.**

I have told you about the night before my third surgery and now I will tell you what happened after the surgery. They took me in and had me in surgery for over five hours. Afterwards, I was told they had to remove part of my intestine due to almost complete strangulation from adhesions that had formed because of the infection. They literally removed every organ in my abdomen and removed the infection and adhesions from them before replacing my organs. When they finished the second surgery, the surgeon had not gone through all the layers of my abdomen. He believed the infection was on the first and second layer only and had not permeated through to the third layer, affecting the organs. I feel that if they had done a CAT scan in the first place, they would have found the extent of the infection. I also found out that I had three major strains of infection attacking my body: staph, strep and E.coli. Either one of these infections alone could have killed me! The combination of the three was almost impossible to treat. I made it through the third major operation hanging on to life but I was gravely ill. My recovery was slow and hard and the pain was again horrendous. I had tubes placed throughout my stomach area for drainage and each day, the doctor would come in and pull each tube out about an inch. They called this "advancing" the drainage tubes. This was so painful that when I would hear the doctor coming down the hallway, I would tense up and tears would stream down my face. There was also a tube down my throat to keep my stomach empty and this tube remained there for a week. I could not eat or drink anything. I did not miss the eating but my throat became so raw from the rubbing of this tube that I would have killed for something to drink! It ended up with me having more pain from the tube than from the surgery. I remember crying and crying because of the throat pain; the pain medication did not seem to affect my throat. Finally, after about four days, they gave me a solution to put in my mouth and let drip down my throat to numb it. If only they had thought about this medicine four days earlier!

I remained in the hospital for about two weeks. After the tubes were removed from my stomach and the tube down my throat was removed, I walked and walked to try to regain my strength. When it came time for me to go home, I was still very weak, but eager to get back to my children and husband. My in-laws had taken baby Jeffrey to New Mexico, where they lived, and they took care of him there while my parents helped with Sandra. This allowed Jeff to go to work and spend as much time with me at the hospital as he could. The day after I returned home, Jeff flew to New Mexico, picked up Jeffrey, and brought him home to me. It was a happy reunion, but it was still very difficult for me to take care of him. I had lots of help, however..

After being home for about three days, I started hemorrhaging. This was a female-specific problem and I notified my doctor. I went in to see him and he put me on medication to control the bleeding but it continued. I was recovering from all of the surgery, but I continued to be very weak due to the blood loss from my hemorrhaging. The doctors could not figure out what was going on. Finally, a friend of ours who is a reconstructive surgeon spoke with my husband and told him he felt the doctors who were taking care of me were not getting to the root of the problem. He suggested that I leave El Paso and travel to Houston where there were more specialized physicians who could possibly figure out what was happening to me. The arrangements were made and I traveled to Houston to see a specialist in women's medicine. This doctor looked over my complicated history and then examined me. He concluded that I needed to have additional surgery to clean out my uterus. We scheduled the surgery for about a month later and I had to take an extreme amount of iron to replace the iron in the blood I was continuously losing.

5-17-2007   **173 lbs.**

I traveled back to Houston to have the fourth surgery, after spending the month trying to build my body up. We arrived the day before surgery and settled in. The morning of the surgery, they came and got me early to wheel me to the operating room. When I woke up after the operation Jeff was by my side. He told me the doctor would be in to see me later. When my doctor came in, he told me what he discovered during surgery: an extreme amount of calcified placenta remaining in my uterus with more signs of infection. He was unable to take care of everything in this surgery. He then broke the bad news: the only way to rid me of all of the infection was by doing a complete hysterectomy! The damage to my female organs was too severe to salvage. The reason he did not do the hysterectomy during the surgery he had just performed was because it would not be a simple surgery and I was still too weak to undergo such a drastic procedure. The decision was made to place me on massive antibiotics once again and to build me up with extreme amounts of vitamin C to promote healing. This would help me through yet another major surgery.

Jeff and I were sent home and for the next five weeks I was confined to almost complete bed rest. My diet was high in healthy foods, and I took the antibiotics and large doses of vitamin C to promote healing. The plans for my fifth surgery, the total hysterectomy, were in place and I would travel back to Houston for the operation.

While I was still at home, I did everything the doctor told me to do but I remained sick with a low-grade fever, hemorrhaging, cramping and severe back aches. I was bloated around the middle but had lost a considerable amount of weight. I felt weak and truthfully, I did not feel like I was gaining any ground, but nonetheless I wanted the date of surgery to hurry up and come so that I could get it over with and get on with my life. Finally, that day arrived and we were off once again to Houston.

Upon arriving in Houston, the hospital was waiting for me and they got me settled in within a few minutes. When I saw the room they had assigned to me, I was impressed. I had a huge private room with a beautiful view. Memorial Hospital is a beautiful facility. The hospital at that time was top notch with the finest facilities the medical profession had to offer. It was beyond the hospitals I had seen; I could not believe it. El Paso is a large city and you would expect it to have the same quality of medical facilities as any other big city. There was absolutely no comparison, however, even when comparing the people who worked there. Their attitudes exuded professionalism while retaining human compassion, something so desperately needed in the medical profession. I did not come across one single person who was not happy to be working there and who truly cared for every patient. It was refreshing to feel like I was a real person with feelings, and not just a complicated case. I do not want you to think by my comments that I always had inferior care in my hometown hospitals, because this is not the case. However, it did seem like my needs were met more at the out-of-town facility.

5-18-2007   **173 lbs.**

My surgery was on a Monday and I was not scheduled until late in the afternoon. My doctor talked with me to explain everything he was going to do. I felt confident with him because he was the chief of surgery and a head professor at Baylor College of Medicine. He was an older gentleman with a terrific bedside manner. I made him promise that they would not put a nasal gastric tube down my throat; this apparatus had caused me so much pain after the surgery in El Paso. He understood how scared I was because of all I had been through, and he handled me gently. I went into surgery at six p.m. and was not through surgery until midnight. I ended up back in my room around two in the morning. Later in the morning, at about seven, the nurses had me up sitting on the side of my bed. I was groggy and, yes, it hurt a lot, but I was not as badly off as I expected. After a couple of hours, they got me up and let me walk to the restroom. I was able to clean up by standing at the sink and grooming myself. I had IVs in me but they put a line in my neck, sub clavicle, so it freed my arms. With this, I did not have to worry about my veins collapsing. My poor arms had suffered enough from the previous surgeries. My doctor came in later that morning and he told Jeff and me what he had found during surgery: my uterus was riddled with infection and had calcified; there were multiple adhesions throughout my female organs; another part of my intestine and my appendix had to be removed; there was a lot of intestinal resection that was necessary; I was a mess! He was surprised at how much damage he had found and then told us it was a complete miracle I was alive. After reviewing his findings, he concluded that during the first surgery, the tying of my tubes, the surgeon had nicked my intestine causing the contents to pour into my abdomen, resulting in the infection. I had peritonitis, better known as blood poisoning, and with the three strains of infection, I had almost lost my life. He was amazed no one caught the problem in the beginning. If they had, it would have spared me of all the suffering and my near-death experience. He did, however, feel confident he had thoroughly cleaned all the infection out and even though he had removed organs and infected tissue, he was positive I would finally start to heal. We listened to him in amazement and thanked him for his honesty and care. We also thanked the Lord once again.

It was amazing how I felt the next few days! Even though I was sore from major surgery, I actually felt stronger than I had felt in months. I could feel my body responding to the antibiotics and the fact that all the infection had been removed from my abdomen. I took very little pain medication actually, taking only pills instead of shots. I would walk up and down the corridors and walking felt comfortable for the first time. I was gaining energy and my appetite was returning. My doctor let me eat a regular diet the day after surgery and I was able to keep everything down and looked forward to my next meal. I could actually taste food for the first time in a long time. This hospital offered a gourmet menu so there was a wide selection to choose from. My doctor was very funny; he would time his visits about the time meals were being served, and while sitting and visiting with me, if something was on my tray I did not have room for, he would "mooch" off me. It was hilarious! We developed a friendship during those days I was under his care. I would time my walks when I knew he was coming in and he would actually walk with me up and down the hall while we talked. Jeff ended up having to leave for home two days after surgery, so I was left there to heal while he was at home working and taking care of the children. My doctor knew I was all alone so he went out of his way to spend as much time as he could with me, making me feel comfortable and not alone.

After a week in the hospital, I was released, but I had to stay with friends in Houston for another week until I was cleared to travel back home. I am so thankful we knew people who lived there and the fact they offered their home to me while I recuperated. They both worked during the day, so I had peace and quiet and could rest. It was great! After the week was over, my doctor cleared me to go back to El Paso. Jeff flew a private aircraft to pick me up and soon I was home with my family and friends. I was so happy!

The next few months were a healing time for me as I got back into the swing of my life. I enjoyed my baby even though we had been separated for such a long time. I did, however, notice Sandra being very clingy to me. At first, when I got back home, she was standoffish towards me. She had become so accustomed to her daddy taking care of her she initially shunned me. I think she was afraid of getting close to me again and then something happening which would take me away once more. When she realized I was not going anywhere, she did a complete about-face and would not let me out of her sight! I could not get away from her! Even when I went to the restroom, she would stand outside the door banging on it to get in! I had to take her with me everywhere to keep her from getting hysterical. Before too long, we had to seek professional help to deal with what Sandra was going through.

5-21-2007   **173 lbs.**

Unfortunately, my nightmare did not end with the hysterectomy. For the next few years, I suffered from many infections and it eventually settled in my left kidney. Continuing to have abdominal pain, I soon realized the extensive kidney infections led to a condition known as infectious kidney stones. The pain from this condition was horrid; I struggled to make it through each episode. I continued to go in and out of the hospital for the next four years having surgery upon surgery to deal with the massive infections. When the doctors had just about reached the end as far as knowing how to treat me, they came up with the idea to place a tube in my left kidney, through my back, and to run an antibiotic solution through the kidney daily. This was to try to flush out the infection. It was a radical procedure but I agreed to it because we had reached a point where no matter what we tried, I was not responding. The experimental surgery was scheduled and I tried to remain hopeful.

I have to say, out of all the surgery I had had up to this point, this surgery proved to be the most painful! I remember my mother being with me after surgery and my pain reaching a point where I was screaming so loudly due to the extreme pain that she went charging out of my room and demanded the nurses get in contact with my doctor and have my pain medication dosage increased. She could not stand seeing me suffer to the extent I was suffering. I thank her so much for her attitude because she got action and I was too weak to fight for myself!

This particular kidney surgery worked for about six weeks until my kidney ended up rejecting the tube that had been placed in it. I went to the doctor's office daily where they had a medication solution to inject into the tube to rinse out the kidney and try to rid it of the infectious kidney stones. This was an extremely painful ordeal as my kidney would spasm as the medicine was being flushed into it. I dreaded the daily ritual.

5-22-2007   **172 lbs.**

At about the end of a six-week period, I awoke one Saturday morning with extreme pain in my bladder area. It was so bad I could hardly walk! I placed a call to my kidney doctor and waited for him to return the call. Soon when I went to pee I was to discover I had a wire coming out of my body! I was naturally horrified. I placed another call to my kidney doctor and he eventually returned my call. He asked me to meet him at his apartment, which was only about two miles from where we lived. I had to drive myself there because Jeff was out of town. We had hired a housekeeper/babysitter to stay with the kids so I took off to my doctor's place alone. Looking back on this later, I realized just how bizarre it was for this doctor to request I meet him at his residence. At the time, however, I was so concerned about the wire that was coming out of my body that I did not pay much attention to anything else! I arrived at his apartment and he asked me inside. He then went to examine my back where the tube was sewn onto my skin, keeping it in place inside my left kidney. He clipped the stitches loose and started to move the tube around. I almost passed out! I was leaning over his kitchen sink where he asked me to stand and the pain from the tube moving around inside my kidney took my breath away. I yelled out! He steadied me, walked me over to the sofa, and had me lie down. He kept repeating to me "Please do not pass out! Please do not pass out!"

The doctor realized the problem was more than he could handle outside a hospital setting. He should have realized this when I called him in the first place but he did not! He decided to make a run to the nearest hospital about a mile away and get the supplies he needed. Yes, he actually left me there in incredible pain, by myself, on his sofa while he took off to the hospital! He probably was only gone for about 10 minutes but it seemed like a lifetime, as I lay there alone. The doctor returned with many supplies and again tried working on me while I lay there, on his sofa, in pain. Tears were rolling down my face. I was frightened, but up until then, I had trusted this doctor. He genuinely seemed to care about all that had happened to me. We were both soon to realize that my problem was much bigger than he anticipated. I needed to be in the hospital so he could take me back into surgery to remove the wire. He told me what his plans were and then told me he only had his motorcycle there at his home to drive because his girlfriend had borrowed his car. He asked me if I could drive the short distance to the nearest hospital and even though I was afraid, I told him I could. I did not want to have to wait for an ambulance to get there and it seemed stupid at the time to call 911 for such a short trip. The doctor got on his motorcycle and I followed behind him on the minute-and-a-half trip.

Upon arrival at the hospital emergency room, everyone there started to hustle, and before I knew it someone was wheeling me into the operating room. They did not put me completely under anesthesia because the doctor needed me awake to some extent during the surgery. He ended up having to remove the tube from my kidney because it had rejected the foreign object inside of it, and due to constant cramping the guiding wire, placed inside my kidney to help guide the tube into place, had come out my urethra. The doctor was not prepared for what he found! The constant spasms had made my kidney "eat" the wire and it escaped my body the only way it could! The pain was so bad because the wire was attached to the tube, which was inside my kidney. What a nightmare!

As I lay there in the operating room, my mind was so overwhelmed by all that was happening it was difficult to relax. I was scared and my condition was very painful. *Why is this happening to me? This* kept racing through my mind. Once again I was in a crisis due to either incompetence or a very bizarre treatment.

So here I was, being worked on once again because something was not done right in the first place. This doctor, I am sure a very competent physician, made some bad choices for my care and now I was suffering the consequences. I lay there, my body falling apart and my spirit suffering greatly, as the doctor tried to put me back together again. I was far too sick to give much thought about the whole situation, but after I was released from the hospital for the umpteenth time, I started exploring my thoughts and just how angry I was. As my mind started to clear, I knew I could not let this go; I had to take some type of action and hold these doctors and nurses accountable for the mistakes they made. I did not want any other person to go through what I had been through and if I could set them straight, I would. I made a vow to myself as well as to my children who were robbed of their mother for what ended up being most of the time they were growing up. I vowed that those individuals who misdiagnosed me and treated me poorly would have to publicly acknowledge their mistakes and apologize to me, as well as lose their right to practice medicine; that is if you can call it that. They certainly practiced, and they practiced on me!

After the second kidney surgery, I remained in and out of hospitals because of infectious kidney stones. I was taking medicine all the time such as antibiotics and pain medication in ever-larger doses because my body was gaining high tolerance to these drugs. My purse became a walking pharmacy and every couple of hours I had to take some type of drug to help me feel better. The problem was, the drugs were not working very well. Remaining in a vicious cycle of pain and medicine, my mental outlook was failing me. It was taking a toll on my whole family.

While going through the turmoil of my medical condition, I decided to seek legal counsel. After asking friends about recommendations for me to talk to, I finally decided on an attorney. Jeff and I went and met with her, and she assured us I had a major malpractice case on my hands. I ended up hiring this attorney and the wheels were set into motion; the lawsuits were filed. I filed against the hospital where I had the first surgery and I had to file against my original doctor because he was in charge of the original surgery, even though I felt he was not the *main* one responsible for my condition. He had left me in the care of the other doctor who misdiagnosed me and it ultimately fell back on my original physician. In the beginning, I was unhappy due to the fact I had to bring suite against Dr. M.O., but later on I discovered that he was not willing to claim there *was* a major mistake made, and my suing him became easier as time went on.

I have suffered all of these years due to the mistakes these doctors made. There is no monetary value to one's life. Not all of the money in the world would make up for the pain and suffering I experienced. There is also the suffering my whole family experienced due to their negligence. Nothing can bring back the time I lost with my children, not to mention the loneliness my husband experienced every time I was hospitalized. Our whole lives were disrupted. After the morning of August 13, 1982, life as we knew it would never be the same again and my health would never be the same again. To this day, those memories are still at the forefront of my mind, and no matter how hard I try to get over it, they are still there, haunting me on a daily basis; years and years of therapy have not erased them. I have walked through my life since the incident, but there has always been a shadow lurking behind, reminding me of that day. My prayers have been answered inasmuch as I am still here to enjoy my family and my life, and I try to forget, but I know all of this has made me a stronger person. There were many things I faced through these years. I think that because I have gained strength through adversity, I have been able to persevere through it and have emerged a stronger person because of it. I have always tried to find the good in every situation. If I have to focus on the good of my medical situation, it would have to be the fact that I have become closer to God through it all. My faith was tested repeatedly and I always looked to God for the answer and the strength to carry me on. He has always been with me and has kept me safe and alive.

I do believe by looking at my story, others can look back on their own situations in life and realize that God has carried *them* through as well. Even those who do not fully believe are most likely to focus on a situation where they as a person had no control, but something brought them through it, to live and tell about it. When they realize this, they have to know there is something stronger than themselves who has acted in their best interest. It does not take a rocket scientist to realize this! God works in his own way. Sometimes it takes baby steps to get us to believe, and sometimes we are hit over the head to make us stand up and pay attention, but always, it is God's love that sees us through the darkest of times. We are made in His image. He loves each one of us, and for me His love is apparent to me each day I draw breath into my lungs. He has given me my life, and for this, I am truly thankful. I praise Him, every day.

THANK YOU LORD!

CHAPTER TWELVE

TO SUE OR NOT TO SUE... THERE WAS NO QUESTION!

5-30-2007   **172 lbs.**

I have never been the kind of person who thinks you should run out and file a lawsuit against somebody, unless, of course your life has been at stake. My life had been put in extreme danger due to negligence and I felt if I did not do something to ensure my future as well as my children's future, I would later regret it. In addition, I needed to know no woman would go through the same things I did due to this negligence. All these factors weighed on my mind and after giving it considerable thought I made my decision.

Before I go on any further, I want to say if I had to do it all over again, knowing what I know now, I am not sure I would make the same decision. I say this because of the way our legal system works and the fact that lawyers can be as cutthroat as possible in order to win their cases. Even if you are an attorney, I do not apologize for this statement. You know what your training and profession allow you to do in the name of justice and defending your client. That is why we, the public, hire you. Unfortunately, the average person has no idea how attorneys work to make their cases and defend their clients, until they find themselves in the situation of a litigation. Up until my own experience, I thought if you were an innocent person, wronged by someone else, especially in the health profession, you were entitled to be compensated for that wrong. I was soon to find out just how cruel our system can be when a hotshot lawyer finds it necessary to prove his or her case, no matter what the cost. I learned the human factor is completely removed and the money factor steps in. This is unfortunate for those of us who have suffered irreversible damage at the hand of others and then are made to feel it was somehow our fault. I cannot say, in good faith, this practice is okay; I feel it is cruel and unjust in what is supposed to be a *justice* system. When did the tables turn and when did we say it is okay to make the victim the one responsible for whatever tragedy they have faced? What happened to victims' rights? If you have asked yourself this question, I am almost positive you must have been faced with some kind of legal issue that has made you feel inferior, even though someone else harmed you or a loved one. If you have never asked yourself this question, rest assured you or someone you know will one day be faced with a situation where you will be able to look back on what I am saying and realize I speak with first-hand knowledge. I have been through it, not once, but twice, and believe you me, it was two more experiences I would call some of the worst things that have happened in my life!

5-31-2007   **172 lbs.**

I do not want you to think I am against the legal profession because this is not the case. I know there are a tremendous number of ethical lawyers practicing in our great country. Everyday life can make us at any point need legal counsel, whether it is in business or personal affairs; sometimes we need "legal eagles" to help rectify an issue. I have used many attorneys in my business as well as in my personal life. Basically, I have had good luck when it comes to working with lawyers in these instances. However, when it comes to a personal injury case, or medical malpractice, my dealings have been anything but pleasant! I have been put through the ringer, and this is why I made the previous statements.

During my period of failing health, I made the decision to file a lawsuit against those I felt were responsible for my mishap. My family encouraged me to do so, as well as my friends. At first, I was slightly hesitant because I really knew nothing about lawsuits of this nature and I just wanted my life back and things to get back to normal. Yet, after my continuing pain and suffering, as well as that of my babies and the rest of my family, I gave it great amount of thought and decided to check into the possibility. Nothing, especially a monetary award, could make up for the time I lost with my children and husband, or the pain and suffering I had been through. I knew my health issues were going to continue for the rest of my life and insurance or no insurance, it would become increasingly difficult for me to afford health care.

There was no way to predict what the future had to offer as far as my health was concerned. I knew there was permanent damage to my body as well as psychological issues from everything that was going on. My body was damaged, my psyche was damaged, and Sandra and Jeffrey had been many weeks away from their mother because of my illness. I, like everybody else, had no way of knowing what lay ahead for us as a family, but I knew I was sick, that my kids and my husband were suffering, and I was the one who had to take a stand. It had to be me no one else could do it, so I made the decision to find counsel and seek damages. For whatever it was worth, I had to at least try to secure a future for my family without being inundated with rising medical bills and destroying my family's financial outlook.

6-1-2007   **172 lbs.**

After talking with friends, and upon their recommendation, I found the attorney who I felt was the most qualified to handle my case. We made an appointment with her and went in to discuss everything. After talking with her for over an hour, she informed us that I had an excellent case against the hospital and the doctors involved. In fact, she told us she would be able to retire after winning the case with her third of the settlement. This is how confident she was in the lawsuit. We signed the necessary papers and the wheels were set into motion.

My attorney helped us find doctors who could help me through my various health related crises. In fact, she was instrumental in finding my doctor in Houston who took care of me and did the hysterectomy. She was very motivated in the beginning; she requested all of my medical records and continued to do so each time I was hospitalized. It took months to collect all of the documents from the original hospital where I got sick. We also discovered something else during this fact-finding period. It was brought to our attention that the hospital required proof of medical malpractice insurance before any physician was allowed to practice at their facility. My doctor, the original surgeon, did not have any malpractice insurance, and was in direct violation of the hospital's policy.

As I stated earlier, I did not want to sue my original doctor because I felt if he had been in town when I first got sick, he would have correctly diagnosed my problem and would have treated me accordingly. Nevertheless, because he was the original doctor in charge, I had to sue him and then he could go after the others if he so chose to do so. It still made me feel uneasy about involving him but my attorney explained to me that this was the only way. We also had to sue the hospital, which was not a hard decision for me to make, especially after finding out they allowed this doctor to practice there without malpractice insurance. They opened themselves wide open for the lawsuit.

During the discovery phase of my suit, I was allowed to review copies of my medical charts and I spent hours doing this. I was soon to discover all of the mistakes and just plain "crap" that was on my medical chart at the first hospital. There were things recorded in there that did not happen, things not recorded that did, and many flat-out lies! There were even pages missing with absolutely no explanation of what happened to them. I made extensive notes for my attorney of exactly what I remembered and I questioned my family and recorded their recollections of what took place from day one. We spent many hours going over my notes.

My attorney brought in a partner for my case after a few months; they worked as a team. He was a good-looking smooth talker, which, I was told, would help me when it came to a jury trial. She was the spitfire who would push herself right up to the point of being called down by the judge. He would then step in and smooth everything over, scoring points with the court as well as the jury. This had worked well for them and they were very successful with this strategy.

6-2-2007   **171 lbs.**

The attorneys started contacting medical experts who could testify to the fact that I was mistreated and misdiagnosed. I was soon to find out that some doctors have a kind of unspoken honor where they will not testify against each other. It was hard for me to believe that ethical people, or persons who should have been ethical, would not take a stand and admit there was wrongdoing in my situation. This really hurt me. I thought doctors take an oath: "First do no harm," when they graduate from medical school. I did not know that sometimes they stand up for each other even when it is apparent a mistake has been made. I thought facts were facts, regardless. Soon I discovered we were having a hard time finding an ethical physician who would take a firm stand and admit under oath that many mishaps occurred during my care, or lack of care. When things would start to look hopeful, something would halt the process.

My medical files had to be sent across the United States in hopes of finding our expert witness. Our attorneys would tell us they were hopeful with "this doctor" or "that doctor" and we would eagerly await their response. Then, the attorney would call me and tell me the chosen doctor had backed out. The doctors would never come right out and say they did not believe wrongdoing took place but there was always some excuse as to why they could not join our team. This was very frustrating, to say the least.

Before long, a year had passed, and then a second year passed and so on, while I continued to be sick and facing surgery upon surgery. I actually had thirteen surgical procedures in the period of three years, and I grew to hate my body because of all of the scarring from the multiple surgeries. At this point in my life, I had no control of what was happening to my health, but I soon found out I could take some control of my body, or at least how it looked on the outside, by starving or purging. Before long, even though I had scars underneath my cloths, I possessed the thinness of a super model and I loved all of the attention I was receiving with my new body. My modeling days were always present in my mind. The truth of the matter is that I truly hated my body. I was abusing it by starving, but at least it was *my* choice and I had control. Everyone thought my pencil-thin body was the result of all my surgeries and continued health problems. They were none the wiser.

My attorney called me one day and told me she had good news. She had found an expert in New Mexico who was willing to look at my records and meet me in person. This was a first in the case. My files were sent to this doctor and then an appointment was set. We drove to an area right outside of Albuquerque where the doctor had his practice. He was a cardiac surgeon. I was not quite sure why they found a heart surgeon to do this but this doctor explained everything to me. He wanted to check me out and fully examine my cardiac function, which he did. After doing so, and running many tests, he called us into his office and told us he was very concerned about my heart health as well as my kidneys. This was all because of the one antibiotic I was given when discharged from the hospital; the strong antibiotic my nurse neighbor injected for me. He explained how serious this drug is and he told us the serious side effects it is known to produce. He told us it causes heart muscle deterioration as well as serious kidney issues. Of course, I was having the serious kidney problem already but I was not experiencing heart trouble. However, the physician told us it could happen at any time; yet another alarm went off in my mind. I did not think I could not handle much more.

6-4-2007   **171 lbs.**

We now had our expert witness; this doctor was willing to testify on my behalf. The time came for our depositions and Jeff I went in together. I did not know Dr. M.O. was going to be with us in the room, let alone his attorney. The hospital also had legal representatives present. This made me uncomfortable, to say the least. The attorneys took Jeff's deposition first. It was lengthy, about two hours. Each attorney had a chance to question him. Then it became my turn. It was bad enough listening to Jeff talk about what had happened to me because his emotions overcame him several times. They then started questioning me; I was not prepared for what followed. Before I knew it, everything was looking like it was *my* fault for getting sick in the first place. I could not believe what was happening. In addition, there sat my attorneys, remaining quiet the whole time. I was expecting them to pipe up and say something but they did not. I had to sit there and be run over by the other attorneys. I had never been in a deposition before so this was all new to me. My lawyers told me to be truthful and strong. That was all they said, not preparing me for what was taking place.

I must have been questioned for about thirty minutes when they started saying things that were just not true. Dr. M.O.'s attorney looked straight into my eyes and had the gall to tell me that I never wanted my baby! This attorney spoke directly at me, telling me my doctor said I tried to abort my son! It still angers me to think back on this. I broke down in tears and told them that was a big fat lie! Anyone who knows me knows I would never do anything like that; I love children, period! I do not believe in abortion. For them to sit across from me and say such blatant lies was appalling. *How could they say this? How could they get away with this?* I screamed to myself.

I answered the question through tears and when I did, I looked at Dr. M.O. directly. He put his head down, staring at the table. He could not even look at me because he knew those statements were big lies! I was shaken up at this point, and it was hard to continue. We took a few minutes' break and then started again. We had arrived there at nine in the morning and we did not leave until after four p.m. that afternoon. We broke one hour for lunch and that was it. Going through this ordeal for six hours was as bad, if not worse, than the actual mishap. I had to relive the terribly painful experiences all over again, but this time I was left to feel like it was my entire fault instead of that of the doctors who put me in the condition to begin with. When I left there, I was drained, completely and emotionally. There was nothing left of me and I felt like I had been run over by a freight train. I felt like I had just been raped by a bunch of lawyers. I also felt like my attorneys did not prepare me properly for the ordeal. Maybe they were going for my raw emotion and wanted me unprepared for that reason; I do not know. Whatever the reason, I felt it was very unprofessional for me to be unprepared for what took place during those depositions. I was now questioning if I could withstand a trial if it went that far. I knew the trial would have to be much worse than this was experience. My nerves were now on end. I was scarred, exhausted and just wanted it all to be over!

6-5-2007   **171 lbs.**

After the depositions were over, I needed time to regroup. It was such an emotional strain; it took me a couple of weeks to get over it. Then the time came for our expert doctor's deposition. My attorneys made all of the arrangements and he was to fly to El Paso on a weekend and stay at the finest hotel in the downtown area. We thought everything was going along fine. After the weekend was over, my attorneys contacted me and told me the news. Evidently, this physician had a problem with drugs. He had been under the influence for the whole weekend. They suspected it was cocaine, but could not prove it. He was a complete mess and there was no way they could take his deposition in this condition. Evidently, my attorney told him to go home and get sober; he was ticked off, and that was the end of that! We did have some papers, his interrogatories, in which he gave all of the information about my condition and how he felt the other doctors did harm to me. The only problem was if he were called as a witness, and he would be, and he was on the stand messed up from drugs, it would be all over for us. We therefore could not use anything he said. Once again, we were back to square one.

One phone call finally ended the seven-year ordeal I went through with this lawsuit. Our family moved to California before a court date was set. Then, we received a set date. A continuance would be ordered and then we would get a new date and another continuance. This cycle went on for over a year. It was wearing me down. I just wanted my day in court and to have it all finalized so I could go on with my life. I was dealing with serious health issues each day of my life and because of these issues, I had constant reminders of everything that happened to me and the aggravation of this lawsuit was messing with my head big time!

The final court date was set, and it looked like this was going to be it. We were to go to court on a Monday in 1989. My attorneys coached me on what to wear to the courthouse, nice but simple, possibly something in navy, and they told me not to wear makeup or curl my hair. They told me to consider a simple ponytail or possibly a bun. This was *so* not me! I never went anywhere without makeup and my hair was *always* curled. I guess they did not want me to look too good as it might have given the jury the wrong impression. As I said, I had never been involved in a lawsuit before. I felt my case was compelling enough without getting so worried about my personal appearance, but I agreed. After all, they were the experts and I hired them to do a good job.

The day before we were to catch a plane back to El Paso, my phone rang. It was both of my lawyers on a conference call, and they told me we had an offer on the table. I listened, a little bit shocked, as they explained that the other attorneys had gotten together and agreed to settle out of court for a mere one hundred thousand dollars! We originally sued for *one million*! We originally agreed we would not settle for anything under five hundred thousand. So here we were, four hundred thousand dollars off! Immediately, I told my attorneys that I did not want to settle for this amount. After all, when they took their third, after they took their expenses out of the settlement and I paid medical bills that were pending due to the suit, it would leave only a few thousand dollars left over. At the same time, I was unable to get medical insurance because I was such a high risk, so a one hundred thousand dollar-settlement did not leave me any funds to pay for upcoming medical expenses. Even the expert we had who ended up not helping us wrote a letter saying it would not be possible for me to get health care and the expected cost of my upcoming medical bills would be "prohibitive for any wage earner!" After I expressed my opinion to my lawyers, they began wavering, telling me that we were taking a big chance going to trial! Of course, there was no certainty we would win, but I felt we had a chance. After talking with them for over twenty minutes, I was worn down. I actually agreed to settle out of court!

6-6-2007   **171 lbs.**

After the settlement and expenses were paid, I ended up with seventeen thousand dollars. I paid off as many medical bills as I could, but I could not pay everything I owed. My medical insurance was exhausted and my major medical was exhausted. There was not much I could do about the situation so I ended up having to file bankruptcy. Fortunately, I could file as an individual and not affect Jeff's credit. This was the way it was back in 1989 in California. Things may have changed since then but I managed to handle it this way. It was a hard decision for me to file, but I had no other choice. I was drowning in bills.

That year, 1989, was a particularly bad year for my family and me. It started out with my dad undergoing open-heart surgery for four bypasses. He actually had the surgery right after Christmas 1988 but his recuperation extended into the new year. My mother was very ill also and I was worried about the toll my dad's health would take on her. In February, a very close friend of Jeff and myself was flying from El Paso out to California to surprise Jeff on his thirty-fifth birthday. Unfortunately, he never made it out of El Paso. He was killed instantly when the twin-engine airplane he was flying had mechanical trouble right after take off and he crashed into morning traffic on the interstate; we think he was trying to get away from all of the innocent people on the roads but ended up crashing short of the airport. This was a horrible accident. The out-of-control airplane crashed and burned, killing our friend and his two passengers. There was also one automobile involved and other casualties as well. It was horrible. Don was Jeff's best friend and I had to be the one to break the news to Jeff. This almost destroyed him. Then in March of 1989, Jeff had an almost fatal heart attack at only 35 years old. All of the stress and things that were happening took its toll on him and he almost lost his life. This was a very traumatic experience for all of us.

I settled the lawsuit in May, then in June of that year I changed careers. Even though I was happy with what I was doing, the money in the new opportunity was too much to pass up, so I took the new job. It is one of the worst decisions I have made in my life. I hated myself for being sucked into the glamour of more money. Then, in July of 1989, my mother was told she was dying due to liver cancer. We lost her three weeks later. After this, I filed bankruptcy in August and settled it in September. This was a very difficult thing and a very humbling experience. Therefore, as you can see, I had six very emotional traumas happen to me in a matter of nine months. I often wonder how I kept any type of sanity, but the truth is I was slipping downhill emotionally, unknown to most. I will talk about this issue further in another chapter, but now I want to tell you about my second experience with a lawsuit.

6-7-2007   **171 lbs.**

In November 2000, my daughter, my grandson and I were driving down a street close to our home. Sandra was behind the wheel in her brand new vehicle. Suddenly, a truck came out of a private driveway not paying attention to ongoing traffic. He hit us, and we ended up flipping three times, end over end, landing down the street in the opposite direction of which we were traveling. Somehow, I was able to get out of the car and get to the back seat to check on my grandson who was only three months old. He was safely fastened in the car seat and slept through the whole accident. Thank God for that! I, however was injured badly. There were many broken ribs and crushed disks in my back. My daughter Sandra was bruised up pretty badly as well. We were all taken to the hospital by ambulance.

Because of my severe injuries, my daughter and I decided to sue the man that hit us. He was driving someone else's vehicle and he had no insurance of his own. Because of this, the woman who let him drive her truck was then responsible. We found out she was insured by the same company that insured me. We sought legal counsel and called a firm that was highly recommended to us. We set an appointment and went in to discuss the case with them. Once again, we were told we had a heck of a case and they could not wait to get started on it. They were very excited; I assumed because they thought they would not lose the case. We hired the firm and started proceedings. The head attorney for our cases asked each of us to bring to him our current insurance policies so he could go over them. We did so the following day at his request. Within a week, he asked us back to his office. He informed us we had a "big" case and we would sue for about three hundred thousand dollars.

With all the medical problems I had from the accident, I soon used up all the personal injury protection insurance coverage Sandra had on her policy. I am still not clear on why the other person's insurance did not take over in the first place, but nonetheless, my coverage came from my daughter's policy. I ended up having to seek out a neurologist to take over my care, so I chose a local doctor and he exhausted all my insurance coverage. I found out his ethics left a lot to be desired. He has had numerous legal actions brought against him and I was soon to learn that he got patients addicted to drugs, pain medication and nerve medication so they kept going back to him for the pills. If that was not bad enough, when he exhausted all insurance coverage, he dropped his patients like hot cakes! This made me outraged! When he used up my insurance, he threw me out of his office, yelling at me to go home and get on with my life. I was so angry and upset that I decided to file a complaint against him. My lawyer told me that when he went to go visit this doctor about my case, the doctor spent the full hour talking to him and then had the nerve to charge me five hundred dollars! Of course, this fee would have to come out of my portion of the lawsuit. I was infuriated by this and refused to stand for it. My lawyer told me not to worry; it would be taken care of.

6-8-2007   **171 lbs.**

This lawsuit ended up lasting four years! It was unbelievable what we ended up running into. Our depositions were set and I was very nervous about the whole thing, especially after what I had been through years before with the other suit. Before I go into this further, I have to tell you what happened with our attorney. He became very ill and ended up having bypass surgery. He would be out of the office for months, so our cases were turned over to his partner. It seemed that up until his partner took over, not much was being done. After the new attorney took over, things seemed to start happening. He told us he wanted to get it done so he filed for a court date. Then the judge who presided over our case ordered mediation.

This deposition was not as bad as the one I had before, but it was still uncomfortable. Going through something that happened four years earlier was difficult especially because of the trauma I went through during and after the accident. We went in, sat with our attorney, and across from us sat the lawyer for the man who caused the accident, as well as the attorney for my insurance company. It was weird having to sue my own insurance company because I never had any problems with them in the past, but nonetheless this is how it played out. The attorneys asked us questions and they stayed pretty much true to form compared to the interrogatories we had done at an earlier time. The only thing they focused on was the fact that I have lupus; they insinuated my injuries might not have effected me as badly if I did not have this disease. I felt this had no bearing on the initial injuries. The fact that it may have taken me longer to heal from the injuries could be discussed, but the facts were the facts! If I were a perfectly healthy individual, with no health issues whatsoever, given the same circumstances I would have still been injured the same way! Of course, we did not set out that day on our drive into town to be involved in a terrible accident due to someone else's negligence! No one sets out to be involved in a wreck. We hashed it out repeatedly and even though the procedure was emotional for me, I made it through not feeling as bad as I did with my first lawsuit.

The lawsuit continued dragging on, even though the partner of the law firm was now in charge. I started making phone calls to their office daily, trying to push them along. After all, I was getting extremely tired of waiting. Finally, the date was set for the mediation and we were ready, or so we thought! I want to remind you that we were suing for three hundred thousand dollars. What happened was we got into the conference room of our attorney's office, and the mediator came in the room with an offer. He handed it to our attorney, excused himself, and allowed us to have a discussion. Our attorney looked at the offer and then tells us we should not consider it; it was very low. He then handed us the offer. We sat there, speechless, and then, it sank in! There in my hand, in front of my face, was the figure of seventeen thousand dollars! One *ridiculous* offer, for *both* of us! I looked at Sandra, she looked at me, and we both looked at our attorney and the words found their way to my lips! "This is a mistake, right? It's supposed to be one hundred and seventeen, right? There's a "one" missing... right?" I swallowed hard.

It's an amazing thing when the person you are talking to and asking a question of starts to clear his or her throat. You know at that very second, they are trying to answer you without exposing whatever it is they don't want you to know. Well, the throat clearing started and the hidden statement became very obvious. There was also a lot of shifting in chairs and a lack of eye-to-eye contact!

Our lawyer sat there, rather still. He had a dazed look on his face. The silence deafened the room and you could cut it with a knife. He stumbled, searching for words. Then he cleared his throat, and in a very matter-of-fact voice said, "Well, it is a low figure. I know you can get at least twenty-five thousand dollars, but yes, this is a real offer; a starting point for us to work with." We sat there in total "kick in the teeth" astonishment!

"What do you mean we can get at least twenty-five thousand? We are suing for three hundred thousand!" I blurted out. He looked at me with a sheepish expression and then said, "Well, um... you know your insurance policy only allows you up to... um... twenty-five thousand dollars. That is... um... your underinsured limit."

"What are you talking about?" Sandra and I both said out at the same time.

"Your partner told us we were suing for three hundred thousand dollars! He made this deal with us and said we were not going to settle for under one hundred thousand!" I exclaimed.

The attorney looked at us awkwardly. The room was so quiet you could hear a pin drop. We sat there with both our mouths open, awaiting an answer. He was struggling for words but after a few seconds, which seemed like 10 minutes, he spoke. "Well, um... I don't know why he told you this. It is falling back on your insurance policy as well. There is twenty-five thousand from the other parties' policy and twenty-five thousand from your policy. We cannot sue for over what the policies show for coverage!" He quit speaking and we sat there in complete disbelief. Here we were, four years down the road from when we hired this firm to represent us. Years earlier, we had complied with our first attorney's request to deliver a complete copy of our insurance policies so he could review them. He then, several days later, after he reviewed my injury reports, told us we were suing for three hundred thousand. I am no genius and have never claimed to be, but if he reviewed the policies finding out everyone's coverage limits, how did we get to a figure of three hundred thousand when we could only get what the policies allowed in the first place? Does this not seem a little strange to you? Let me say this, it did to us; we were livid, infuriated, disgusted, appalled, and many more things I choose not to express in this text!

After sitting there incredulous for a few minutes, still trying to grasp what our lawyer had just informed us, someone had to break the silence. That person was Sandra. "This is complete crap!" she so eloquently blurted out. I followed with "There is no way in hell this is happening!" We were both enraged! We sat there waiting for some reassurance from the man sitting across from us, anything, even a comment or something. Then a thought crossed my mind. Possibly, I was dreaming! Maybe this was all a nightmare! I then pinched myself and it hurt! Nope, this was for real; the real deal, and it looked like I was being taken once again. Stupid, naive me, once again I went to someone who gave me unrealistic possibilities, and once again, here I was, at the mercy of someone else holding the cards. I trusted the attorneys we hired to handle our case and be assiduous to our cause.

6-11-2007   **170 lbs.**

Before I keep writing about the lawsuit, I want to recognize that yesterday, June 10, 2007, marked the second anniversary of my sister's passing. I was in St. Louis to be at my adopted daughter's wedding reception Saturday evening. I dreaded Sunday though, because I knew it would be a very difficult day for me as well as for my dad who traveled to St. Louis with me. We were able to spend part of the day with family and then traveled back home to Kentucky. We shared memories, cried together but also laughed at reminiscences involving Sheri and us. It was a bittersweet day.

Now, back to my story of the lawsuit. Once it finally sunk in what we were up against in mediation, we had to move on. Of course, we were still devastated by what we just learned. Our attorney had no explanation as to why we were told a much larger figure in the beginning and then led on for four years thinking we were suing for that amount. Sandra and I both ended up breaking down, because it just did not seem fair. We both had massive amounts of medical bills due, not knowing how we were going to pay them off. Beside this point, we had to counter the offer and send the mediator back to the others and await an answer. It did not take long to get their bottom offer and our counsel advised us to take this offer because the opposing side was not going to go any further. Therefore, we accepted the offer. It was a far cry from what we originally expected. As I mentioned earlier, we were in Sandra's brand new car and it was totaled. By the grace of God we escaped this accident with our lives, but by looking at the car, you would never have thought anyone walked away alive. Her insurance only allowed a certain value for the vehicle so, in other words, she could not replace her new car without adding three to four thousand dollars to the settlement. Her monetary recovery was mere peanuts and she owed more on the car than she received from her insurance. She ended up having to buy a used car to replace her new one. I thought the whole thing to be utterly ridiculous!

My own recovery was peanuts as well. By the time you pay the lawyers and pay expenses, a huge chunk is taken out of your proceeds. I ended up with about seventeen thousand in the end. I used it to pay bills, and as for the injuries I sustained, I still have continuing problems with my back. There is shoulder pain that radiates down my left side from nerve damage. I fractured three vertebrae: T3, T4 and T5. Even the expert doctor our attorney sent told me he had the same injury from an accident years before, stating you never get over it. I have not as of yet, but I am still hopeful.

My friends and family were outraged at how this case was handled. I contacted the State Legal Board and sought help from them because I felt the case was mishandled in the beginning and I wanted to file a complaint against the firm. They were very gracious and listened to me when I explained the situation. Unfortunately, all they could do was check into the matter and write letters allowing the attorneys to know there was a complaint against them. It looked like there was nothing I could do. I asked if I could file malpractice charges against the firm. Again, it was going to be difficult to find someone to stand up and go against his or her peers. I then had to decide if the hassle was worth it to me. After looking back on all the years I wasted being tied up in litigation, thinking the system was completely fair, I decided to stop where I was and put it behind me. I did this and I am much happier for doing so!

6-12-2007   **170 lbs.**

Because of what I experienced through these lawsuits, I hope I am never involved in any type of litigation again. The emotional toll they put on me was rough and hard. Then there is the "hurry and wait, hurry and wait" period where you feel as if nothing is being done on your behalf. The anticipation of finality goes on for such a long period that you reach a point where you just want over the whole thing done with. Attorneys count on this happening so they can get away with smaller settlements. They wear you down and then zoom in for the settlement, knowing you are most likely going to accept a much smaller figure so you can move on and not be worried with it anymore. Dragging a suit out for four to seven years tends to do this to a plaintiff. I know I am not the only one who has been through this. Many more have been in my shoes and I have to wonder how many hundreds of thousands of dollars have been saved by this practice.There is something else that really bothers me. There are the most absurd cases making their way through the court system, with people being awarded millions of dollars because they burned themselves with hot coffee or someone else looked at them cross-eyed! It literally makes me sick to know these individuals are awarded gigantic sums of money while others, like me, are given a mere pittance to shut us up when we have been severely injured due to someone else's negligence. What makes this fair? Why is our system this way? There is nothing, as far as I am concerned, that can justify these practices and we, the taxpayers and voters, need to rally for change. Those injured because of negligence need to be taken care of when they have ongoing problems, either physically or financially. Our laws need to be more serious to protect the injured and their families, not just getting away with spitting a few mere dollars their way to shut them up. We need not reward suit-happy folks and punish those who are really hurt and seek compensation. What is it going to take? Where do we start? I plan to start paying more attention to our judicial system and place my vote where it is going to matter the most! How about you... do you agree? Please do understand; I am grateful for what the Lord has given me. I don't want to seem like I am not, but I would be lying if I said these situations did not leave me a little bitter for a period. I have since moved past the bitterness and have forgiven those individuals who were involved. This was hard at first, but my faith has grown and I know the only way for me to move forward is to let all of it go. This was a hard lesson. I had to pray about it for sometime until I found the answer. There is a saying: "Let go and let God." This is relevant to so many areas of our lives. If we learn to live by this, we end up being much happier individuals and we are able to get many more things accomplished in our everyday lives, as well as our spiritual lives. How much easier it is to encourage another human being when you do not have resentment hanging over your own head? If you are clear, your inner light shines, allowing one who is in need of spiritual lifting the chance to bask in that light God has given you. We learn inner growth and spiritual growth by surrounding ourselves with those who are on the same mission. This is why I try to keep negativity at bay and surround myself with upbeat people. It just so happens that my circle of friends is also seeking spiritual awareness and growth. There are times that I will meet someone struggling, for whatever the reason. Isn't it great to be able to *first* be a good listener and then be able to offer encouraging words to this person? This is especially true if by some chance, you have possibly lived out a similar situation and can show you have survived in spite of it.

I truly believe the axes we bear are obstacles when we refuse and keep hanging on to them. I feel if we "let go and let God," we are axe free; others gain from your clarity. Even though I had bad things happen to me and these things were unjust, by letting go of it all I am free to witness others' struggling through bad times. Just remember, we never walk alone! If I can share my trials and victories with others, everything I have been through in my life will have been a teaching ground for me. I definitely know I have never walked alone! The good Lord has always been with me through it all! The path he has chosen for me has possibly been for me to experience these things so I can help others through what I have learned. The writing of this book may be one of those ways I am supposed to help others. I feel this in my heart, so it must be true. I believe I was led to do this project for some profound reason. For me, it goes beyond the challenge from my son. Jeffrey did challenge me but it had to be put in his mind for some reason, right? Do I believe it came from the Lord? You had better believe I do, because this is making me stand up and be accountable for my choices as well as learn about who I really am deep inside; no smoke and mirrors! Can I help others by talking about my misgivings and myself? I certainly hope I can.

"To everything... turn, turn, turn... there is a reason... turn, turn, turn..."

CHAPTER THIRTEEN

RELATIONSHIPS, RELATIONSHIPS, RELATIONSHIPS... OH MY!

6-13-2007   **170 lbs.**

As I start this chapter, I want it to be understood that I am no expert on relationships! In fact, I am quite the contrary. I am probably the last person who should give advice when it comes to matters of the heart. All I can say though, in my own defense, is that I have had more than my share of experiences in relationships. If anything, I can probably tell you how *not* to do things. If this helps you out, great. If not, please say a silent prayer for me because after you read this chapter, you will surely agree... I need many!

I will start by saying that I have never had any problems meeting the opposite sex. I was an early bloomer, so to speak, and boys started noticing me early on. They gave me a whole bunch of attention at an early age and sometimes this attention did make me a little uncomfortable. While still in junior high, I had a teacher on whom I had a gigantic crush. He was young, good looking, and he was involved in music, my heart and soul at the time. My best friend and I harassed him unmercifully in class and we ended up giving him a nickname, which consisted only of the initials C.T., for Choir Teacher! We talked about him constantly and wrote notes back and forth about him; our other friends had no idea who or what was our constant topic of conversation. You may have guessed, we were more interested in choir than any other class; gee, I wonder why!

This young teacher ended up becoming a really good friend to my family. He knew I had an extreme interest in music and he went out of his way to help me in any way he could. He taught me how to play the twelve-string guitar, and we even ended up becoming singing partners performing for senior citizens' centers and children's homes. We spent endless hours with each other in my family's living room and den, working on different music and perfecting our act. Most of this happened during the summer between the eighth grade and my freshman year in high school. As the summer wore on, I still had a major crush on this man but I was also involved with many friends, and had many boys that were prospects to be a boyfriend. What I did not know, however, was the fact that my teacher friend had started developing strong feelings for me.

My best friend and I, like all little girls, talked, gossiped and dreamed. We dreamed about growing up, getting married, and having children. When I talked about my dreams, C.T. was always my husband. We lived in a big house, surrounded with musical instruments everywhere. We whistled and sang to our two children, who I already had named; you know how young girls are! This was all a fantasy, of which girls have many while growing up; the princess and the prince stories... it was all greatly exciting to pretend about these things, but then something started changing, and my relationship was not quite the same with C.T.

6-14-2007   170 lbs.

It did not take me long to figure out that my teacher friend was starting to think about our relationship a bit differently than when we had first started working together. After all, we met when I was in the sixth grade. I was now moving on to high school and I did not look like the normal freshman or normal fourteen-year-old girl. I was very "mature" for my age and I looked even older when I dressed up. It was fun to pretend I was involved with an older man, but I was not quite prepared for how I felt when the older man started showing more than just friendly behavior toward me.

I remember well how all of this started happening. Our family took a weekend trip up to our mountain home in Mayhill and my parents invited him along. He had become a very big part of our family and my parents treated him as such. He always joked around, saying he was going to wait for me to grow up and then we were going to run away together. We would all laugh and joke about it. After all, he was the age of my older sister. There was a ten-year age difference! We made the trip to the mountains and had the weekend all planned. He came equipped with his guitar and I had mine as well. After we arrived, he and I took a walk and ended up in the gravel pit up above the farmhouse. We sat and talked for a long while and he started expressing his true feelings towards me. He did nothing inappropriate other than just talking to me, but it did make me feel a little strange; suddenly my friend was telling me that he was falling in love with me. Even though he knew I was very young, too young to handle any relationship, he wanted me to know that he would wait for me until I got old enough to marry him. Wow! He was serious! When this subject was joked about, it was funny, but now it had become all too real for me.

From that moment on, I started backing away from my friend except for during our performances. I started dating and after school started, I was so busy with school activities that I had little time to spend with C.T. Later on, I met my first serious boyfriend, Brian, and we went together for sometime; this is the boy I wrote about in a previous chapter who got himself involved in drug trafficking. C. T. and I remained friends for many years until I moved away from El Paso. He sang at my sister's wedding and was my escort during the festivities. We even have a picture of him and me walking down the aisle of the church with him having his fingers crossed as if to say "hopefully, someday!" I actually ended up getting married before him and he sang at my own wedding as well. After marrying, he and I performed several other times in the years that followed. I went to his wedding several years later and then we lost contact with each other. I still have fond memories of the many hours of music we shared and all that he taught me musically. He gave me an early appreciation of opera as well as all classical music and for this, I thank him. My family continued to love him and after I got older, I told my parents about him sharing his true feelings with me at such a young age. I do not think they were surprised because he always made it known that he loved me. They trusted him and they trusted me. He would have never intentionally hurt me. We were kindred spirits with a tremendous age difference between us. If it would have been years down the road, perhaps me at twenty and him thirty, you never know how it would have ended up. That was not the case, however, and our lives ended up going different ways, as so many of our relationships do when we are young. We meet, we love, we end, then we move on.

6-15-2007   **170 lbs.**

I dated different boys throughout high school. With the exception of Bryan, most of my boyfriends were much older. I guess because I was far more mature in many ways, I found older boys more appealing. The summer of my sophomore year, I met someone who was working for my dad at his construction business. With me having a severe knee injury and facing surgery, this man wanted to talk to me because he had been through two knee surgeries himself. He asked my dad if it would be all right if he spoke to me about my upcoming surgery. My dad agreed because I was very scared and the young man set up a time to talk to me about the surgery. He explained to me what to expect after surgery, but one thing stuck in my mind: he showed me his scars and told me to tell my doctor not to mutilate my leg the way his were. I remember him telling me I had far too pretty of a leg to leave such a nasty scar to live with. The young man's concern made an impression on me. After I had the surgery, he came and visited with me while I was in the hospital and I started looking at him differently from that moment on.

There was a huge age difference between us. He was in his mid-twenties, and I was sixteen. We never looked at our age as being an issue, though. That summer, we started spending large amounts of time together. I was lifeguarding at a friend's pool and we would spend everyday together after he got off work. He and his best friend would come to the pool and hang out with my friends and me. We hit it off so well, and we started to fall in love. Pretty soon, we spent every waking hour we could with each other. We got along so well that even my friends could tell it was turning out to be more that a casual relationship. My parents did not know for quite some time that we were spending as much time together as we were. Finally, he approached my dad, his boss, and told him he wished to date me. My parents were a bit against it at first because of our age difference, but eventually they gave in because my dad knew he was a good young man and my parents both trusted me as well. They had raised me to be a good girl so they had that confidence, knowing I could handle myself. We were allowed to go out because they felt he was responsible and would protect me; they were right. We both came from good moral families and they had to trust in God I would be treated like the lady I was. He *did* always treat me like a lady and I soon fell quickly and furiously in love with him. I knew he was the one I would marry someday.

As he was older, he had been in a serious relationship before, even engaged at one time. However, the wedding never happened and he shared the story with me. I felt badly after he explained the situation around the breakup. He told me the only way he would ever be engaged again was if he first made darn sure it was what he wanted. By what he told me, he had been cheated on during his engagement and he was the one to cancel it. He was hurt terribly.

6-16-2007   **170 lbs.**

After dating exclusively for a few months, I was sure I had found the man of my dreams. We had become best friends as well. I adored his family and I know they loved me. The time came when he proposed to me and I accepted. We scheduled our wedding for the next summer after I got out of school. Then, we had some tragic news. His mother was diagnosed with bone cancer and was not given long to live. The news was very disturbing to all of us. She wanted to be a part of the wedding badly but she started failing fast. I then found out I had enough credits to graduate from high school early, and I could leave after the fall semester so we moved our wedding date up to March. Unfortunately, his mother passed away the end of January. This was a very sad time for all of us but we went ahead and kept the March wedding date because many things had already been ordered, such as invitations. It was a very sentimental time for everyone involved in the wedding.

On March 8, 1975, I was married. I was 17 years old. I know what you are thinking, that I was way too young to get married, and I was. Even though I was much more mature than other seventeen-year-old girls that I knew, I was still very young. I thought I had it all together and that my life was all planned out. I would go to college, have two children, a boy and a girl, and we would live happily ever after. I planned on being the best wife possible so my husband would continue to adore me. We would have the great house, with a swimming pool of course, a dog and a cat and anything else we wanted. This was the plan at least; then life came! My husband wanted me to stay home and not go to school because he wanted kids almost immediately. I wanted a baby also and decided I should try to get pregnant. We tried and nothing happened. Month after month of disappointment started wearing me down.

2007-2007-2007   **170 lbs.**

When I could not get pregnant, I decided to go on with my plans of college, as well as working full time. School and work kept me busy. I also decided to continue with my singing and started working with a local band on weekends. My schedule was completely full and I started drifting away from my marriage. I wanted a lot out of life but my husband was content working for my dad and continuing on the same course. This drove a big wedge between us because I wanted him to have more ambition in life. He had the opportunity to take advantage of the G.I. Bill and go to college, but he chose not to. I considered this foolish because he could get an education free but chose not to. I had to pay for my schooling and I looked at him as being lazy and unmotivated. Even with our age difference, I felt I was the more mature one in the relationship. Our differences ended up becoming more than an issue. They became the ruin of our marriage.

I decided I could not live this way anymore so I took steps to end the marriage. My mother stood by me and understood my reasoning, but my father did not understand. He became angry with me. I had other personal reasons why I wanted to end my marriage but I was not willing to share these reasons with my father. A wedge came between us but I moved ahead and did what I needed to do with my life. It was my decision, and no one else's, and I had to be able to live with my decision. I knew I would be better off in the end even though the breakup was difficult.

My husband put me through a lot of emotional turmoil. After his mother passed away, his two little sisters lived with us almost full time for the first year. I was seventeen when we got married and I was not equipped to be a full-time mother to two young girls who were 10 and 12 years old. I wanted to help as much as I could and I became extremely close to the girls, but full-time motherhood was difficult with children this age. When we started the divorce, I had to distance myself from his family because he made it so difficult on me. He tried everything he could to get me to change my mind and he used the girls to try to get to me. This was very unfair for those little girls, not to mention me. I knew he was heartbroken at my decision to end the marriage, but I could not turn back. I had to do what I thought was best for everyone involved but most of all, I had to be true to myself.

I ended up becoming very bitter towards my husband because of the mind games he tried to play; I hated feeling this way as it was not me. When the time came for him to be served with divorce papers, he dodged the sheriff so I ended up having to trick him and serve him myself. This was not easy. I ended up moving away from El Paso to New Mexico to distance myself from him while the divorce was pending. That move proved to be the beginning of my next major relationship.

While I was separated from my first husband, I met two men I went out with socially. I was modeling for Harley-Davidson at the time, and met many new people during this experience. A friend of the family introduced me to a young wealthy rancher who lived part-time in the city and part-time on his ranch in Arizona. We hit it off immediately and ended up spending lots of time together. He had been married once before as well, and he had a small son from his marriage. He was still in court fighting for full custody of his child and the stress of his custody battle put a strain on our relationship. Then, when I found out he did not want to have any other children, I broke it off. I cared for him and it broke my heart to call it quits but I was not willing to give up my dreams of what I wanted out of life, once again. In my first marriage, I was expected to bow down and go along with what my husband wanted for our life and I ended it because of this expectation. I was not willing to get into another relationship where I did all of the compromising in order for it to work out. I do believe in compromise but not when it is completely one sided.

I casually dated another young man who I met through my Harley-Davidson experience but we ended up just remaining friends. We never went out completely by ourselves. My best friend and her boyfriend were always included in our plans. The four of us spent evenings going to the dog races in Mexico and playing pool in our apartment's game room; we all lived at the same place. It was a new singles apartment complex and most of the tenants were airline pilots, flight attendants, and young business professionals. We had a blast living there, and made many friends with fellow dwellers.

My sister Sheri was then living in Albuquerque. I had a chance for a modeling assignment in Albuquerque so my best friend and I set off one Friday afternoon to New Mexico to check it out. We arranged to stay with Sheri and had a full weekend planned. Halfway between El Paso and Albuquerque sits a small town called Truth or Consequences, New Mexico. This is usually the stopping point for people traveling between the two big cities. We stopped in "T or C" to fill up with gas and get a snack. As we pulled back onto the interstate, a red Trans-Am whizzed in behind us at a high rate of speed, and then passed us as if we were sitting still! I was traveling at 55 miles per hour, the set speed limit at the time. I was driving a brand new car and the dealership had told me to drive it gently during the break-in period. This bright-red Trans-Am almost ran over me and then passed me, leaving me in his smoke! I realized there was a C.B. radio antenna on the top of the red car and I picked up my C.B. mike and yelled out on the heavily used highway channel, "How 'bout the idiot in the red Trans-Am?" My girlfriend started laughing and then she said, "Forget the car! Did you see the *driver?*" Of course, I was not paying attention to the driver. I was highly insulted that this guy almost ran over me in order to fly past me as if I wasn't moving at all. His driving had a lot to be desired! As I was thinking this, a voice called out from the C.B. radio.

"Did you call the driver in the red Trans-Am? I had my radio off and as I reached to turn it on all I heard was 'red Trans-Am!'"

I hissed back, "Yeah, I was calling you! I'm in the maroon and gold car you almost *ran over* as you passed me!" I was indignant.

"I'm sorry," he replied. "I'm a little upset and not paying too much attention as to how I'm driving. I apologize."

His voice sounded sincere. His voice also sounded quite "cute." It looked like I was going to let him off the hook!

6-20-2007   **169 lbs.**

I did not know that on that November day in 1977 I was destined to meet my future husband and the father of my children soon after a two-and-a-half hour drive down the interstate, talking nonstop on the C.B. radio. You know what they say about destiny; it was meant to be. I know without a doubt, we were both supposed to be on that interstate, in the same location, at the same time, so our lives would intersect. As you can tell, it all came into play and both of our lives changed on that day.

That day, the young man proved to be an excellent conversationalist. We talked about everything on that stretch of highway. I learned that he had just gone through a difficult divorce and was actually just leaving an auction of his business when he entered the interstate in such a fury. From the sound of it, he had really been through the ringer. I told him about my own divorce and what I was going through and he sympathized. We talked about our families. We talked about our education and we talked about our friends. Before long, we were approaching Albuquerque and Jeff, as we now knew him, asked us what our plans were the next afternoon. We told him we would be free around two o'clock. He asked us to a barbeque out in the country at around four in the afternoon at a bar owned by a friend of his. He gave us his phone number and asked us to call him the following morning and he would give us directions if we wanted to attend. We agreed.

The following morning at around 10 o'clock we placed a call to Jeff and his roommate answered. He told us Jeff was not in but he gave us the directions on how to get to the barbeque. We made plans to attend and went out there that afternoon. When we arrived, Jeff was not yet there so we waited for him in my car. He arrived and did not see us. Another female saw him drive up and she got out of her car and went up to him. About that time, he saw us sitting in the car and he hurried her inside. He then came out to where we were. He started apologizing to us and said he had a situation on his hands. We figured the female was his ex-wife and we graciously excused ourselves and told him we were not into causing problems. He apologized again and asked us if we would meet him Monday morning for breakfast before we left town. Normally I would have not given him another chance to explain why we were being gracefully un-invited to the barbeque, let alone give him another chance to enjoy our company! I could see on his face, however, he was truly humiliated and I saw something in him that I liked in spite of what had just happened. I told him I would call him the next evening and let him know if we were going to meet him for breakfast the following morning. I did not want to seem too eager; I wanted him to sweat it out a little! He gracefully agreed to await my call and we then left.

My best friend was furious at the fact Jeff had hurried us away. I was not very happy but I figured there had to be a logical explanation for his behavior. After talking with him during our ride the day before and him telling us about everything he had been through with his ex and all, I just figured he was caught in a jam and I, of all people, was not into making a scene. I could have gotten extremely angry and called him a big jerk and left, but I felt there was more to this story than met the eye. My friend just laughed at me and said something to the effect that I was already hopelessly hooked! I did not think it was *that* obvious, but there was *something* about him, maybe his charm, maybe his extraordinary good looks, maybe it was the fact we could talk so freely, even though we had just met. Maybe it was the fact that his life sounded like it had been so exciting. I don't know, it was probably a combination of all of the above, but I knew I was not willing to write him off, at least not just yet! I felt he deserved another chance, a chance to redeem himself and at least suffer overnight and the next day to see if I was going to call him back Sunday evening!

6-21-2007   **169 lbs.**

We went on about our business and yes, I did call Jeff back late Sunday evening. I told him what time we were planning to leave town the following morning and suggested he meet us at a local pancake house on our way out of town. The plans were made, and he would not dare to not show up! After all, we were being quite generous in agreeing to meet him after the barbeque fiasco.

The next morning we arrived at the restaurant and Jeff was already there waiting for us. Seeing us walk in the door, he met us and escorted us to our table. One of the first things I noticed was the fact that he acted every bit the gentleman, pulling out our chairs for us as we were seated; this was very nice. I am a lady and I expect to be treated like a lady. As the meal and conversation progressed, I also noticed his good table manners; you could tell he had been raised right. This was important because I am very particular. We enjoyed each other's company and Jeff vowed he was coming to El Paso to see me soon. He had a business trip scheduled to California and when he told us when he would be returning, I told him about a Christmas party that was scheduled at our apartment complex, which was also going to be their big grand opening celebration. I said if he planned his trip to El Paso around that date, he could escort me to the party. He agreed and said he would be there! We had a nice visit during breakfast and then had to say goodbye so we could get on the road back home. If Jeff made it in for the party, it would be a month before I would see him again. I believed him when he said he would be there to take me. He seemed sincere.

The next month went by quickly because I was very busy with Harley-Davidson and the local dealership. My full-time job was taking up most of my days and the modeling was an evening and weekend affair. We spent an excessive amount of time working on portfolio shots as well. My photographer ended up being one of my best friends and we spent countless hours together. I could always count on him to set me straight if I needed to be. He also watched out for me when it came to dating and relationships and he was there while I was going through my divorce and suffering. He was not willing to let anyone else put me through turmoil. I guess you could say he was the big brother I never had. He was married to a great woman and even though he was a big flirt, he never crossed *that* line. When I returned from New Mexico, I told him about the man I had met and his guard immediately went up.

"You picked up this guy on the highway!?" he scolded.

I had to explain to him that it was not quite *that* bad! Yes, we did meet on the road but it was as if we had known each other for a very long time.

"Serial killers can be nice guys too!" he continued.

He had a point. Normally, I would have run in the other direction but not this time. Had I met my destiny?

The month continrued to be busy. Modeling, working full time and a social life kept me on my toes! Soon it was time for the big party at our complex. The day before, my phone rang at work and it was Jeff. He assured me he would be in El Paso the following afternoon and would call me when he and a friend of his arrived. He was traveling with his best friend's son. I told him I was looking forward to seeing him. The next day at work, I received a bouquet of flowers. Without opening the card yet, I knew they were from Jeff because that was just the kind of guy he was. To my surprise, when I opened the card, the flowers were from the man I had dated before, the rancher. He knew about the party before he left town to be on his Arizona ranch. In the card, he expressed the fact that he would arrive at my place at seven p.m. to escort me to the party. I was astonished! I had not talked with him in two months! Then, within about an hour of the first bouquet of flowers arriving, I received a second bouquet! Again, as I went to read the card, I expected them to be from Jeff. And once again, as I read the card, I was in for a second shock! This bouquet of flowers was from my soon-to-be ex-husband who I thought did not know where I lived, let alone know anything about the big party! In his card, he expressed *his* desire to escort me to the festivities! So here I was at work, with two huge flower arrangements sitting on my desk, in complete and total disbelief about who sent the flowers! Then, within thirty minutes, another florist showed up at my office with yet another bouquet! I opened the card cautiously and finally found Jeff's message inside the card telling me how beautiful he knew I would look that evening. Here I was with three bouquets of flowers, three invitations and there was only one of me to go around! It was not a hard decision though. I had promised Jeff I would go with him and in a way it infuriated me that my ex-husband and ex-boyfriend just *assumed* I would go with them to the party. Did they think I had no life? In the cards, each one said they would be at my place at seven p.m. sharp! Now I had a situation on my hands! Each of them was going to be on my front doorstep at the same time, and I did not want a scene. As I tried to figure out how to handle the situation gracefully, Jeff called me to see if I received the flowers. I told him what had happened and he told me not to worry about it, so we made plans for him to arrive at my place early to beat the other two! Sure enough, Jeff showed up at my door early, and when the other two showed up, within seconds of each other, I politely explained that I had made other plans and I also told each of them they should never assume a woman is sitting at home waiting for their "when the mood strikes" attention! By the looks on each of their faces, I think they got the message. Jeff and I went to the party, and then went to a local nightspot and closed it down! Afterwards, we sat up the rest of the night in my apartment talking with him cracking jokes, keeping me laughing and in stitches; I had a tremendous time. We hardly got any sleep that night and I had an early modeling call at the local Harley dealership. Jeff agreed to stay in town to watch me work and I felt good that he wanted to learn a little bit about what I did in my world. I can openly say that I was falling for the man I had met on the road the month before.

6-26-2007   **169 lbs.**

Christmas came and went, and I had the opportunity to move to Albuquerque. My sister decided to share her home with me and we became roommates. I had modeling opportunities there and found a full-time job as well. Moving away from my hometown was not easy to do, but I needed a change in my life. My divorce was not final and I needed to distance myself from my husband because he was not making my life any easier. This also gave me the chance to get to know Jeff better. The move was a good decision for me at the time.

As soon as I settled in, Jeff and I spent a lot of time together. My mother accompanied me on my first trip to Albuquerque during my move and she had the chance to meet Jeff. Afterwards, I remember her telling me that because of his good looks and charm, women were never going to leave him alone! She liked him instantly and told me that as long as I could handle this fact, she supported us getting to know each other better. I was truly amazed at her reaction, but I think she saw a drive in him that would make him successful through life and she liked that. I also think she saw the undeniable chemistry between us and she was seeing me happy for the first time in a while. Well, I had *half* the battle won! There was still my father's opinion, and because of his closeness to my soon to be ex-husband, I decided to hold off before making any formal introductions. Jeff and I needed time to get to know each other and explore our relationship before I carried things any further.

For the next four months, Jeff and I were inseparable. He took me to Arizona to meet his mother and step dad. We hit it off instantly; they were charming and it was very apparent Jeff came from a strong family with values and love. His father was his roommate in Albuquerque and they also were very close. As each was a bachelor, they loved to go out and have fun together. Jeff's dad was truly young at heart. He was also extremely good looking and had lots of lady friends surrounding him at all times. His money did not hurt either; he could afford to take off and travel with any one of his lady friends and always show them a good time. It was easy for me to see where Jeff got his charm! His mother and father both possessed the talent of winning you over with just a few words. I often kidded Jeff and told him if I had met his dad first, you never know what may have happened!

My divorce became final in March of 1978. Jeff proposed to me that very same day and I accepted without hesitation. We set our wedding date immediately for May 13, 1978. To our surprise, my sister and her boyfriend also announced their engagement at the very same time and set their wedding date to be exactly two weeks before ours! Our parents learned of Sheri's engagement and wedding date one weekend shortly after that, and then Jeff and I made the trip to El Paso the following weekend to break our own news! Boy, what a double whammy we presented to our parents! They did not see it coming nor did they have the chance to react too much because there was no time; there was five weeks until the first wedding and seven weeks until ours.

It all went better than I expected with my dad regarding my upcoming wedding. I expected him to throw a royal fit, but after we explained our plans, Jeff's future and the fact that either we would be married with all of their blessings or we would live together, he readily agreed. Of course, we were not going to live together without being married but Dad did not know that! He gave us his blessing and then he expressed his desire for grandchildren as soon as possible; that is, after the wedding and a following nine months!

6-27-2006   **169 lbs.**

On May 13, 1978 Jeff and I were married. The day before our wedding, Jeff completed his training and received his private pilot's license, which he had been working towards for several months. His plans were to continue flight training and become a corporate pilot. The day after our wedding, I had a modeling assignment for Piper Aircraft at a local airport, and we then left New Mexico for Oklahoma where Jeff enrolled in flight school to continue his training. This was a big move for us. We were going there on the promise we would have no trouble finding housing close to the school. When we arrived in Oklahoma, the school gave us a sheet of paper with rentals listed on it and we were then on our own; it was quite unnerving for us. We had a U-Haul trailer with our belongings in it and we had to find somewhere quickly. We ended up renting a very small place about a mile from Jeff's flight school. We thought it was great at the time but looking back on it now, it really was a dump! Oh, to be young and in love!

Sometimes our judgments are a little clouded by the newness of a great love. Jeff's mother came to visit us about a month after we moved in, and when she took one look at the place her exact remarks were "My kids are not living in a place like this!" If it was one of my kids and I saw they were living in a little dump like the one we rented for sixty-nine dollars a month, I would object too! The Oklahoma stay only lasted for about five weeks. I got ill shortly after moving there, and Jeff's school was a big disappointment; they promised him things they could not deliver. Jeff became disillusioned and with me being ill and unable to work we made the decision to go to Arizona where his mother and step- father lived, to complete his flight training there. They had a guesthouse on their property so we could live there rent-free until he completed school. This decision was not hard for me because I did not like Oklahoma; I lived in fear the whole time we were there because of tornadoes! I had never lived in a place where weather was a safety issue and I'm sure this had a lot to do with me getting sick after we moved there. I never rested. My eyes would stay glued to the TV as tornado warnings flashed across the screen almost all the time. I wanted to go back to the Southwest where I felt safe and family was close by.

We made the move to Arizona and things were much better there. Jeff was back in flight school and I found a job without trouble. I also continued modeling whenever I got the chance. Then, two months after we got married, I found out I was expecting our first child. We were excited and scared all at the same time, and Jeff vowed to be through with school by the time the baby was born. Shortly after us finding out we were pregnant, we decided to move to El Paso so I could be close to my mother because she was ill and I needed to be with my family. My father offered me a job, and Jeff was able to transfer to a school in order to complete his training. It was hard to leave his parents, but they understood my need to be close to my mom.

2007-2007-2007   **169 lbs.**

Two days after our daughter was born, Jeff opened up his own flight school. He completed all of his training including what he needed to be a flight instructor. Flying was big business at the time. It seemed like everyone wanted to take flying lessons. With the cost of fuel in Mexico being what it was, he would get his fuel over the border and because of this low cost, he could offer lessons cheaper than in cities further away.

The first year we worked at the business together, with me keeping the books and running the office while he flew. We bought a twin engine airplane so he could give multi-engine instruction as well as single-engine. The business was located at a little private airport set apart from the international airport. A friend of ours owned the little airport and he had planes that Jeff could use. There was no twin-engine plane, however, until we purchased one. It was quite funny when we went to a local bank to ask for a loan on the airplane. They informed us they had never loaned money on an aircraft before! Nonetheless, there is a first time for everything, and they funded us the money. One of Jeff's students who wanted to take multi-engine lessons decided to go in with us on the deal, so he became our partner.

We got plenty of use out of that plane when Jeff was not training someone in it. On weekends, we traveled to New Mexico and Arizona to visit Jeff's family, and we usually had someone going along with us for the ride. I have to tell you, I was, and still am, deathly afraid of flying! Commercial aircraft are not that bad and I can tolerate commercial flights if I have to, but small airplanes scare me to death! I have to say though that I have spent many hours in a small plane and the only pilot I ever trusted was Jeff. I knew he was an experienced and safe pilot and I trusted him with my life, as well as Sandra's. She was flying at three days old and experienced many, many hours in an airplane with her daddy. At one point though, I finally decided I would never get into a small aircraft again and since then, I have not! My decision came about after we experienced a terrible flight from Oklahoma to Texas and, after finally arriving in El Paso, as I was exiting the plane, I became tangled up in the seatbelt and fell to the ground, breaking my knee. I swore at that very moment that would be my last flight in a small plane, and I meant it! I took it as some kind of sign or something. Jeff never complained about me not wanting to fly any more and even if he did, I would have held firm in my choice.

After about a two-year period, aviation fuel costs went up tremendously, and it hurt the business. Jeff had been training with an airplane mechanic who worked at the airport and he in turn became certified to work on aircraft. Deciding to close the school down, he moved over to the big airport and started working on planes, making good money. He still taught flying, but his main business was aircraft repair and inspections. The first year he met the man who ended up becoming very important to our family. Before long, Jeff left the mechanics business and took a job with this man's company in hopes of them buying a corporate aircraft and him becoming their corporate pilot. This man ended up becoming like family to us and tragically, he was the friend who was killed in his airplane on his way out to see us in California several years later.

7-3-2007   **168 lbs.**
Jeff worked for this company for about three years, but the company never bought an airplane for him to fly. He worked at the company as head of mechanics for their road construction division, but even though he made very good money and had excellent benefits, this was not what he wanted to do. Someone else he had met at the airport who had a small aircraft Jeff worked on, bought a major company in California, saving it from bankruptcy. They started talking one day and this man told Jeff he needed someone to go out there and run this company for him. Jeff was looking for a change. Jeff and this man both had a love for flying, and one thing led to another; before long, this man offered the position to Jeff, offering many incentives to make the move.

I remember when I heard about this; I was in the hospital. This whole event occurred about three years after my illness when our son was born and I was in and out of the hospital frequently. Jeff had told me of the company in California and about Paul, the man who owned it. Paul also owned a major corporation right there in

El Paso. Because I had been so ill, I really did not take things too seriously when Jeff met someone who promised him a big chance to fly. He met people on a daily basis who talked about hiring him as a corporate pilot; this was not much different. He would go to California and run the company, pulling it out of trouble, and then they would concentrate on purchasing a corporate plane. Anyone who met Jeff could see his potential; he ran his own business before his first marriage broke up and he had opened the flight school after Sandra was born. He has amazing business sense and his intelligence has always carried him through in any situation. He has always been a go-getter, and this is obvious when you meet him. He has a charismatic personality and the charm to go with it. When unsure, he can talk his way through any situation. As I was lying in a hospital bed, Jeff came in to visit me, and during the visit he informed me he made the decision to make a move to California and take the position. I lay there in shock! I knew him well enough to know he was serious. Now here I was, sick, with uncertainty about my future because of illness, and there was my husband telling me he was planning a major move to another state! Not only were my roots there in Texas, but my business was as well; I was a partner in a major construction and development company with my dad. I lay there watching Jeff's lips move, hearing what he was saying, but not comprehending it at all. He continued by saying he had given it a lot of thought and he believed I could stay behind, sell our two houses, finalize the business and then join him.

When I look back, I realize this was the point where our marriage started to fail terribly. Not to say that we did not have some problems before this point, but this seemed to be the time I lost some of my respect for our marriage. Jeff made a major decision about our future without considering what this decision would do to my career and to me. The fact that I was sick was a big issue; I wanted to be close to my parents during this time. During my recurring hospital stays, they helped with the kids. I also had a nanny/housekeeper who the children adored and because of her age, I knew she would not be willing to make a move out of state. Jeff was asking us to change our whole lives because of *his* choice and did not give me an opportunity to think about it. It was a done deal; he was moving!

7-5-2007   **168 lbs.**

After Jeff made the decision to move to California, I was not left with much of a choice if I wanted to save my marriage. We discussed the fact that I would stay in El Paso for a year, settling our real estate by selling our two homes, and also settle my company business. We had major contracts going and I could not leave my dad high and dry. I was also on the board of directors for Associated Builders and Contractors and this move would force me to turn in my resignation. This saddened me because I had put in many, many hours and two years with the organization, and still had two years remaining for my term. I was the first woman elected to the board and I enjoyed the service immensely. The loved me because I was instrumental in bringing in many new members to the association. I also brought in record amounts of money in the fundraising activities I chaired. Not to "toot my own horn" but the association benefited greatly by me being on the board. Bringing new and fresh ideas to the group was exciting, and I think my fellow members appreciated my hard work and dedication. This was apparent when I was honored with the Member of the Year award in 1984, as voted on by the membership!

Jeff packed up and left Texas. We commuted back and forth between California and Texas on weekends. One weekend he would return home, the following weekend I would fly to California. He lived in an apartment until we decided where we wanted to live. I also needed to sell our homes before we could buy another. The agreement was that I would take a year to finalize all of our business in Texas and then the kids and I would move on to California. At least, that *was* the agreement that lasted for about two months! Then, Jeff started calling me and put demands on me to move immediately. I couldn't, and this made my life very difficult. I understood he was lonely out there by himself, but after all it was all his idea in the first place. What say did I have in his decision? None!

After a short period of time, my life became a living hell as I endured daily calls from my husband demanding us to hurry and get out to California. This infuriated me to no end. I had so many things to do that the last thing I needed was pressure from Jeff. My health was an issue too; the stress did not help the eating disorder I suffered from. I felt my body weight was one of the only things I could control. Jeff's demands were completely unrealistic and it got to a point where I dreaded his daily calls because we would end up fighting. Then when weekends would come, we would make up. Each time, however, a little piece of me died. The pressure was becoming too much.

Four months later, Sandra and I made the move. I had sent Jeffrey out to his dad the month before. He was not in preschool yet and I needed to be free of caring for him during the day so I could pack up the household. I also needed to do some repairs on the home we lived in to get it ready and turned over to the real estate company I hired to lease it. Deciding to lease made better sense in case things did not work out in California. I thought I possibly had a job there with Associated Builders and Contractors as their organization's executive director. For some reason I do not remember, either they decided not to hire me, or I decided the money was not enough. At this time, I was used to a hefty paycheck. This type of association could probably not pay me what I thought I needed to live in California. I had to pay for childcare, endure the major cost of living in that part of the country, and buy a home, smaller than what we were use to, for fifty thousand dollars more than we paid for our large home in Texas. The cost of living in California was atrocious, but I did not go to work right away. I took my time and that ended up being a good thing because my mother had a second heart attack that May and Sandra and I went back to Texas so I could help out. I spent the summer in El Paso taking care of her.

After the summer was over, we went back to California. I started trying to find a job that would satisfy my career aspirations. This proved to be difficult, living in a strange place, not knowing anybody, and especially trying to find something that could even slightly compare to what I had in Texas. I was used to being my own boss and keeping my own hours. I wanted to continue doing something in the construction field, but I did not know what. A couple of months passed by and the holidays started approaching. I did something crazy; I found an ad in the newspaper for a jewelry salesperson to work in various shopping malls around the Southern California area, selling gold jewelry. Gold chains were fashionable during this time and I really needed something to do, so I contacted the company. As luck had it, I got the job and it was great fun! The people I worked with were a riot and I made great commissions. It was different and something I had never done before. In fact, it was my first retail job.

While working on this job, I continued watching the newspaper and went through employment agencies for the perfect employment opportunity. Right before the holiday season ended, I ran across an advertisement for a public relations expert. This stirred my interest. I called and arranged for an interview with this company and found out they were a real estate magazine dealing with new home sales in the Southern California area. They needed someone with great construction knowledge and public relations experience. So where do you think I ended up? You guessed it; that job was made for me!

Jeff went on with his career and I proceeded with mine. We both worked very hard at our respective careers, which took time away from each other and our children. We hired a live-in housekeeper/baby sitter to help with the home and with Sandra and Jeffrey. I do not know when it started happening, but Jeff and I started growing apart from each other. Jeff is a neatness fanatic, so I would go behind our house cleaner making sure everything was in its place when he came home from work. I dealt with a lot of pressure because of my full schedule and then when I returned home, I had to make sure everything was to his liking. Looking back on it now, I would have done things differently. There was absolutely no reason to put myself through this. He could have stepped up to the plate and given me more help at home but he didn't.

The strain started taking its hold on me and I started resenting it. His hours at work started increasing, which meant I was left to take care of the kids and all of their extracurricular activities. It always felt like my career was not as important as his, and I was expected to drop my plans to be at home when he was not. In earlier times, this would have been the case but we were living in the 80's and times had changed. Two-career families were the norm, and we needed both paychecks to live in the custom we had grown into. Living in California dictated we both work in order to compensate for the pleasure of living there. Looking back, I would have been happy staying at home with my children. I would have easily given up my career to be with my children more but it was always understood, I would work as well. Why, I cannot say, but this was the expectation that was required of me. I would have been perfectly happy being a stay-at-home mom, watching my kids grow up.

I always had a hard time standing up to Jeff. He could guilt me into many things. Even when my heart screamed *no*, I usually gave in to him. I truly resented this. It showed weakness on my part and controlling behavior on his part. As time went on, I started resenting him for his controlling ways. It ate away at me, day by day, and it became increasingly hard for me to hold in my resentment. I can honestly say, I never really stood up to him and told him exactly how I felt. I am sure that my submissive behavior added to his control issue. Those who know me as I am today will probably not believe that I was a little submissive creature who let someone else take control of me. I never took a firm stand and shouted, "There's no way in hell I'm agreeing with that, or doing that!" I've grown so much since the time Jeff and I were married.

Jeff and I loved each other greatly; there was never any question about this fact. Sometimes, however, love is not enough. You have to be compatible in almost every aspect of your lives in order to make things work. We have always been each other's biggest fans when it has come to supporting one another and I know Jeff can accomplish anything he puts his heart to, and I know this feeling is mutual. We have always supported each other and it is this way even to this day. I believe in him, sometimes more than he believes in himself, and I am sure he would tell you the same thing. We both have the gift of meeting others and making friends easily. In this aspect, we worked very well together, and in situations of internal doubt, the other has always come to the rescue to reassure the doubtful one assuring the other they can do anything if they put our heart into it. Not a day goes by on my part when I want to pick up the phone and call Jeff to tell him how my day is going because I know if it's bad, he will encourage me, and if its good, he will say "Good job!"

7-16-2007   **168 lbs.**

Jeff and I stayed married for 13 years. We realized that we were two people who could not live with each other regardless of how much we loved one another. We separated several times, but then would get back together; each time it was a little more difficult. At one point, we actually filed for divorce, lived apart for several months and then stopped the divorce proceedings. After this, we decided to renew our wedding vows and had a second wedding on the date of our twelfth anniversary. It was lovely. Unfortunately, our marriage the second time around was worse than the first. We were both miserable and even though we wanted to stay together for the children's sake, it became more detrimental with us fighting all of the time. At one point, Sandra asked me why I stayed with her daddy. I guess this was the question I needed to realize that our choice to try again was actually harming the kids even more. The decision to leave the marriage was an extremely difficult one for me; I loved my husband with all of my heart but in many ways

I did not like him. The constant arguing and fighting wore me down and I know it did the same to him as well. I actually think we became addicted to each other. We could not live together, but we could not live apart. We were each other's bad habit!

At the end of our marriage, I decided the only way we were going to break our cycle of addiction to one another was for me to pick up and move back to Texas. I made the move, and within a month Jeff had decided he also wanted a change. He decided to move back to El Paso, where I was, and open a business. I found a home for him to lease that was not too far from my apartment, so it would be easier on the children to spend time with both of us.

7-20-2007   **168 lbs.**

After about three months of me living in El Paso, I started getting extremely sick again. I started having seizures and the doctors could not determine why I was having them. They ended up medicating me so heavily that I was not able to live by myself. I moved back in with Jeff so he could take care of me. I did not have anyone else in town and I needed to be close to the kids; we shared joint custody. He was amazing in respect that he let me move back in with him. I know our relationship was unconventional to say the least, and the fact that the man I had left months earlier agreed to take me in during a rough time in my life was hard for some people to understand. Nevertheless, this is what you do for family and we were still a family, despite divorce proceedings. At that point, our divorce had been final for only a month or so and Jeff still wanted to reconcile. We agreed to live together until I could get back on my feet. My health reached a point where I ended up filing for disability because it was certain that my working days were behind me. With all of the medication, continued seizures and other health issues resulting from the previous things that happened after Jeffrey was born, it was apparent I could no longer hold down a job. I do not know what I would have done without Jeff. He truly came through for me.

About a year went by and Jeff decided he was going to move

across town, closer to where his business was located. I made the decision to move with him. We had the kids enrolled in a private Christian school where they experienced more of a "hands on" teaching style. Sandra was in a public school until this point, but there was a tremendous amount of gang activity, even at the junior high level, and we did not want her in this environment. I was feeling a bit better at this point and thought I still needed to separate myself from Jeff because we were starting to fall back into our old habits once again. We were also living in a mobile home, and it was tight living as opposed to what we had in the past. Jeff's business was mobile home sales and we were living on the sales lot in a home he bought. We were soon to find out there is a *huge* difference between a twenty-five hundred square foot home and a mobile home! We were also in the sand hills and our kids were used to having a large yard to play in. We had to watch for snakes and such; we could not just turn them loose and let them play. The close living situation was becoming unbearable for me.

7-21-2007   **168 lbs.**

Jeff and Sandra had a hard relationship. He was much harder on her than he ever was on Jeffrey. As she became a teenager, his reigns pulled her in even more, and it was difficult for me to watch because I felt he was being much too hard on our daughter; their constant fighting was wearing me down. She was starting to rebel against her dad and I could recognize the warning signs. Sandra was watching her little brother get away with everything, as far as their dad was concerned but when it came to her, if she even *looked* at him wrong, she was grounded. I knew the combination of Sandra's personality and her father's personality was a combustible combination at this time in her life but she was going to be a teenager in spite of him. His constant hard approach to keep her under his thumb was only making matters worse and I knew if I did not separate the two of them, it would be detrimental to Sandra. She was a good girl, but she was also a typical young teenage girl going through those awkward years of not being a woman but also not being a little kid anymore. She was definitely head-strong but her dad often made her out to be the worst kid ever. In so many ways, the two of them are just alike, hard-headed and stubborn. I did not want Sandra's spirit broken, however.

My dad told me about a place in Kentucky where kids could go and sing, and perform to a full audience with the chance to go on a live radio show. Sandra was showing great potential with her singing and performing talents, and I wanted to make sure she had the opportunity to excel. With the difficulty I had handling Jeffrey and his little "big" temper, and Sandra and her dad's conflicts, I made the decision to move Sandra and myself to Kentucky. This was difficult leaving Jeffrey behind with Jeff, but I could not handle the child, and Jeff could. Jeff could not handle Sandra, but I could. I also needed to be away from Jeff because we would have ended up back in a full-blown relationship with the same results, miserable and fighting all of the time.

7-22-07   **169 lbs.**

Sandra and I moved to Kentucky in November, 1992. It was very difficult being away from my son, and Sandra missed her dad and little brother, but I did what I thought was best for my family at the time. Jeffrey still attended the private school in Texas and I enrolled Sandra at the local junior high. The separation of our family was lonely in the beginning but after we were settled in, Jeffrey was able to come visit us during his winter break so we got to spend two weeks with him the first month we were there. He and I had a great visit; I spoke about this in a previous chapter. Jeff and I talked almost daily so the kids could talk to each other. When Jeffrey went on his spring break, Sandra was on hers as well so we traveled back to Texas and spent a few days together. We stayed with Jeff. He was dating someone but when he found out I was coming to visit, he broke it off with the woman he was seeing. I felt bad for her. I was also dating someone I met in Kentucky. Jeff talked to me once again about reconciliation and once again, I told him that I could not go through with it. I ended up cutting my visit short because I started feeling uncomfortable.

The man I was dating at this time was an escape from my relationship with Jeff. I was lonely. I started dating the first man I met in Kentucky, and it proved to be the biggest mistake in my entire life! He asked me to marry him three months after we started dating and I accepted, like a fool. He appeared to be the kindest, gentlest man in the world and I fell for his kindness and passion. He also claimed to be a Christian and knew a lot about the Bible and its teachings. This appealed to me. Before I knew it, I was under his spell. Big mistake! We got married after only knowing each other four-and-a-half months.

I will not go into a lot of detail about this marriage because I cannot talk about it and stay sane. It ended up being one of the darkest times of my life, and I am lucky to be alive after being involved with this person. He was dark, manipulative, and mentally abusive. My daughter endured months of his mental abuse, though unknown to me at the time. He had brainwashing capabilities and he tried his best to influence everyone he met. Everyone thought he was charming, except for two of my friends who told me not to trust him. He was in law enforcement and one friend warned the other friend that he was the type of guy who could "blow your head off" and get away with it! I saw nothing alarming in the beginning, and it actually took me one year before I realized how dangerous the man was. At one time, he and Jeff actually met each other and got along fine, but Jeff told him if he ever did anything to hurt Sandra or me, he would answer to Jeff. At one point, I witnessed this man verbally abuse my teenage daughter and I also uncovered some very serious details about his life before I had met him. It scared the hell out of me and with good reason. The minute I heard his abuse towards Sandra, I made him leave and told him I never wanted to see or hear from him again. That was it! I lived in fear for many, many months and both Sandra and me went to counseling, and I immediately filed for divorce. We were only married for one year or, should I say, lived together for one year. The divorce took two-and-a-half years to complete. It still makes me sick to think about this man and what he did to my daughter and me. I made a very bad judgment call in this case and we both paid the price for it. I am still so sorry for what I put Sandra through, even though I was unaware of his evilness.

7-24-2007   **168 lbs.**

At this point in my life, I was uncertain about my future when in romantic relationships. I did not trust most men I met due to the horrific experience I had just gone through. After a few months, one of my close friends, Kip, told me she had someone she wanted me to meet. He was someone who she had worked with and she thought of him as a really nice guy who was as lonely as me. I told her I was not interested, but she insisted! She had been with me the whole time I was going through the fear of my last marriage and she knew how untrusting I was, but she kept after me to at least meet him and go out to dinner. She thought we would be good for each other, and she knew he would treat me well. After protesting for a few weeks, I finally agreed.

John and I hit it off immediately. He was involved in the music industry and, because of my love for music and the excitement of it all, we seemed to have lots in common. We met at his mom's home during a cosmetics party she and his sisters were putting on. Kip was involved in the cosmetics business and she had booked this party with them. John ended up coming in at the end of the party so he could meet me; Kip had arranged this.

The next few months were great. John and I spent almost all our free time together. I started helping him in his music business and we grew very, very close. I found myself falling for him hard, but at the same time, my inner alarms kept going off and the trust issue kept rearing its ugly head. I knew he was falling in love with me, and even though I was very much into him, I started fearing I would go down another bad path. John is the type of person who expects his mate to be completely involved with his family because they are so close. I am the same way, but there has to be a happy medium where time is spent with both families. We hardly ever spent time with my family and I guess in a way, I started resenting the situation. I suddenly started finding myself pulling away from him. I would find any little thing he did irritating, and now when I look back on it, this was my way of getting out of the relationship without being very honest. John is very possessive, not in a bad way, but I am very independent and I was afraid the combination would make our relationship die. I broke it off after seven months.

The ending of this relationship actually did hurt me greatly. I missed him and missed the excitement we shared together in everything we did. We traveled, we shopped, and we were always on the go. He always showed me a great time, but my health was an issue and it was hard for me to explain to him exactly how my illness affected me (in a coming chapter, I will tell you about being diagnosed with lupus). John wanted us to travel as much as possible, but I also had Sandra to consider. She was fifteen and needed me around to keep her grounded. John did not have children, so I felt it was difficult for him to relate to being a parent. Anyway, my decision to break it off left me feeling empty inside.

After the break up, I needed to discover who Karen was, who *I* was, without a boyfriend or a husband. I decided to stay single and get my life back on track. I needed to heal from my breakup with Jeff and the ending of our marriage. I needed to heal from the disastrous marriage I had to the lunatic who could have destroyed my life for good. I needed to heal from just breaking up with someone I truly cared for and loved even though I would not allow myself to just give in and see where it would go. I just needed time to find *me*!

8-1-2007   168 lbs.

I spent the next few months in no relationship and instead enjoyed my friends. My health hit some rocky roads with the lupus and my kidneys were suffering. I rested as much as possible, and between doctors' appointments, I enjoyed my teenage daughter, as she was becoming quite the young lady! I was unaware that at the end of that summer, I was going to meet my fourth husband.

Yes, you read correctly! I said *"Fourth* husband!" By no means was I trying to keep up with my favorite soap opera, *All My Children*, and the famous Erica Kane! When I got married the first time, I expected it to last a lifetime. The second time, I of course expected it to last, and the third we will not even talk about. To this day, I do not recognize it as one of my marriages. I have left that one year blotted out of my mind. After that nightmare, I swore I would never get married again; I was wrong.

On August 5, at Libby's, the place that Sandra sang most every weekend, I met Jimmy. His cousin, who I knew from the establishment, came up to me and told me there was a guy who wanted to dance with me. I told her "No way!" She was persistent until I finally agreed to go into the auditorium and met the man. She led me up to a table full of people and this person had his back turned to me. She tapped him on the shoulder and as he turned to her, he saw me and turned beet red; I could tell he was embarrassed! The people at his table were giving him a hard time by teasing him. Later on, I found out this was his family. In addition, this is when I found out that the girl who introduced us was also part of his family. I found out they were actually cousins!

Jimmy introduced himself to me, and it was obvious he was shy. He did, however, ask me to dance. We hit the dance floor and danced several numbers while talking. He told me he was in the rental business, real estate, and owned several pieces of property. He also told me he was a plumbing contractor and he built some of his own rental properties. We made small talk for the rest of the evening and he then asked me if he could take me out dancing sometime; I agreed. I gave him my phone number and he told me he would call me the following Friday to make a date. He seemed like a nice enough man. I was not accustomed to giving out my phone number, but because of the recommendation of his cousin, I felt he was okay. He was handsome, shy and very soft-spoken. He was dressed like a weekend cowboy, boots and all, and he had a black hat sitting on the table where his family was sitting. My first impression of him was that he looked like Travis Tritt, long hair and all.

Jimmy kept his word and did not call me until the following Friday. We talked for over two hours on the phone! It was August 11. We made a date for the next day. August 12 came and it had to be the hottest day of the summer! He came to my house to pick me up at about five in the afternoon. I had asked him the previous day if he would inspect a home I was looking at buying; I needed him to check the plumbing to make sure there were no unforeseen problems. We left my house and headed to the other property. It was so hot that we were both sweating profusely. He even stopped at a convenience store and went inside to change shirts because of the heat and sweat! We then headed to Nashville for our first date.

8-3-2007   **168 lbs.**

The date proved to be somewhat eventful! To start things off, when we arrived at the restaurant we were confronted with a homeless woman who needed help. The story she gave us was that her home had burned down the previous day and she was trying to get back to where her children were staying in a shelter. She did not ask for money but simply a ride to where she needed to go. I quickly realized that the man I was out with for the first time was a special man. Without giving it a second thought, he escorted her inside his vehicle and we took her to where she needed to go. He then gave her fifty dollars and even though she was not going to accept it, he insisted she do so and then wished her luck. I was blown away by the generosity and kindness he showed to this total stranger. Most people, especially out on a first date, might not have given the woman a second glance, let alone go out of their way to help her while their date was waiting. This impressed me and showed me that this man was possibly worth the effort it had taken me to get up enough nerve to accept the date in the first place.

The rest of the date was terrific! We had a great dinner and then went to the Opryland Hotel and strolled through the gardens. It was a romantic evening amongst the lavish greenery and garden atmosphere. We rested at one of the nightspots, enjoying a cold drink and talking non-stop for a couple of hours. We learned about each other, and it was apparent we enjoyed each other's company. We left the hotel and endured the drive back home in the bitter heat, even though it was close to midnight. Jimmy escorted me to my front door, said goodnight, and expressed his desire to see me again; I agreed. He gave me a gentle kiss goodbye and then left. My head was swimming the rest of the night and into the next day. I very much enjoyed the time Jimmy and I spent together and could not wait for him to phone me. He did call me that evening and we made plans to see each other again the coming week.

We dated for many months and always had a great time together. We spent many evenings at home playing cards with Sandra and her boyfriend, and I was grateful for the way Jimmy always included her in most of our plans. Even though she had her own teenage life going on, he always made her feel like she was a part of us, and this was extremely important to me especially after my previous relationships. Jimmy grew to love Sandra and he was always kind to her.

After dating for about eight months, Jimmy took me on a picnic to the river in Clarksville and he proposed to me. I told him we could be engaged, but it would be a long engagement because I would not remarry until Sandra graduated from high school and went off to college. I had made this promise to my daughter after the disastrous third marriage. I told her I would never put her through anything like that again and I needed to make darn sure I knew who I was involved with before I took another plunge. Jimmy respected my wishes and understood my thinking; we agreed we would marry two years down the road.

8-4-2007   **168 lbs.**

The next two years were full of family and friends. We both grew close to each other's family and tried to spend equal amounts of time with both. My family liked his family and vise-versa. We even did many family things together which included both sides of the family. About six months before our wedding date, I started planning a big wedding because it was a first for Jimmy, and his sisters wanted to make sure he had a *big* wedding experience. Jimmy and I could have had a simple little ceremony, but the family was not having it, so I knuckled under and started planning. I recruited my sister to design and make my wedding dress. She had six months to accomplish this and she seemed to get into it. I gave her no guidelines. It was up to her how I was going to look on my wedding day! Jimmy and I continued planning and in a way, it was a lot of fun. As the date came nearer, all of the nerves and stress did find us but we held tough and made it to the wedding day.

8-7-2007   **160 lbs.**

The night before our wedding, my sister Sheri flew in from Phoenix with my wedding dress. I had not even seen it in pictures! She met me at a friend's seamstress shop, and when she unveiled the dress to me, I took one long look at it and started crying! It was the most beautiful wedding gown I had ever seen, and to this day, I have never seen one come close. I stood there staring at it and could not believe my eyes! The best designer in the world could have not created this gown. It was worth several million dollars to me! The fact that my sister designed this masterpiece meant more than anything she had ever done for me, not to mention the fact that it was fabulous! Everyone in the shop sighed in amazement at the beautiful work and detail the gown had. No one had ever seen a gown of this magnitude, and never will again. It was one of a kind. Each bead and all of the lace were antique and Sheri shopped and saved all of these for many years before I requested she design and make my gown. She did not know what she would do with all of the things she had been saving for many years until I asked her to make my dress. Then it all became clear to her. This was how the fine lace and beads were to be used. It would be her creation, a gift of love for me.

Wedding days are always hectic and ours proved this fact! It all started two days before the wedding when members of Jimmy's church decided a certain song could not be sung during our wedding. We had asked one of my best friends, Lucio, to sing our song, "Unchained Melody", during the ceremony. Talk about nit-picking: the church members were upset with some of the lyrics! "I hunger for your touch", one line of the song, was forbidden to be sung in the church so they banned the whole song! We could not believe their silliness or at least what we thought was silly. They wanted to then scrutinize everything we were doing and we finally told them we were going to move the wedding ceremony away from the church. We would have it at the place we were having the reception. With this threat, they backed off, but we still could not have our song! I respect the house of the Lord and would never do anything I felt was disrespectful in the church. This, however, seemed so ridiculous to me that if it had not been for Jimmy's mother, I would have gladly changed the site of the ceremony. This was her church and she would have never told us not to have "Unchained Melody" in the service. However, because of some of the church members having nothing better to do than question our ceremony and screen it for inappropriate content, they found something and then ran to her to stir up a fuss. Everyone knows this beautiful song and I do not know anyone who thinks the song is inappropriate. It is a love story told in song. It was *our* love story.

After settling the problem with the church, or should I say some *members* of the church, we reluctantly agreed to go on with the church wedding. I was very uncomfortable, however, with the whole situation. To save family peace, we agreed to go on as planned. The wedding day arrived and our ceremony was held up for almost an hour because Sheri had to put some last minute touches to my gown. Fortunately, after she and the gown arrived, the ceremony went off without a hitch. Afterwards, we all went out to the reception site where we had a huge 1950s-style dance party, costumes and all! Everyone had a blast and Lucio and his band played for the reception. The buffet and great party went on until the wee hours of the morning and then we escaped unnoticed to head to our honeymoon destination.

8-8-2007   168 lbs.

Jimmy understood my health problems in part because he was also ill. Jimmy has a severe heart problem and since the age of 25 has been under close doctors' care. He is one hundred-percent pacemaker dependant. They really don't know why he suffered, at such an early age, a health problem that they never have been able to diagnose. He has baffled medical personnel and was even in Vanderbilt Medical Center under experimental drug therapy for many, many months. He almost lost his life to this illness. I think because of his own problems, he can identify with mine.

After being married for a very short time, I realized just how different our backgrounds were. He comes from a big country family and I come from an upper middle-class family. Even though we were together for three years before we got married, we never lived together because neither of us believed in this. In a very short time, I realized just how different our worlds really were. I had to move to where he lived and this was very difficult for me because of the living situations. His family surrounded us, and we were living in a little house he had just built. He had promised me a big home but instead he placed this little house on a tiny piece of property he owned and I guess he thought I would be content with this arrangement; I was not. Sandra lived with us until she went off to college and Jeffrey came to live with us also. The house only had two bedrooms and the smallest bathroom I had ever seen! It was so small that a friend of mine told me it was the only bathroom where you could take a bath, brush your teeth and sit on the toilet, all at the same time! This is no exaggeration; you could not open the bathroom door fully because it hit the toilet. The worst thing was that the bathroom was right in the living room! Thin walls, thin door... you get the picture! This was all there was to the house, except for the kitchen!

I had never lived in conditions like this before. I had moved out of a very large two-story home to an area out in the country. We were surrounded by junky rental properties Jimmy owned and the bizarre tenants who occupied them, plus Jimmy's entire family. Soon, I started to feel isolated. I became restless, then sunk into a deep depression. My health could not take the strain and my lupus was running rampant. I am sure Jimmy thought I would adjust eventually, but I did not. This was normal life for him; he saw nothing wrong with it and I think he was oblivious to my feelings. Also, I did not feel safe where we were living because of drug activity going on around us. This scared me. I did not want to be around this type of environment and I always felt uneasy. There was a different class of people living out there and I did not fit in. It was not where I wanted to be and it ate at me constantly. I needed to be back in my own comfort zone, feeling safe and not secluded.

Something else I discovered is the fact that Jimmy's lifestyle was difficult for me to understand. I have always been with men who are "neat freaks" and this is the farthest thing from Jimmy's persona! I knew he was different to some degree by the way he normally dressed. Jimmy never folded clothes, never ironed (if it was wrinkled he would wear it anyway), and so forth. I just figured it was because he had been a bachelor for so long; I thought he just needed a good woman around to keep him presentable. I tried! Because he was constantly doing some type of construction on one of the houses, I expected him to be sloppy during the day while working. What I did not expect was the fact that it just did not matter to him how he looked! He was such a strikingly handsome man but his sloppiness took away from his persona. I bought him new clothes and he would wear them outside to work in, and they would be ruined immediately! This really ticked me off when he'd do this! We would go out in public and I wanted to be proud of him, but he made it difficult for me to do so. Family and friends would make comments to me about what total opposites we were and this made me feel self-conscious. It was completely embarrassing for me every time we went somewhere.

Before I go on any further, I have to say Jimmy was, and is still, a great guy! His loving nature and compassion for others is evident in all he does. Being a very loving person, I know he loves me with all of his heart and he is easy to love. We have always been able to talk, laugh and cry together. This is important. Nevertheless, our differences in living together are more than I could handle. I love him and I trust him with my life but our upbringings are so different, we could not seem to cohabitate together. I am sure my neat freakiness drives him crazy also. It is not one-sided by any means!

I tried to keep things in their proper place, being a good house-keeper, but he would go out of his way to make a mess. When I stop and think about it though, it is possible he was never taught to care for his living conditions the way I was. I went into the marriage with expensive things like china, crystal, and sterling silver flatware. Within about six months, my china had been broken, my flatware had been used to stir paint, my crystal was taken outside, broken or lost because he could not wash out a mason jar and fill it up with his drink of choice. He had no respect for my things; this bothered me and I would fuss at him but it never did any good. His ways became a major problem for me.

8-9-2007   **169 lbs.**

Jimmy and I stayed married for six years. There were difficult years, but there were also some very happy times. I married a good man whose major downside was he was sloppy! This was a main factor in my unhappiness, but there were others. I always felt some of his family did not care for me too much. He always told me he did not discuss our problems with his family but I feel he did, and this made me angry. I felt our business was *our* business and no one else's. I feel a husband should always stand by his wife. This made me feel like I was not his top priority.

I mentioned the fact I did not feel safe where we were living and the area was very trashy. Low elements seemed to rent his properties and some were involved in drug activity. The dirt road going into our home was like Grand Central Station at all hours of the night; I assume this was drug related. I begged Jimmy to move away form the area but he refused. The last straw was one time at about three o'clock in the morning when a state trooper started banging on our back door, which happened to be right by my bed. It woke me up from a deep sleep and when I opened the door, this cop was standing there demanding to know where one of Jimmy's relatives lived. It scared me and made me think about what kind of area we were living in. The next evening, about fifteen officers from several city and county offices surrounded our area because some of the family's kids and their friends were making pipe bombs and setting them off! I was the one who called the authorities because I wanted this element removed from there. At this point, I had made up my mind that I had enough of the environment and made plans to leave. I knew Jimmy would not go with me because this was all he knew and he was not going to budge, so I left him and we divorced six months later. This was a sad time for both of us but I had to do this to protect myself. This was the only answer.

8-13-2007   168 lbs.

I moved in with my dad. This was very difficult to say the least! With him in his 80ss and me in my 40s it was a hard combination. He treated me like a child and it drove me crazy! When I was a teenager, he did not keep tabs on me as much as he did this time around. I dealt with it until I absolutely could not stand it anymore and then I moved out into a home of my own. I thank my dad for giving me a place to live but the time came when I had to stand up for myself and do what was right for me. I found a home I wanted to buy and I held out until I could afford to do so. When I finally moved into my house, I was very happy! For the first time in my life, I was buying my own home and I did not have to answer to anyone else! This has been a great experience for me. I do what I want, when I want and my home is clean! I decorated the home to reflect my own personality and I can change it anytime I want, without having to get someone else's approval. It's great! The truth of the matter is, I really like living by myself! I don't have to worry about cooking and cleaning for anyone else, and this is fine with me! To be perfectly honest, I do not enjoy cooking anymore. It is hard to cook for one or two people and I paid my dues when my family was growing up. Now, it's the microwave or out to eat! I still cook for special occasions but with Sandra being a chef, I pretty much leave all of the cooking to her for family events. This is what she loves to do and I love the fact that *she* loves doing it!

Jimmy and I have remained very good friends and we still see each other quite often. We travel together; go out to eat, to the movies, and more. He then goes home and lives however he likes, without me to listen too, and I can enjoy my beautiful home and not be embarrassed if anyone drops by to say hello!

8-14-2007   **168 lbs.**

As I come to finalize this very long chapter, as I wrote at the beginning, I am the last person to give advice on affairs of the heart! After reading through this chapter, I'm sure you agree with me. I have made many, many mistakes in relationships and I am the first to admit it. Truthfully, though, I can say when I fall in love, I do it wholeheartedly and I do not fall "out" of love. Every person whom I have been involved with in my life, with the exception of the third person I married, I still love deeply. Now I know, some of you are probably questioning this statement and the validity of it, but I swear it to be true. I still love my former husbands! I credit this to the fact that I have been involved with some extraordinary men in my life. They have all had something special to offer. I love all of them in different ways, but nonetheless I love them for the love they have given me and all of the things each has taught me.

When I look back to when I was a girl, I had really high standards, which I still do, and my moral values were, and are, high as well. I never believed in living with someone before marriage and when I fell in love, I wanted to marry that person so I could express my full love for him. I'm sure you can guess that this included the physical aspect of the relationship. I was a virgin when I got married the first time and for this, I am very proud, simply because it is my belief, not a way to pass judgment on someone else. I wanted to be able to give my husband my complete self when we got married. This was a big deal to me and I would have not chosen for myself any other way. When the relationship did not last, I wanted to be able to fall in love again and re-marry, giving my new husband the same consideration I had for myself the first time. By not living together, this was my way of being as true to my beliefs as I could. This carried on through the rest of my relationships. I felt that if I was not going to be in a truly committed relationship, marriage, then sex was not going to happen. If I had let this belief fall apart, I would be un-true to myself and I am my toughest critic. I guess in a way, you can say I agreed to marriage easily, because I held quite high expectations of myself. I was not going to compromise when it came to my belief on marriage and sex.

I do not want to get into a religious debate here. I consider myself a Christian, but as a Christian I am human and I have more than a fair share of faults. You've read about some of them here in the pages before this. I ask my Lord for forgiveness daily and the strength to do better. As a Christian, I know He forgives me my wrong doings but He expects me to use better judgment the next time and learn from my mistakes. Being a Christian does not mean I can go along doing the same things wrong day after day, month after month, year after year and keep asking for forgiveness and all is well. Being a Christian means I first admit I need forgiveness, ask for it, and then learn from His answer. If I look back and apply this to my relationships, I have to realize that I have been given great men in my life, have learned from each one of them, have made mistakes, asked for forgiveness, and have been granted that forgiveness. Now it is time for me to put a stop to the cycle and learn what all of these years have gotten me and why I am alone today.

To start with, I am alone by my own choosing. I want to be

alone right now and I need to be alone right now. The reason? I need to learn who Karen really is. This is true; I do not know myself very well! I especially did not know myself very well when I ended my last marriage. I had always been somebody's daughter, somebody's wife, somebody's mother, and somebody's grandmother. Who was Karen? Hell if I knew! The time had come when I needed to take a long, long look at my life and I had to be perfectly honest with myself. This is hard to do but as they say, the buck stops here. Well, who is Karen anyway? The truth was, and still is, a bitter pill to swallow.

8-15 2007   **169 lbs.**

I have learned some very valuable things during my self-discovery. Most of these things explain why I have had such trouble with my relationships. To begin with, Karen is a very selfish person. I hate to admit it, but I am just plain selfish! I want things my way, when I want them; I want to do what I want to do, when I want to do it, and I don't like to compromise when I feel it will not suit me in the long run. Whew! That's a revelation! Boy, is it ever hard to admit to myself, let alone others! Now I have to say, it is not that I have not known this all along, it's just that I have never had the courage to come forth and say so. However, at this time in my life, what I have been doing before has not brought me peace and happiness so I have to reevaluate and come up with the reasons why I have been so unhappy and made others unhappy as well.

Another crucial part of who I am is the fact that I am stubborn and hard headed. If I get something in my head, it is next to impossible to get me to see it differently. When my mind is made up, it is made up and that is all there is to it! This cannot be good on any type of relationship. I know in my heart, a relationship has to be give-and-take to work but unfortunately, *I have always wanted to be on the taking end of the equation!* I am not talking about things such as gifts and such; I am talking about emotions. I am always willing to be on the receiving end, but not to willing to be on the giving end. Communication comes to mind here as it is my biggest fault of all. I can almost sum up all of my problems into one neat little category which involves all of the above: I am not a good communicator when it comes to what I want, what I expect and what I need! I tend to shove my feelings so deep inside, they are all covered up by everyday life. They sit there stagnate until the festering starts coming to the surface, bubbling up with anger and resentment because the other person cannot read my mind to know what is wrong. This is my selfish behavior. It is very selfish of me to expect my partner to know what I need, want or expect. It is also very stubborn of me to not be open and honest with my partner and then get angry when they cannot read my mind. The stubbornness comes in when I keep getting the same results and not changing a thing about my behavior because it cannot possibly be me causing the problem! My stubborn nature does not allow me to be wrong even when I know deep down inside that I am.

Honesty is hardest of all when you have to face yourself. Why is it so easy to find fault with others before we evaluate ourselves and see what needs fixin' in our own corner of the world? I guess it is human nature. I am not content with this answer anymore. I know I need a lot of work. I have hit rock bottom more than once in my life and each time, I vow to do better but do I? Not really. I put a bandage over the problem, hoping it will heal underneath, and I make all the right motions and say all the right things, but the truth of the matter is I have not done what my Lord wants me to do. That is, to *love myself*! I say I love my Lord but how can I truly love Him when I do not truly love myself? The answer is I cannot. I look at myself and I see a big jumbled-up girl who wants so desperately to be loved, wanted and needed, but I do not know how to handle it. I push others away. Possibly, it is because I am afraid I am going to screw up yet another relationship. I know I am mixed up. I know I am one big chunk of insecurity and it all falls back to me not loving *me*. I am intolerant to imperfection in myself, and there is no one more imperfect than I am. I put on a persona of someone I've come to know all too well. She is confident and carefree. She is smart and a people person. Ha! The real truth be known, I've never been confident. I have never felt smart and I put on a false persona when it comes to being a people person. Other people make me feel even more inferior because I see them as being successful, and then I put myself down for my shortcomings. I envy those who seem so intelligent. I long to be the same way. I put on a face to cover my insecurities and most people never realize just how self-doubting I really am. In the years of creating Karen, sometimes I started to believe in my own "creation" and this has made it even harder for the real me to survive.

At this stage in my life, I have decided enough is enough, and I have to come to terms with whom and what I really am. This will not be an easy process. After all, the Karen I have created has taken me 49 years to master. I know I have to start from birth and make my way through the years upon years of lying to others and myself about who I am. There is only one who knows the true me and He being my creator, wants me to love myself. I know I was created in God's eye. In his image, He gave me life. I know He wants me to forgive myself of all of the things I have done to hurt his creation. It is hard to do so. The guilt I feel is a heavy burden. I have to learn to lay this guilt at the Lord's feet and ask Him to dispose of it for me but the truth of the matter is I feel guilty asking Him to do so. Does this make any sense? The Lord knows what is in my heart and even in my weak human frame of mind, I know He knows how to sort through the bad and get to the good that is buried there somewhere. It is hard to feel unworthy yet know you are worthy by your faith. This is humbling to say the least.

In conclusion, the moral of this chapter is simply this: I have loved and I have been loved. I have certainly been loved more than I have ever loved myself. God has seen to it that I have had beautiful men in my life who have put up with me and loved me in spite of myself. He has seen to it that they, each in their own way, had the patience to deal with me on a day-in, day-out basis, and not lose their minds. I, in turn, loved each of them in their own way. I know we learned from each other and I would not change these relationships in any way other than changing any hurt I caused.

Relationships always have two sides and even though I take huge responsibility for my shortcomings, I also know other issues were involved. This is life. I know I am not one-hundred percent at fault for the downfall of my marriages, but if truth be told, I feel I am at least ninety percent responsible. I am not an easy person, and I am a hard person to live with. I am a hard person to get to know. I make people think my life is an open book but I have more secrets than the CIA! What you see is *not* what you get!

So where do I go from here? I'm not quite sure except for the fact that I am a work in progress and until I can feel good about myself I will not get involved again with another unsuspecting gentleman who thinks I am all I appear to be. I cannot go into yet another relationship without knowing what I truly want out of life. If I do not know who I am, how do I know what I want or what to look for? The scariest thought of all though is that I probably already found what I want, had it and then threw it away. How will I get through this revelation? I am almost afraid to dig deeper, as I think I already know the answer.

CHAPTER FOURTEEN

MY DAD, MY HERO!

8-20-2007   **168 lbs.**

As I embark on this next chapter, I realize I will have many things I want to say. I only hope my message is clear and you as the reader can identify with some special person in your life who has given you as many joyous memories as my father has given me. He has always been my rock, my strength, and most of all, my *hero*.

The story has been told to me at least a thousand times. During the 1950s, my dad suffered from an extreme bout of depression. He went from doctor to doctor and they could not find out what was wrong with him. He was given medicine and sent on his way. He, my mother and my sister lived in the home he built with his bare hands. All of the love he had to give was poured into that house at 237 Columbia Avenue in El Paso. At this time, my sister Sheri was 10 years old and she had begged and begged for a baby sister. Being the only child, I guess she was lonely. My parents obliged her, and soon I was born.

As the story unfolds, my father made it know that I was his reason for living! My birth gave him something to look forward too and I became "daddy's little girl." He has told me many times how I saved his life. The one thing I have learned through all of this is the fact that sometimes, or should I say all of the time, it is hard to live up to such a feat. The pressure was on from the very beginning!

My father never wanted sons. He wanted girls and the Lord blessed him with two. Now, this is not to say that Sheri and I were not tomboys growing up, because we were, but we still were allowed the graces in which little girls thrive. We got to do all of the girlie things right along with the boy things. We hunted, we fished, we raised 4-H animals, we each had a gun, we target practiced; just about anything boys could do, we did and most of the time did better! My uncle, my father's little brother, had three boys and it seemed whenever we were all together; it was boys against the girls. We learned to be tough simply to survive! Boys will be boys, so we had to work extra hard to stay on top of any given situation. Of course, my father and his brother always had some type of bet going as to which kids could outdo the others. This was always in great fun and we learned many valuable lessons on how to take care of ourselves.

Being one of four boys born to my grandparents, my dad had a hard life in many ways. As a child, he fell ill a lot and the emotional stress from being sick for such a long time carried into his adult years. He has never gotten over having to spend many weeks in the hospital with diphtheria and scarlet fever as a child. Many fears developed during this trying time in his young life. He has told me stories of how afraid he was when his parents had to leave him home for some reason. If they had to go somewhere, he would wait down the lane to their home, crying for them. His brothers tried to console him any way they could, but to no avail. He always panicked. He has told me how he and his mother would sit up at night making potato chips just to keep him busy and calm. His mother tried anything she could think of to ease his anxiety.

During the time my father and his brothers were growing up, his father did all he could to keep food on the table. They were raised in Central Texas and they raised most of their own food. They moved many times as a family and my dad and his brothers attended several schools while growing up. I have been fortunate enough to go back to the areas where my father grew up and see the schools he attended. There is so much history there and I only wish I could record the many, many stories he has told me of their experiences while growing up. These tales are packed with excitement, history and just plain ole' malarkey but are interesting, to say the least!

In July of this year, last month in fact, we were fortunate enough to attend my dad's 67th high school reunion at Rochelle High School in Rochelle, Texas. The festivities took place on July 7, 2007. There were over one hundred attendees from many different graduating classes! My dad's class was the oldest there, with four of his original classmates in attendance. This school hosts a reunion each year but this was the first year my dad attended. We had wanted to go every year but there has always been some reason why we could not go. This year I put my foot down and told him we were going, come hell or high water, and yes, we found the "high water!" This part of the country has had more rain this year than its share, water and mud everywhere. It rained almost the whole time we were there!

The reunion was a blast! I was able to meet some of my dad's classmates as well as visit with relatives I had not seen since I was a child. We had a great time and my dad's friends made him swear he would attend again the next year. They also made me swear I would bring finished copies of this book, as they are all excited for this project and for me! Jimmy went with us and after the reunion we traveled around the area with my dad telling whopping tales about his upbringing. You have to wonder how many of the tales are true, but knowing my dad and his brothers, I'm afraid most are! After all, boys growing up in the country equals trouble waiting for a place to happen!

8-24-2007   **168 lbs.**

My dad and his brothers grew up during the Great Depression. I, and those who are my age and younger, have no idea what this must have been like. I cannot imagine the feeling of such despair around me. However, I also believe that my dad and all of the others who experienced it first-hand did not know the meaning of a bountiful and plentiful world.. They had to adjust to their environment. He has told me stories about making their own toys out of acorns and walnuts. They each represented farm animals when he and his brothers played as ranchers. They also made army tanks out of empty thread spools, pieces of soap and a rubber band. I can remember as a child he thrilled me when he made such a toy for me to play with. It was much more interesting than any store-bought toy I had at home. I could spend hours sitting on our hard-wood floor making the little spool travel across the living room. My dad and uncles had to entertain themselves somehow. Their ingenuity kept them busy and adventurous. When they were not outside playing or in school, they were hunting for wildlife to either eat or to trap and make a few bucks for spending money. They also had many duties on the farm with the livestock and everyday general care of the place. I know my grandparents tried to keep the boys as busy as possible to keep them out of trouble.

When I was a child, we traveled to the old homestead to visit my grandparents at least once a year. I would go out and spend hours swimming in one of the old tanks or I would somehow be involved with some of the animals. I wrote before about visiting my uncle Charlie at this very same place years later after my grandparents passed away. He and my aunt moved there and kept the place until my aunt passed away after my uncle several years ago. When my Dad and I recently traveled back to his home area, we went by the old place and it is sad to say it is vacant and all grown up with vegetation. There are, however, plenty of cattle on the property. My aunt left the place to a friend of theirs who took care of her during her last few years of life. Even though it is run down, I could still remember myself there playing in the water and I am sure my dad could hear the echoes of three boys playing, hooting and hollering and see many flashbacks of years before.

My father, Richard McCoy Dye, was born October 8, 1921, the third son of Uriah Baxter Dye and Flora Pluenneke Dye. His older brothers were Charles Dye and Lankford Dye who passed away at a young age of eight. Herbert Thomas Dye was my dad's younger brother by two years, and the closest to my father. They remained very close until my uncle's passing in 1999. Herbert and Richard

(Dick) were very competitive with each other all of their lives. It was always "who can outdo who" whenever they were together. In my life, I have never seen two people that are more stubborn when it came to each other. They fought all the time, mostly arguments and such, yet no two brothers have ever loved each other more. If they were apart by geography, they were planning the next visit together when they could aggravate each other once again! I know my sister and I always had a lot of fun when the two families were reunited. We were close to our cousins, Tommy, Ricky and Larry Don. As I stated before, it was always a contest of whose kids could outdo whose! It was always "boys against the girls!"

8-28-2007   **167 lbs.**

Before I go on any further with the story, I have to take a break and address something that still involves my father, but is a detour from the story. Sometimes some things happen that take us off base and we have to reevaluate our course. This happened last Friday, the last day I wrote for you. I was at my daughter's house watching my grandchildren that afternoon. The town Sandra and her family live in, Hopkinsville, Kentucky, is about a half-hour drive from my home. My son-in-law, Jimmy, was expected to arrive home around five in the afternoon. I placed a call to my dad right at five to tell him to meet me at a favorite restaurant, S & J Cafe, halfway between where I was and where he was at home. Sometimes we go there Friday nights to enjoy catfish or a big steak, the restaurant's Friday-night specials. He answered the phone and he started talking, telling me he had not done much during the day and he was just getting ready to go to the post office to get his mail. About that time, I heard my son-in-law drive up and I told my dad Jimmy had just arrived. For some reason, I did not follow through with my original plan of asking my dad to meet me for dinner. I made a conscious decision to tell him I was on my way home; I do not know why. Perhaps it was the fact that he asked me if we were going to S & J for breakfast the next morning, a typical Dye-family Saturday morning ritual, and we discussed the fact that we would. Because I had a scheduled meeting to attend Saturday morning, and I had already decided I was not going to attend, we agreed to keep our plans. In addition, my dad and I had been out Thursday evening for my son-in-law's birthday celebration dinner and two nights in a row were unusual for us, so I said nothing about him meeting me again for dinner out. We finished our conversation and hung up. I started driving home after about five minutes.

While driving home, the radio station I was listening to played about three of my favorite songs back to back. I tend to crank up the volume when listening to good music, and this time was no different. I drove, sang along with the radio, and escaped my busy day of keeping children. My cell phone, in my purse on the front seat, went unnoticed on the short trip home. When I got inside my house, I immediately took my cell phone out of my purse and put it on its charger. At about that moment, the phone buzzed to tell me I had unanswered calls. I opened it up and on the screen it showed four missed calls, so I went into my menu and checked to see who tried to call me. It showed "FATHER" and "SANDRA-HOME." I then looked for my home phone and my caller ID showed my dad's number, four calls, within a minute or two of each other, but he had left no messages. I knew something was wrong so I called him. There was no answer, so I left a message and told him I was home and to call me. Within a minute, my phone rang and my dad on the other end was hysterical.

"Beegee has been hit by a car down the road and I'm afraid he's dead by now!" he screamed. I froze while a chill went up my spine.

"Where is he?" I questioned, while trying to make sense of what he was trying to tell me. He went on to tell me, while sobbing uncontrollably, that his best friend in the world, his beagle pup Beegee, was probably dying in a soybean field up the road from his house. I told him I was on my way, I flew the two miles to his home in what felt like 10 seconds and met him in his truck, and then we took off up the road. He stopped, and I stopped behind him and jumped out of my car to get to him. He was so visibly shaken it scared me. I knew I had to try to find his dog as quickly as possible. He was hit and then ran into the field, my dad had told me on the phone, so I headed out into thigh-high soybeans searching for what I hoped was only an injured pup. I searched franticly, knowing time was not on our side. It had already been at least half an hour since the accident. I combed through the vegetation praying I would find Beegee soon. I called for him constantly but got no response. We were about a half mile from my dad's house so I started focusing on the fact that the pup had possibly tried to make it back home. I took the field row by row, searching. I looked up and realized my dad's neighbor Chris, and his son, were walking up towards where my dad was; this gave me a brief sense of relief knowing my dad had someone up on the road with him to help calm him down. I kept up my frantic pace, hoping I had not overlooked the injured animal. I had been searching for at least twenty minutes, with each minute bringing less hope, when I turned and started my search in a different direction. Within about fifteen seconds, I spotted a white and brown figure lying between rows up ahead of me. I yelled out "Beegee!" as I ran towards him, but when I got upon him and knelt down, he was not moving. Tears streamed down my face as I looked for any sign of life, and then I reached down and picked up a lifeless friend, gathered him in my arms, and started my way back up the hilly soybean field to where my father was waiting with his neighbor. He was watching for the sight of me with hope that I found his injured friend and was bringing him to the truck so we could rush him to the vet. But this was not what I was doing. I was carrying a dog's lifeless body, not noticeably mangled or broken, but obviously so severely internally damaged as to cause the young pup's untimely death. I cried all the way to the embankment of the highway where I had to try to walk up a steep grade with the heavy pup. I was exhausted; I fell to my knees. The temperature was at least 103 degrees, with a heat index of about 106. I had been sick the whole week with a severe lupus episode and had been taking massive steroid injections to help halt a massive rash all over my legs, stomach, arms, back and face. I did not think I could go any further. I knew I could not carry the dog up the steep bank with me, so I placed him down on the ground and I crawled up the bank and then had to drag the pup up after me. I placed him in the back of my dad's truck and then turned around. My dad was making his way toward me with a questioning and anticipating look. I just shook my head... "no".

Grief. G.R.I.E.F. A five-letter word. As far as I am concerned, it should be one of those angry *four*-letter words, the ones that are used in an angry frame of mind when you feel the need to lash out! Yes, grief is an *extra letter*-four-letter word for me. I've lived it, I have witnessed it, and it is just plain terrible as far as I am concerned, or any one is concerned, for that matter. Well, here it is, up front in my face once again. This time, I have to watch it tear my father apart. Grief is bad whether you are going through it yourself or you have to witness someone you love go through it. It is a helpless feeling. It is an angry feeling. It is an empty feeling. It is a guilty feeling. It is a feeling of total despair. We all have to experience it one or more times in our lives, but unfortunately when we get older it seems to affect us in a much more exaggerated way.

8-29-2007   167 lbs.

My dad will be 86 years young in October this year. He is still young at heart in so many ways. He hates the fact that he is getting older as we all do, but for him, it is extremely difficult because he has always been so strong. He lives alone, with me a few miles away. He drives, he gardens, he builds, and he watches his birds that come to him for food every day. Hummingbirds are his favorite; they give him hours of enjoyment, as he can sit and watch them every evening outside by his deck. One thing will be missing however, his little spotted beagle. Beegee was his pal and his confidant. He was his companion and most of all, his best friend. The pup arrived one day after a hunter had been to my dad's property hunting with his pack of beagles. For some reason, the pup did not want to get back into the truck of his owner and other dogs. My dad realized he was left behind and he did not know who the owner was. He figured that the man would return for the pup but he did not. My dad started feeding the puppy and tried to befriend him. The pup was skittish, but he welcomed the food. He started warming up to my dad within a few days but still did not want to be touched. My dad kept working with him, gaining more trust each day. He was falling for the beagle pup. He bought him the best food he could find and gave him scrumptious table scraps (which by the way, I am totally against) because he wanted to fatten him up. Before long, they were a man and his dog! They became fast and furious friends, with the ultimate trust between them. I have never seen my dad take to a dog like he did this pup. He has always loved dogs but this was a special relationship, a friendship not to be taken likely. He chose the name Beegee as an abbreviation for "beagle". It stuck and that was his new name. The hunter returned about two weeks later, but agreed to let Dad keep the pup because he could see how fond he was of him. I think he sensed there was no way in heck he was going to remove that dog from Dad's place, at least without a fight! Beegee always went "hunting" with the hunter and the other dogs when they came to visit, but then he always returned to his new home, with my dad. He was truly a man's best friend!

Beegee and Dad had a routine. He greeted my dad each morning outside his bedroom window as if to say "Good Morning! Come outside and play with me!" My dad would go out and Beegee would lay down for his morning tummy rub. In the evenings, while Dad sat outside watching the hummingbirds, he always had a bag of cheese cubes to feed the pup; this was an everyday ritual. It was their time to bond for the day. When my dad fed his pup the last bite, he would say, "That's all Beegee," and Beegee would turn around and lay down close by. He never begged; his manners were quite incredible.

For the last year and a half, this has been the life for a man and his dog. You could tell they had a very special bond. It was almost like they both needed someone close by to take care of them, and this is why they found each other. Even though my dad has two indoor cats that are comfort and company for him, Beegee was entirely different. Cats are so independent, they seem to act like they really do not need you to care for them, but this little beagle dog needed one-on-one care and love. I truly believe they were sent to each other by God's infinite wisdom.

My dad's place is not fenced in and he lives close to a very busy highway. His biggest fear for Beegee was him being hit by a car. Not owning the property he lives on, he could not realistically fence the place in. Beegee seemed to be pretty car savvy and avoided them most of the time. For the first few months, he would try to chase Dad every time he left the house, and Dad would stop the vehicle, get out, and scold him until he turned back. However, as my dad approached his house, back from where ever it was he went, he could always count on seeing Beegee lying in the ditch by the road, waiting for his master to return. He would then run back to the house following Dad with a wagging tail and a happy puppy smile, as if to say "Great! You're back! Where've you been? I missed you!" After a while, my dad pretty much broke him of chasing his truck when he left, yet the fear always remained. He said he would have premonitions of his dog lying out in the middle of the road after an accident. Dad did not believe in chaining a dog up so this was not an option. I have to admit, I always had an uneasy feeling about them being close to such a busy highway. I suggested tying Beegee up only when my dad was going to be gone and letting him loose when he returned, but he did not want to do it; he wanted Beegee to be free. I worried about the situation and I just hoped for the best.

Last Friday was a nightmare. It has been a hard few days. I am worried about my dad. After the accident, Dad sobbed uncontrollably the rest of the evening. I stayed with him as much as I could. I was feeling helpless as to what to say or do to ease his pain. I called Jimmy and told him what happened and asked him if he could be at my dad's place very early the next morning to dig a grave for the pup. I was afraid Dad would be outside in the extreme heat trying to dig in the hard ground to bury his friend. The weather here has been relentless. Extreme temperatures in the triple digits have caused several deaths in the surrounding area and I worried about my dad's health. Jimmy agreed to be over early the next morning to get it done so Dad was not out there in the heat. At least that was the plan. He arrived early and, of course, my dad was out there in the already-great heat, digging away. Jimmy took over and finished the job. Dad was still sobbing off and on. We went to breakfast to try to get his mind off it for a while, but to no avail. Later in the day, we went to Nashville to the Wilson County Fair to see a close friend of ours perform with his band. This has been an annual event for years, and I was hoping this would help keep his mind off the pup, but I was wrong. It was a miserable trip and not everyone knew how to react to my father's extreme grief. I have to say I was starting to get aggravated because I had never seen him act this way before. Even at the death of my mother and most recently my sister, he never told me he could not go on with his life and would never get over the tragedy. Yes, he grieved, but not the way he was carrying on this time. My friends could tell I was getting upset, mostly because nothing anybody said or did made a difference. But when my dad told me he was angry with God for doing this to him, I almost lost it. He also told me he would not be attending church the next morning because of his anger. With my faith, it hurt me to hear these words. I drove the whole way back to Kentucky having to give myself an attitude adjustment and get over myself so I could deal with my dad in a proper way. We arrived at my home and I kissed him goodnight, went inside, and asked the Lord for help.

I got up Sunday morning and got myself ready to go to church. I called Dad at about nine, thinking he might have reconsidered and decided to go to church. He answered the phone crying. He told me he had been up since seven, woken up crying and could not stop. My heart sank; I felt helpless and did not know what to do or say to comfort him. I told him I was worried about him, his frame of mind and I told him I felt helpless. I quickly made the decision that I needed to go be with him instead of going to church.

I arrived at his place and when I saw him, it worried me even further. He was drawn and pale. His eyes were swollen and red. He was sitting at the kitchen table, so I pulled up a chair and sat with him. He told me he did not know if he would live through this. I opened my mouth and my words came without thought. I explained my faith and my trust in it. I told him we will never have the answers here on earth but I had to believe there is always a brighter horizon ahead. Without getting too philosophical, and in a way I think he understood, I told him why I did not think God purposely made this tragedy happen and directed it to him and this defenseless animal. Dad sat and listened to me and asked me questions. I answered him with love and certainty and he seemed to start calming down as he listened to me. After a while, I told him I was going home to get my computer so I could read something to him from this book that he had not heard. I returned and started reading the beginning of this very chapter about him. Dad listened and smiled for the first time in two days. I then read some other passages from the book and after I was through, he started talking about the book and how great he thought it was. He also started thinking about other things I could add. He then for the first time said he was hungry and wanted to go out and get something to eat. We then left to go out and get lunch. After I got home, our pastor called me to check on us and said he had just left a message for my dad. I had talked to Pastor Will the previous afternoon and told him what had happened. He was concerned and said he would talk with my father. I told Will what had taken place that morning and how I was able to calm Dad down a little. He told me he thought I said and did the right things. I started feeling more hopeful about the situation.

8-30-2007   **167 lbs.**

Up until yesterday my dad had still been really torn apart by all of this, but something happened yesterday morning to kind of give him a new hope. In the early mornings, since he buried Beegee, he has been going and sitting by the pup's grave while he has his early morning health drink of honey and vinegar. Yesterday morning was no different. He went out there and sat down. Within a few seconds, his neighbor's little Scottish Terrier, Happy, came over for a visit. Happy was Beegee's playmate. The two dogs spent many an hour romping and playing. Happy had been looking for his buddy every day. After Happy said hello to dad, he went over to a pile of dirt and broken concrete pieces sitting next to the grave and he started smelling around. My dad watched him and then realized there was something there in the weeds and debris. He got up, looked to see what Happy was so interested in, and soon saw a big bird under a steel table. The bird, a hawk, was definitely injured. He had his legs stretched out behind him and he was resting on his underbody. Dad took a long stick and held it out to see if he could get the bird to move. The hawk stretched his wings out and flopped about so my dad backed off. He sent Happy home and waited for me to get there for my morning visit. He told me about the injured bird and I immediately went to see about it. I found him on the opposite side of the debris from where Dad told me he was. I did not want to touch him, but I knew he needed help. I went back to the house and got him water, and when I set it down in front of him, he started to drink immediately. I went back inside and started making phone calls. I knew there were people who rehabilitated these birds and I thought they were a protected species here in our state. I started with my veterinarian, who directed me to the next county's animal shelter. The animal shelter directed me to Fish and Wildlife, who never answered the phone. I then placed a call to our local game warden. He was out of town but I was able to contact him on his cell phone. He told me he would try to get in touch with someone and have him or her call me back. The rest of the day was phone call after phone call, trying to find someone close enough to help. Finally, by about nine last night it was all arranged for me to bring the hawk to the town where my daughter lives, today, to meet a rehabilitator. I went over to my dad's last night, put the injured hawk in a pet carrier, and took him home where he stayed the night with me. The bird remained calm when I talked to him, and he never tried to bite me. It was as if he knew we were trying to help him and he did not seem to be afraid. I felt bad because the rehabilitation people did not want me to try to feed him and I knew he had to be hungry but I also felt they needed to wait until they had a chance to evaluate his injuries. When I met the rehabilitator this afternoon and turned over the care of the injured bird, I knew he was in excellent hands, and they promised to keep me informed of his progress and care. I actually shed a tear or two when they drove off with him. As they briefly examined him, before transferring him into their carrier, they told me that they did not think his legs were broken. There were no visible injuries so we think he is just badly bruised. My dad lives close to the railroad track and when I talked to our game warden yesterday, he told me many of these hawks are hit by trains. When Dad found him, he was less than 10 feet away from the track. We feel for certain this is what happened.

By now, you can guess that I always try to find the good in bad situations. This was part of the talk I had with my father on Sunday when he was so distraught about his dog. I told him yesterday I thought the injured bird was directed to him for a reason. I firmly believe this. Today, when I got back in my car after the transfer of the injured hawk, my radio was blaring out a song with the words, "God is watching us... from a distance...". Coincidence? I don't think so! I have to believe all of this happened for a reason. I called Dad and told him about the bird's transfer and the fact that it went well and then I told him about the song playing on the radio. He chuckled and said he had to agree that something good had happened. I know he is still grieving over his pup but we have made progress. He told me he had just spoken with Chuck, the man who owns the property where Dad lives and he told my dad it was okay for him to put a fence up. This has to mean Dad is thinking about getting another pup, not to replace Beegee because there'll never be another Beegee, but to have a friend, a companion, a confidant who will give Dad unconditional love and who

Dad will love unconditionally. Do I think God is watching us? You had better believe it!

9-5-2007   167 lbs.

When I think back about growing up, I think about all of the times I spent with my father. We have always been very close, and he was always my "knight in shining armor" when I was a little girl. I could just about finagle anything I wanted from him without much difficulty. I used to leave him little notes all around the house, telling him how important something that I wanted was and how it was going to make my life or our lives easier! He got a big kick out of my creativity when it came to finagling. I always made a good argument for my case. Dad had a hard time refusing my requests and this has continued through the years!

Because Dad grew up around animals, he saw to it Sheri and I had that same privilege. He and our mother were very involved in 4-H as leaders and teachers. We always had horses, cattle, lambs, and chickens up at the farm in Mayhill. Sometimes we had one or two of our horses stabled at our house in the city so we could ride everyday if we chose. Our friends would always join us on horseback, whether on our horse riding double, or on their own horses riding alongside of us. Not all of our friends were fortunate enough to have a horse, so we rode double a lot! Dad always made sure we took good care of the animals by teaching us the proper care of them. We had to be responsible in order to keep them, so this was great motivation. I have to confess though, there were times in the morning I would be in a hurry to get to school because I was running late for some reason and my mom would feed them for me. I still have nightmares about this and it is always the same dream. I forget to feed one of my horses and remember three or four days later, only to go out and find a starving animal with its ribs sticking out and all. I am horrified in the dream! Of course this *never* happened but I guess my guilty conscience for leaving my mother to feed my horse when I was too busy to take the time and do it myself has left a big mark on me and I pay for it quite frequently in my sleep. I do not know if my dad ever knew, or if my mother ever told, but I still feel badly about it. It has left a gigantic impression on me!

When my father graduated from high school, he had all intentions of attending college. He was already registered at John Tarlington Agricultural College (now Tarlington State University) in Stephenville, Texas when he was called into the military. He joined the Army and went to officer training school, coming out as a Second Lieutenant. He served in Saipan, Iwo Jima, and on the island of Oahu ending up as a captain. He then settled in at Ft. Bliss in El Paso where he met my mother. Shortly after their marriage, he left the military and decided to go into the construction business where he remained until he retired.

I remember when Dad became president of K&D Development and Construction Company, Inc. in the 1970s. Up until then, he was Vice-President of Karam Construction Company when they decided to incorporate and change the name of the company. His peers felt he was the best choice for the presidency and they voted him in. I was very proud of him being vice-president, but when he became president of his company, I was even more proud. I know that I was the only kid in my school that had a father who was head of his company. I did not go around advertising this fact, but word got out and I paid for it with lots of jealousy and resentment. I did not understand this as I was very proud of my dad. I guess I thought everyone else should fall in line and feel the same way!

My dad was very successful in his career. People trusted him and he was honored by serving on many business boards throughout the years. His involvement in civic and business organizations led him to always give whatever the cause a fair and honest approach in whatever they were trying to accomplish at the time. People respected his honesty and fairness. His employees witnessed his fairness daily when dealing with him. They knew him as a man of his word.

Dad's company built many commercial buildings as well as industrial and multi-family housing. Most of the HUD projects in

El Paso were built by K&D. They built Tony Lama Boot Company, Farah Manufacturing, buildings for banks, savings and loan companies, warehousing, apartment complexes, (which were non-HUD), credit unions, supermarkets, shopping centers, and even a solar-heated Olympic-sized swimming pool later on, after I joined the company. I started there in my teens, worked on and off for many years and later on I joined the company as a public relations consultant and secretary, both of which I loved.

My dad has been athletic all his life. He loves sports and has played them throughout his life, doing everything from football, baseball to tennis, and running, biking, hiking, pool, bowling, golf and ping-pong. When I was a kid, he was the one who got me interested in running. He would come home from work and then go out again, running or riding his bike for an hour or two. At 49 years old, he decided to run a marathon in Artesia, New Mexico, which he completed through to the finish line. To understand my father, you must understand his drive to succeed. He never does anything with the intention of quitting somewhere down the line. When he ran the marathon, he literally trained for many months. The week before the race, he had us take him twenty-seven miles out of town and drop him off. Wearing combat boots with thick heavy hunting socks, he decided he was going to run the whole way home under extreme conditions just to make sure he could complete the full marathon the next weekend! We waited anxiously at home for him to return. Sure enough, after about six-and-a-half hours, he came limping up to the door of our home. He had blisters all over his feet. Even though he had them greased down with Vaseline. He had also rubbed his toenails completely off both feet! This did not dampen his spirits though; he continued his training the next week and then he made it to the marathon, determined to go through with it. We cheered him on and, by golly, he finished in the top twenty! I believe it took him a tad over six hours to run the twenty-six and some-odd miles for the second time within a seven-day time frame; we could not have been more proud of him, Even if he didn't finish, we would have been proud of him for the accomplishments he had made up to that point. His determination carried him through the pain he had to have obviously been feeling.

9-10-2007   167 lbs.

Dad, my uncle Herbert, and their friends had a few hunting trips each year. They went deer hunting, quail hunting, dove hunting, pheasant hunting and elk hunting. Deer and elk hunting in Colorado was always a big trip for them, and something they looked forward to every year. When getting in shape for the trip, my dad would spend weeks climbing the Franklin Mountains close to our office building. This was his endurance training preparing him for the week in Colorado. He always wanted to make sure his little brother Herbert was not in better shape than him! Then the time would come for the hunting trip. My uncle and cousins would travel from Kentucky to meet my dad and some friends. They were gone for about a week then returned home with all kinds of tales. One had to wonder how much truth was spoken in these stories, especially coming from Dad and Herbert, who usually had whoppers to tell about themselves and each other!

Being in good physical shape was a necessity for my father. He always has watched his weight and up until recently, he exercised frequently. He had both knees replaced three years ago and since then, his balance is not very steady. I think by being bow-legged for so many years, when he finally got straight legs, it threw his balance completely off. This has deterred his desire to continue with his exercise routine, which usually was biking or walking. I worry about him falling. He has had several bad falls since surgery, which has resulted in a few trips to the emergency room with many stitches and a few broken ribs. Thank the Good Lord this is all the injuries he's had as there were a couple of falls that could have been very severe.

I remember taking Dad to my orthopedic surgeon for the first time regarding his worn-out knees. I wanted my surgeon to do his surgery because I trust him greatly. He had performed surgery on my right knee months before. I told the doctor to imagine the worst knees he had ever seen in his career, multiply that by about thirty, and this would give him an idea of just how bad my dad's knees were! I also told him if Dad were a few feet taller, a freight train could drive straight through his legs! The doctor laughed! Then, when he did meet my dad, x-rays had already been taken, giving him the chance to look over them before seeing Dad for the first time. He came into the room where we were waiting, looked straight at me and said, "Boy... you weren't kidding, were you?" He then looked at Dad and told him he had the worst knees he had ever seen! He told Dad he did not know how he was even walking and taking the pain. We all talked for a while and the plans for surgery were set as soon as some testing was carried through and schedules coincided.

Dad was quite nervous about the procedure and after a few delays with the hospital and some of their air-conditioning equipment, he was *very* apprehensive. He was beginning to think that maybe he should not go through with the surgery. My nerves were a little on edge also, but I could not let him see that. I knew he had to have the surgery or he would not be walking in another few months. He had the surgery in July, 2004, and was in the hospital for twenty-one days doing in-patient physical therapy. It was extremely rough on him. For the first time in my life, I saw Dad completely dependent on others and myself for his well-being. I knew this was very hard for him. He is not a good patient because he has always been so strong, and for him to be at someone else's mercy had to be rough. I knew he was in an incredible amount of pain because he complained about it and he rarely, if ever, complained about pain because of his high tolerance. He was on extremely powerful pain medication but he still hurt terribly. He kept telling me he could not do it and I kept telling him he would make it through. He was also depressed because he did not think he would ever be the same again. I encouraged him, as did other family members and friends. Dad eventually recovered, but not without a rough hill to climb.

IN REMEMBERING THE TRAGEDY OF 9-11, I CHOSE NOT TO CONTINUE MY STORY TODAY AS MY WAY OF SILENT REMEMBRANCE OF THOSE WHO LOST THEIR LIFE DUE TO THE HORRIFIC ACT OF TERRORISM BROUGHT AGAINST OUR GREAT COUNTRY AND ITS PEOPLE ON SEPTEMBER 11, 2001. MAY THEIR MEMORY LIVE ON THROUGH EACH AND EVERY AMERICAN WHO HAS, EACH DAY SINCE, REMEMBERED THOSE WHO TRAGICALLY DEPARTED FROM THEIR FAMILIES AND FRIENDS, DUE TO TERRORISTS WHO HAD NO VALUE OF HUMAN LIFE AND WHO DID NOT HAVE THE CAPABILITY OF EVER UNDERSTANDING HUMAN DECENCY. THIS IS THE SIXTH ANNIVERSARY OF A TRAGIC ACT OF COWARDICE DONE BY THOSE WHO HAD NO PERSONAL STRENGTH TO STAND UP FOR THEMSELVES OR KNOW RIGHT FROM WRONG, AND THEN WHO WENT FORTH BECAUSE OF SOME INHUMAN DICTATOR'S WORD TO COMMIT THIS HORRIFIC ACT ON OTHER HUMAN BEINGS.

I PRAY FOR PEACE. I PRAY FOR FORGIVENESS. I PRAY FOR UNDERSTANDING. I DO NOT UNDERSTAND SUCH EVIL. I PRAY FOR ALL OF THE FAMILIES AND FRIENDS WHO LOST THEIR LOVED ONES. I PRAY FOR THE LEADERSHIP IN OUR GREAT COUNTRY TO ALWAYS DO WHAT IS IN THE BEST INTEREST OF OTHER HUMAN BEINGS, NOT JUST HERE IN THE UNITED STATES, BUT ALSO IN OTHER COUNTRIES. I PRAY FOR EMOTIONAL AS WELL AS PHYSICAL HEALING, FOR ALL OF THOSE WHO HAVE SUFFERED DUE TO THE EVENTS OF SEPTEMBER 11, 2001. I PRAY FOR THE FUTURE OF "...ONE NATION UNDER GOD, INDIVISIBLE, WITH LIBERTY AND JUSTICE, FOR ALL."

When I was about twenty-one, I realized my dad was human like all of us. I always thought he could never do any wrong. I think most girls feel this way about their fathers. When I became an adult, I was soon to realize Dad made mistakes like everyone else, and this was hard for me. He had always been the smart one, the strong one, the best one in my life. I even put him above my first husband and in time, put him above my second husband. This was not fair to either of them. When I took my wedding vows, I took them seriously but my dad was still the main man in my life and it should not have been this way. I know I was wrong. I think that because Dad and I were so close while I was growing up, it was hard for me to cut the ties that bound us together; I am not sure I ever have. There is still a tremendous hold he has on me and I have never understood it, but have had to accept it. I honestly don't think it is healthy for either of us, but at this time in our lives, I do not know how to change this fact. I love him with all of my heart and would not ever want to hurt him.

We have a very complicated relationship and I believe we are co-dependant. Of course, as he gets older, he depends on me heavily and I have to say, it is hard worrying about him and wondering how much longer he will be able to live on his own. I think about this a lot. How will we manage? What will we do? I know I am not physically able to take care of an adult for a long period of time. With my lupus, my strength is limited. I do not have the answers for the future. Dad is still mentally and for the most part, physically strong, so I hope that we have a long time before we have to address these issues.

This chapter is ending, and as I reflect back on my father's life, I have to say he has always worked very hard, loved his family, been a good provider, succeeded in business and most of all, has a sensitive nature about him. I don't know if I have ever known a more sensitive man. He wears his emotions on his sleeve and it is never hard to figure out how he feels about something because he will always tell you. As he gets older, his sensitive nature becomes even more apparent which became apparent after the loss of his little beagle. We all felt so helpless and did not know what to do to comfort him. He has, however, found comfort in the birds that he feeds daily. The hummingbird feeders keep him busy and he enjoys caring for the tiny winged wonders. Dad is now anxious about building a fence around his yard so he can get another pup. Things are looking up! I know he still hurts over his loss, but at least he is looking to a future of loving something else that will depend on him for friendship and care which, I'm sure, will go both ways. Having another living creature love him as unconditionally as Beegee will be a great comfort and great joy for my dad. A boy and his dog or a man and his dog; they seem to be the same to me!

REFLECTION 4

9-18-2007   167 lbs.

During the writing of the previous chapters since my last reflection, I have had to do a great deal of soul searching. Taking a deep look at *me* has been very difficult as I have had to relive some very painful memories. This had been a heavy four-and-a-half months; I have cried many tears while typing away at the computer and sometimes have had to stop for the day to compose myself so I could continue the next day. Do I have any regrets about what I have written? Not in the least. With some of my experiences, if I do not write about them, who will? I feel the issues are important enough even if I have left my raw soul out there for others to judge. As I have stated before, if someone else can identify and possibly feel a little better knowing someone else out there in this big old world has been through something similar, lived through it and come out better for it, then my work is done. I hope this is the case for at least one person who reads about my life.

Summer has been very busy for me; I traveled to Florida with my daughter Sandra and my grandchildren. Sandra had the American Culinary Federation (ACF) National Convention in July and I accompanied her so she would have someone to watch the little ones! It was a great trip, and I was fortunate enough to attend the Grand Ball with her, and I met some very lovely people. Chefs from all over the country attended. A big highlight was meeting Rock from *Hell's Kitchen*! He was this season's winner of the popular TV reality show and he will now have his own resort in Nevada. Sandra and I both chatted with him and had our pictures taken with him as well. I even had him phone my very best friend, Ann Marino, a big fan of his, and he talked with her on my cell phone with her in complete shock! He is a very kind and giving man. Sandra, Ann and I all wish him and his family the best of luck in the future in all of his endeavors.

On the trip to Florida, we made some dear friends whom I am sure we will be in contact with for years to come: Chas (our friend from Chicago), Ed, his wife Erin, and Rick (friends we met in Nashville at the regional conference) and others were great fun to be with. I look forward to attending many more functions with Sandra in the future. She is the current president of the Clarksville, Tennessee chapter of ACF and I am sure she will be a member for many years to come.

We also traveled to Illinois to be at my "adopted" daughter's wedding reception. Wayne, my new son-in-law by "adoption", is a great person and I know he and my daughter Tammy will be happy for a lifetime. They did sneak off to the Dominican Republic to be married, but upon returning home close to St. Louis, they held a great reception for all their family and friends. It was a very nice weekend, celebrating Tammy and Wayne's new life together. Good luck and God bless them, and Tyler and Logan, too! By the way, Happy Birthday Logan! Five years old tomorrow and going on sixteen like his big brother Tyler! He thinks he is every bit as old!

Two weeks ago, Dad and I went to Mississippi with Sandra, Jimmy and the kids for the weekend. Sandra and I went to a concert and Jimmy and Clay, my grandson, went clay pigeon shooting while Dad rode along. It was a good relaxing Labor Day weekend, and it was the kid's treat. We all had fun!

You can see by the dates of my writing that I have been off the job quite a bit lately. Church affairs have kept me busy with meetings aplenty, as we plan our year for 2008. All of us have worked hard in the planning and I think we finally have things underway for a spiritual year full of church family and friends, but most of all, God's work. I am so thankful for my church family and I will never get tired of saying so! We are so blessed to have such a great group of people to worship with and I can never thank God enough for leading me on the path to Trenton United Methodist Church. There was a time, not too long ago that I never thought I would belong to any particular church. I am a very spiritual person but until I was led to my church home, I never believed in having to go to church to believe in God. I guess my years of having to attend a specific church as a child left a bitter impression on me. I had many bad experiences in early life with the church I attended because I was very impressionable and saw too much wrong going on with the adults in the church. It was not a pleasant time for me at all. Now, I do not feel the same way. I love belonging to my church and because the people have given me so much support and love, it is hard to remember my objections to church life years ago. I cannot imagine it any other way now.

In the last four chapters, I have written about pain, hurt, betrayal, love, history and faith. It has been hard, it has been a revelation, and it has made me face some of my own demons. I look forward to moving on and telling you about two main loves in my life. I will also get into the area of my present health with lupus and bipolar depression. I want to balance the good with the bad, because I absolutely believe for every type of suffering I go through in life, there is something out there balancing it out and making me glad to be here to experience it all. Yes, I am an optimist and a very big optimist at that! I always look for the good, hate it when people dwell on the bad and negative (my family can attest to this) and I know things will be okay in the end. Why, you ask? Why not! My motto? Believe!

If you think things are going bad,
And something or someone has made you sad,
Look for tomorrow and all it brings,
Laughter and sunshine and other great things,
Peace and love are yours to keep,
Cherish and own both… keep them deep,
Within you is the chance to be,
Happy and loved… treasured and free.

CHAPTER FIFTEEN

SOMEBODY SPECIAL CALLS ME MAMAW!

I dedicate this chapter to the two special children in my life, Clayton Andrew and Lily Glori-Ann. They give me so much great pleasure on a daily basis that I cannot imagine my life without them. Each day is an adventure, watching them grow and learn. They truly do light up my life!

Sail away my child, and slumber deep
Lay your little head down, in peaceful sleep.

Drift up to the billowy clouds in the sky,
And know, if far away, I am still close by.

Tiptoe in wonder, of everything grand,
Then frolic and play, in a fairytale land.

Many adventures you'll live, through glorious night,
Even with your eyes closed, it is all in plain sight.

For the stars light your way, as you sail the night on,
And as you play till early dawn.

God's gift to you is slumber deep,
As you renew with peaceful sleep.

Where do I start? I wrote that poem last evening after babysitting my two special little ones. I am not sure where it came from, but I knew that today I was starting this chapter about them and it just hit me while on the twenty-mile trip home. What can I say? They *inspire* me! I have had to look over them many times while they sleep, and it is the most precious thing. Such innocence, and not a care in the world; it makes me warm inside. These words above have been, I guess, my unspoken thoughts for them when they close their eyes to rest. Yes, I am a mushy grandmother. There's absolutely no doubt about it! You know what they say, having grandchildren gives you bragging rights and there is truth to that! I thought I bragged a lot about my kids, but when the grandkids came along, that bragging multiplied so many times that I've lost track. I know in my "Mamaw" frame of mind they are the greatest grandkids alive! Of course, I also know, there is not one grandma out there who does not feel the same way about her own little wonders!

Grandparenthood started for me in September of 2000. Our millennium baby, Clayton Andrew, was born on the fifteenth of the month, and he came into this world with a bang. In an earlier chapter, I told a little about his birth and Sandra's complications of latter pregnancy and ultimately, delivery. We were all on pins and needles for the last three months before Clay was born, but fortunately, Clay was born healthy and strong. His mommy was a bit worse for the wear, but she rapidly recovered and they both went home at the same time. The fact that I was present at Clay's delivery was the greatest thing in the world. I got to hold him almost immediately, and the thrill of seeing this little person whom I had prayed for so much in the previous nine months totally overcame me. He was finally in my arms, tiny eyes trying to focus on my face, as I looked down on him with more pride that I could contain. Here he was at last!

9-21-2007   **166 lbs.**

When we were blessed with our little girl, Lily, things were not so easy. Her arrival into the world nine weeks early was a trying time. Sandra's complications while carrying her little girl were life threatening for herself as well as for the baby. I have never prayed so hard in my life. When Lily was born in a labor room with only her daddy and me in the room with Sandra, the silence was deafening. It all happened so fast that no one was prepared, even though labor was induced and the alarms that were attached to Sandra, monitoring her and Lily, started sounding off. The hospital was busy, and there were not enough staff to go around for the four women in premature labor on the OB floor. It was just a nightmare! When our lifeless, teeny, tiny, little girl lay there on her mommy's bed, so still and purple-blue, it had to be the scariest few minutes the three of us have ever, or will ever, experience. The next few weeks after Lily's birth were no piece of cake either. Her premature little body was in constant danger of shutting down. I prayed God to take my life instead of hers if he needed to take someone. I kept constant vigil, visiting her as many times as the doctors and nurses would allow, and I kept reassuring my daughter and son-in-law that their little girl would be all right.

Four weeks came and went and our precious Lily was ready to go home! What a great surprise we all had. It was not the two months we had been prepared for, no, it was four weeks early and almost unheard of for a two-pound, thirteen-ounce birth-weight baby! She was now at the magic number of four pounds and doing remarkably well. We were ready to get her home but I know all of us were still a bit apprehensive. Lily, however, was ready to be loved and held all of the time, and she fought to make the unbelievable progress that she did. She is one tough little cookie and her fight for survival astonished all of us. Today (let me put it this way) she is in charge! There are no ifs, ands or buts about it! If you don't agree, she will make herself quite known and you will soon have to change your mind! She's a force to be reckoned with. When I look at her, I think of an old Bill Cosby comedy routine where he talks about the birth of a daughter. He goes on to say that when this child was born, she came out with a cigar in one hand and a martini in the other, saying, "I'm in charge here!" I remember hearing this back in my teen years and thought it was quite funny. I did not realize at the time that someday, in my own family, we would have a similar experience! Little blond-haired, blue-eyed Lily is the one in charge, and I'm sure in a few months when she is able to talk more, if we don't believe it, all we'll have to do, is ask her! I know she will set us all straight.

Clay and Lily, Lily and Clay... whew! Where do I begin? I will start with Clay, the first born. Clay is quite a handsome child. His great good looks and infectious smile melt my heart, and when he sheds tears, my heart crumbles. I feel his feelings. There is a special bond between us that can never be broken. I always have told him, since he was a tiny baby, that he was my reason for living. He knows this quite well and reminds me of it on a daily basis. The greatest reminder of this was one day, when he was around four years old, and I was depressed and having a hard time. Clay came up to me and threw his little arms around my legs because he could not reach any higher, and said "Mamaw... I'm your reason for living!" It caught me off guard and as I looked down into his big smile and big hazel eyes, whatever I was depressed about melted away right at that very moment. He was, and he knew it! I know even in his tiny little mind he sensed my uneasiness and bad ways. Even if he consciously was not aware of what he was doing, subconsciously he knew I needed to snap out of it and he said what I had repeated to him so many times before, adding the gigantic hug as reinforcement! Boy, that will knock the bad mood right out of you! If it doesn't, there is something wrong!

When Clay was a baby, he and Sandra lived with my husband Jimmy and me while Sandra was going through a divorce from Clay's biological father. She worked during the day, so I took care of the baby while she was away. Clay and I were attached at the hip. I read to him all of the time and I spent countless hours playing with him when he was still small enough to stay on the bed with me. When he became a little older, it became more difficult for me to take care of him because of lupus and a severe back injury from the car accident he, Sandra and I were in. As long as I did not have to chase him around, it was great! When he was up and running, not so great! I was fatigued more every day, and even though I wanted to, it became increasingly difficult to care for him. I started feeling guilty. We did not want him in daycare but

I was not strong enough to keep up with his energy. Little did we know at the time, he was already starting to show signs of ADHD. I know Sandra did not understand why I, at only 44 years old, could not keep up with Clay. I think sometimes she thought I was lazy or did not want to be bothered. She did not understand my illness, as many people do not. This caused friction between us. I never wanted Clay to think I did not want him around because this was the furthest from the truth, so I spoiled him in every way I could. Before too long, Sandra was living elsewhere and she put Clay into daycare with me babysitting on weekends when needed. Then, when I moved away and got my divorce, I bought my house and Sandra and Clay came to live with me again. We both needed the financial help of having two people share expenses so it had its advantages and I had Clay with me to spoil even more.

As he started getting older, Clay's hyperactivity became increasingly harder to handle. It was exhausting to everyone who was around him, because he never slowed down. He was in perpetual motion. Just watching him would wear you ragged! Sandra kept seeking medical intervention, but until he reached a certain age, medication was out of the question. Then there had to be full documentation from teachers at school, and counselors, that his concentration abilities were hindering his school performance. All of this started in pre-school and continued until he reached the point where the doctor would put him on medication. We researched the various medications available and none of us wanted to see our little boy put on ADHD medication, but we knew he would not be able to perform in school otherwise. So, with all said and done, the prescription was filled, the medicine was given, and Clay became a different little boy! The difference was night and day. He calmed down and his loving nature became even more apparent because, suddenly, he could sit still and cuddle and share without feeling the need to wiggle and squirm. We now have our little boy back! He does very well in school and is very bright and curious. Everyone looks forward to him bringing home good grades every reporting period, which he does. Mostly As and a few Bs seems to be the norm. His reading ability is uncanny, and I do believe all the hours I spent reading to him as a baby has helped with this along the way. We cannot say, though, he does not still get into trouble at school! Nothing bad, just talking, socializing and such. After all, he is very friendly! His teacher has to move him sometimes to put a stop to his little blabbermouth, but overall, he does exceptionally well in school. I know there has never been a time I have visited him at school when I have not had someone stop me in the hallway or cafeteria when they realize he is my grandson, and tell me how sweet and polite he is. It makes me beam inside out to know he is ours — our golden boy — to love and cherish. Yes, he belongs to us and we are so thankful God has graced our family with another loving, giving child who lights up the life of everyone who is fortunate enough to encounter him. Clay loves his family, he loves life, and he loves Jesus and says so. He says his prayers every night before going to sleep: "God bless Mommy, Daddy, Clay, Lily, Grandma, Grandpa Jack, Mark, Jaclyn, Jeffrey, Grandpa Walker, Grandpa (Dye), Winchester and Mamaw." In case you're wondering, Winchester is the family's miniature schnauzer. After all, he needs prayer too!

2007-2007-2007   **167 lbs.**

Clay was a happy baby and a good baby who never cried very much. He was, and always has been, very easy going. Lily, however, is going to make darn sure she gets her way; she's a little spitfire! Do not get me wrong, Lily is also a very happy baby; she smiles all the time. She is easy going when the "going" is going her way, and is not afraid to voice her opposition if she is unhappy. Lily will certainly make her wishes well known! Bottle this up in a 19-month-old baby who is just learning to talk and you get "Lily Loud!"

When she was such a little preemie in the neo-natal intensive care unit at the hospital, she was nicknamed "Lily Loud Mouth"! Her lungs were strong from the start! The nurses gave her this name because she was louder and fiercer than all the other babies combined. We got a kick out of her lungpower! Things have not changed a bit. Lily feels very free to voice her opinion whenever she feels it necessary, but this does not mean in a bad way. She laughs very loud, and it is infectious. We are all starting to realize that we have a little *clown* on our hands. If Lily can get a laugh out of you, she will continue on and on to get even more of a response. She always has an audience as she holds court with her antics. This little tiny girl is just downright funny! She keeps us in stitches most of the time. I have never been around a baby or little kid who can make people laugh with just facial expressions like Miss Lily can. She has a constant changing face as she learns how to manipulate her pretty features into some of the funniest expressions I have ever seen. The other day Sandra and I were talking, and Sandra said she knows Lily is going to be the class clown when she hits school. We may even have the making of a famous comedian on our hands! If she keeps up the antics, life for our family will never be dull.

I have the honor of watching my little ones on an almost daily basis. Lily stays with me during the morning and then, in early afternoon, we make the trip back to Hopkinsville where the kids live so I can be at their home when Clay gets off the school bus. After he is home, I make sure he gets his homework done. They have a snack, and then have playtime while I sit down and start working on my writing. This is how I got most of this book done; I wrote while they were playing. Sometimes however, it is next to impossible to work when a seven-year-old and a very active baby girl are on the run! They seem to find countless things to keep them busy! Lily especially finds new and exciting adventures on a daily basis in their house. What was not of much importance yesterday is a completely new adventure today! We keep baby proofing but she keeps finding more and more to explore. It is now almost a constant "never take your eyes off her" experience! I can glance away for a second, and she will have found something she had already zeroed in on and have it in her hand or mouth before I can glance back. Heck, she finds things at my house I never knew I had! Clay is also learning that his toys and other things are of great importance to his little sister. This is starting to teach him to keep his things in his room with the door closed so she cannot get a hold of them. In addition, another thing that has become obvious lately is the two most spoken words of the household: "Lily, no!"

9-26-2007   **166 lbs.**

If you have children, you know that when *they* hurt, *you* hurt. Grandchildren multiply this feeling. In our family, about two years ago, Clay developed a swollen gland on the side of his throat. At first, it was not much of a concern, but after a day or so and it getting more bothersome, Sandra took him to the doctor. This is where the panic started! The doctor was very concerned about the enlarged area and immediately started running tests. He told Sandra that he was not ruling out cancer! As you can imagine, we all freaked out. The next forty-eight hours were painful. I think we all stopped breathing for the full two days. There is no way to describe the fear I felt. I prayed and prayed for his health and I prayed for all of us to have strength during whatever it was we faced. After receiving the initial news, I ran out and bought him the biggest ride-on battery-operated vehicle I could find! I thought he needed a little extra spoiling while we waited on test results. We all tried to carry on with life as normal, but I think we were just going through the motions for those long hours until the results came. The time finally came and the results were negative. The doctor even re-ran tests to make sure there was no chance of error. We were ecstatic to say the least. Our little boy was fine, and all he had was a swollen gland.

I cannot imagine how parents, grandparents and other family members feel when the news is not as good. My heart truly goes out to these families. It has to be the worst kind of hell knowing your helpless child is sick and you can do nothing to make him or her better. I know God never gives us more than we can handle but this would have to be the closest thing I can think of to dispute this fact. All I can say is being faced with the fact that Clay had a serious illness, I needed God in my life at that moment more than ever.

I would have died with worry if I was not comforted by the fact the Lord would see us through this. I hope if you are faced with this kind of tragedy, that you can find comfort in knowing your child is in God's hands. I also believe a sick child can make you show just how much you truly love them because you are more attentive to their needs, wants and wishes. Your whole world revolves around this innocent child and his care. I think it would have been very hard for me if one of my children had been seriously sick, and I had to care for the other child as normal. I would not like to think that the healthy child lacked my attention, but it would have been hard to carry on as if nothing changed. I know there are parents faced with this daily, and again, my heart goes out to them and their families. It has to be the most difficult of situations.

All of us know a family who has, or is going through, this kind of crisis, and I encourage you to lend support in whatever way you can. Remember the other children in the household and do whatever you can to help. Sometimes families are overwhelmed with help and support, but I am a firm believer that there is never too much support. If there is more than one child in the home, even just arranging to pick the well child up from school and taking them for ice cream can make a big difference to a sibling who is feeling helpless and slightly ignored. Also, I recommend taking the child to the grocery store and letting them plan a meal by purchasing the ingredients and then, with your help, preparing it for the family so the child feels helpful and useful. This gives the well child a feeling of family participation and they feel like they are helping in their own way. It also gives stressed parents a breather knowing the other child is not feeling left out.

By no means am I an expert on parenting, nor do I have any experience on the subject but I know when we were faced with the possibility of Clay being seriously ill, many things ran through my mind those forty-eight hours of being wide awake. I thought of almost everything and wondered how we would deal with it all. I planned, I prayed, I planned and prayed even more, and the one thing foremost in my mind was that the Lord would see us through. My wish is that no parent or grandparent has to feel the fear we felt when faced with this, but if you do, please find peace in knowing you are not alone. Many people love to be of help and if you are fortunate to have these angels in your life, take them up on their kindness. Also, know that there is always support in the churches around you. If it is truly God's house, you can always find peace and comfort there, and if for some reason you and your family feel alone, when you lay your head down at night, ask the Lord for companionship. He is always there. He is always in your corner. Never doubt Him.

9-27-2007   **166 lbs.**

Today, Clay was out of school due to a dentist appointment. I arrived at their home around 12:30 to watch him and Lily. Clay showed me some catalogs he got from school for a fundraiser for the PTO. The catalogs have greeting cards, wrapping paper, and other items in them. He wanted to know if I wanted to buy something. This is his first experience of selling anything and of course, I had to cheer him on. I looked through the merchandise and had not quite made the selection of what I was going to buy when I got busy with Lily and my mind was taken off it for a while. Before long, I realized Clay was very quiet and I called out for him. He did not answer, so I assumed he was outside playing. I walked outside and called for him but there was still no answer. I then went and looked in his room to see if he had settled down to watch a movie; he was not there. About the time I was going back outside to look for him, he came running in the house with a sheepish look on his face, carrying his little sales catalogs. He handed them to me and a sheet of paper with a lady's name on it and her order neatly written down, a note to me saying if he needed the money now, let her know, and she would bring it over. I looked at the total sale and by golly, the little guy had sold twenty dollars worth of stuff; I was amazed! He had not even rehearsed how to approach a prospective buyer, nor did I know he knew the products. I told him to go tell the next-door neighbor, his first customer who he hardly knows, that the money was due by Monday the first. He did and she came over and gave me a check for the total. She said he was "quite a salesman" and he was so sweet, she could not refuse. I laughed, and then thanked her. After she left, Clay sat me down and put the catalogs in front of me and said, "Mamaw, what do you want to buy?" There was absolutely no shyness when it came down to money and prizes he might win by the number of his sales! I glanced back through the catalogs and made my purchases while my grandson, who just turned seven a little over a week ago, made sure I did so while he watched. Within one hour, he sold forty-eight dollars worth of wrapping paper, novelties and cards for the holidays. I could not be more proud! It looks like Clay has the "born salesman" gene that so many of us have in this family. When I was his age, my parents always said I could sell snow to an Eskimo! Clay is on his way, too! You cannot imagine how proud he was of his accomplishments.

Every day, my grandchildren amaze me. When I think I could not possibly love them more, I do. My heart is filled with their laughter and smiles but it breaks when they shed tears. All three of us are inseparable. Not a day goes that I don't miss them when they are not around. No matter how tired I am from watching them and sometimes needing a break, I still yearn to be with them. On the days when Sandra does not have to work, I miss the pitter-patter of Lily's little feet running through my house. My dad misses her also because we always go over to his place in the mornings and visit. There have been a few times when I've shown up without her and he actually did not seem too thrilled to see me alone! Of course, I know this is not the true case but he does get disappointed. I know she lights up his day.

These two little people mean everything to me. With everything I do, I have to think about how it affects them and how can I do better. When I am feeling ill from my disability, it hurts me not to be the playful "Mamaw" they want and need. It is very difficult feeling terrible and not being able to take them and do things with them that I wish I could. I know there are times, Clay does not understand why I have no energy and cannot play with him. I try to explain. He listens. His other Grandma is very vivacious and very physically fit. When she visits, they are on the go all of the time. I envy her health and non-stop energy. She is an amazing person and I could not ask for a better other grandma for my little ones. She loves them as much as I do if that is even possible! I am so thankful for her, and I know that what I may lack in physical energy, I make up with understanding and creativity. My grandkids and I do play! It might be with me laying on the bed and us making up stories or silly songs, or it might be with me teaching Clay how to play a little flute toy I bought him, or it might be just drawing, or playing a board game. Whatever it is, I love my time with the two of them. Each day, I watch them grow and grow. Each day, they never cease to amaze me. Each day is an adventure with them, and each day, my love grows and grows for the two most important children in my life. They light up my days, they light up my nights, and they light up my life! Clay and Lily are indeed our family's greatest gift from God. They can never be loved more than we love them and God knew what He was doing when He gave these children to us. They deserve the best in life, as all children do, and I know for myself, they absolutely are my reason for living. I cannot imagine my life without them. They make me stronger in my faith, stronger in my love and stronger in myself. I want to give them the world and everything that they could ever wish, for but in reality, all I do have to offer them is my undying love and devotion. This will never waiver; they will never be without me loving them.

Clayton Andrew and Lily Glori-Ann: your Mamaw loves you more than you will ever know. Thank you God, for this special gift. There is no greater!

IF EVER YOU DO NOT BELIEVE,
LOOK INTO THE EYES OF A CHILD.
IN A WORLD YOU CANNOT CONCEIVE,
LET IT ALL DRIFT AWAY IN HIS SMILE.

CHAPTER SIXTEEN

ALICE IN WONDERLAND MEETS DARTH VADER!

9-29-2007   **166 lbs.**

Hi! My name is Alice... today, that is! Now tomorrow, it might be a different story! Tomorrow my name just might be Darth Vader! There! I said it! Are you thoroughly confused by now? If you are not, than you may suffer from the same disorder I do, and if you are confused, you are probably *normal*!

All fun and puns aside, this *is* a serious subject for me. I am referring to the illness known as bipolar disorder. Myself, like hundreds of thousands of other people in this world, suffer from this unexplainable mental condition. A great deal of research and in-depth studies of this illness are ongoing but there is still much to be learned. As for me, it has been a roller coaster sometimes. Trying to understand this illness and its effects is an on-going process. I learn more each day about my symptoms and myself as I struggle to maintain some sort of *normalcy* in my life. Support from family helps, advice from specialists works sometimes, and the *medications* are a Godsend!

This all started for me back in 1989 and 1990. 1989 was a horrendous year for me. I talked earlier about some of the stressors in my life during this time like my father undergoing quadruple bypass surgery, a best friend killed in an airplane crash, my husband Jeff having a massive heart attack and us almost losing him, me making a major career change, and then the loss of my mother to cancer. All of this happened from January 1, 1989 through July 29 of the same year. Seven months of the hardest things I could have gone through emotionally had left me spent, angry and most of all sad. From August through Christmas, I tried to go on with life as normal, not allowing myself to feel. I went through all of the motions of everyday life, never slowing down and I was burning the candle from both ends. I did not eat and I did not sleep. Friends and business associates could not believe how well I was handling everything.

I was truly an amazing bundle of energy and I put on a "happy face" so no one around me, including my family, saw the suffering I was going through inside. Truthfully, I do not think I even realized just how sad I really was. My mind raced continuously, keeping the darkness hidden somewhere in my subconscious. Sometimes I even amazed myself as to how well I was coping with everything.

10-1-2007   **166 lbs.**

When 1990 came, I started to feel darkness come over me. I struggled to keep on with my everyday life but it became increasingly more difficult as time ticked by. I decided to leave Jeff and move out on my own. We filed for divorce but right before it was finalized, we decided to reconcile and I moved back home. I decided to quit my job to work on my first novel and we took a trip to Japan in April. In May, we renewed our wedding vows on our twelfth anniversary with a second wedding ceremony complete with family and friends. Things were supposed to be turning around in my life, but I was feeling like a caged animal, trying to escape myself. Jeff and I started fighting even more, and my mood was becoming more and more unstable. I was sinking down into a black hole. I went to a doctor and told him how depressed I was feeling and he immediately put me on Prozac, a minimal dose. Depending on the medication to change my mood, even though I knew it would not be instantaneous, did give me some hope. Actually though, it was like putting a bandage on a severed limb. It was enough to cover one tiny problem but not enough to cover the complete problem, leaving me "bleeding" out my heart and soul. I functioned like this for months but my life was steadily slipping away.

March of 1991 came with me breathing, but not living and it all came to a head one morning when I was home alone. The kids were at school, Jeff was at work and I found myself in my living room completely numb. I sat down on the floor and started sobbing uncontrollably. I was in incredible pain both mentally, as well as physically. My mind raced with thoughts of how I did not want to live like this anymore. I wanted it to end. I thought of taking my own life but I knew I could not do this to my family, especially my children. The pain started getting worse, and I felt like my chest was being crushed. I could hardly breathe. I knew I needed to get up and get to the telephone to call somebody because I knew I was in serious trouble. It was as if I was completely paralyzed. It must have been over an hour of me sitting like this, trying to get up and take the first step. I was numb with fear, with fear of the fact that I had lost my mind completely and I would never escape the darkness of myself. I do not know how much time actually passed, but finally I was able to make my way to the telephone and I called my sister Sheri. Within hours, I was on a flight to Phoenix to be with her. I knew I needed hospitalization but I did not know where to start so we decided together that I would spend a couple of days with her because she knew I would be safe there. She knew how to talk to me and she allowed me to talk as much as I needed too. We spent the two or three days with me sleeping because I was completely exhausted and we also just sat and talked when I was awake. I made several calls to facilities back in California and made the decision to go back home and admit myself into the place I thought fit my needs the best. When I arrived back home, I made the necessary arrangements and within one day, I was ready to go commit myself.

10-7-2007 (happy birthday to me... my 50th!)   **166 lbs.**
When I made the decision to go into the hospital, a sense of relief came over me. Yes, I was somewhat scared because I did not know

what was ahead for me, but yet after making one of the most important decisions in my life, calmness surrounded me and I started to relax. I checked myself into the facility late in the afternoon and the first hours were spent going over rules and regulations of the hospital as well as room assignment and meeting the person to whom I would be sharing a room. There were no private rooms in this facility. The whole concept was to get you involved with someone else who was suffering from problems and participating in many group activities, anywhere from counseling sessions to arts and crafts. I was expected to participate in all of the activities so I was not laying around in my room feeling sorry for myself. This type of environment was of great help to me. It allowed me to be with others and learn from them about what they were going through in their lives that led them here. I was soon to realize my problems seemed minor compared to some of the stories I heard. Within a few days, I shifted from a wounded depressed person to that of a friend and confidant to several other people whom I grew extremely fond of very rapidly. I also immediately made friends with my roommate and we identified with each other very closely. Within a week, I felt like most of the people there in the hospital with me had become somewhat of a new family. We knew each other's secrets more rapidly than most people who meet for the first time and many of us shared issues that were alike. Even though the people with whom I was hospitalized with had many different reasons for being there, we all suffered from extreme depression regardless of whatever else was going on in our lives. My nurturing nature took over and I started focusing on the others and their troubles instead of being so consumed by my own turmoil, which had brought me to check myself into this place.

I did not know how therapy works nor did I know that group therapy could be such a revelation. After my first group session, I was aware I was not alone in my depression. The others there were also at their wit's end in their own lives. There were people there who were hopelessly addicted to drugs or alcohol. Some tried to take their life by attempted suicide. There was a girl who was severely abused as a child; during her first semester in college, she suffered a complete nervous breakdown. A woman was admitted so drunk from alcohol abuse; she slept for two days, and when she finally woke, screamed for two more as she went through detoxification. We could hear her screams, and I felt every one of them run down my spine. I could feel her pain through her shrieks. I wanted to be able to go to her and comfort her, but then again, I was afraid because I had never been exposed to anyone like her before. After about a week, she joined the general population of the facility and I realized she was my own age, a total surprise to me. I figured she must have been older; I am not quite sure why except for the fact that I possibly could not conceive someone my own age could be so hopelessly addicted to alcohol. As I said, I led a somewhat sheltered life up until this point. In my mind, alcoholics were older people. Anyone I knew of who drank excessively was usually way over fifty. This shows you exactly how much I really did know. As far as alcoholics go, I had known maybe one or two in my life up until this. I now know there were probably many more, but I was just unaware of their problems by either them hiding it, or by me not wanting to see it, or both. After all, this was "other people's" problems. They could *not* have been anyone I knew!

10-11-2007   **167 lbs.**

During my stay, for the first two weeks, I requested my husband to stay away and not visit me. We were having problems in our marriage and I needed to clear my head before addressing the issues. He did not understand, and he took it as a personal attack. My doctors tried to get him to understand, but he was wounded by my request and it made everything harder as far as we were concerned. When I did talk with him, he scolded me for turning my back on *us*. I tried to make him understand but I know he never did. This was unfortunate, because it only made the pressure on me worse as far as our relationship was concerned. After I got out of the hospital and started feeling strong enough to face facts, I arranged to leave California and move back to Texas. I knew we needed the distance between us while we went through the motions of divorce all over again. Shortly after when he moved to where I was in Texas I know it was a Godsend because this is when I became extremely ill with seizures and needed someone to take care of me. Thank God, he was there.

Years went by with me suffering from bouts of depression, but I always attributed it to the fact I still had some difficult times I was going through. I knew I was suffering from extreme depression, but it really came to a head after the destruction of the third marriage. I spoke briefly about this marriage in the chapter about my relationships and this is all I will say about that marriage. It was horrible, I am lucky to be here and my daughter and I paid the price of the stupid mistake I made. I cannot, however, spend any of my God-given energy on such a bitter memory. Every day I try to forget it ever happened, but the fact is it did. I do believe I am stronger for it today and I must move on.

10-17-2007   **166 lbs.**

For the last several days, I have been very sick with lupus. You can tell, by the last day that I wrote, it has been over a week. Today I am feeling a little bit stronger and I decided that because this chapter is about depression, I needed to push through it and carry on. I do tend to get very depressed when my illness takes over, but I refuse to let it control me. Sometimes, with the extreme fatigue I suffer from with a flare, I can hardly lift my head off the pillow and I have an emotional struggle with myself. I then realize I just have to let it go and deal with the cards I have been dealt, which means not giving in to it but accepting my limitations and living life from this point. It may sound easy enough, but I have to admit it is not always so.

Back to the topic at hand. In 1994, at the time of the destruction of the third marriage, I went into a tailspin. Within a matter of twenty-four hours, life as I knew it turned totally upside down. I found myself scared out of my wits, uncertain about anything I thought was true about my life, and I did not know which direction to turn. The first thing I did was place a call to my family doctor and immediately went in to see him because I was hysterical and scared. My dad was out of town at the time, so it was only Sandra and me. I knew I had to take action to protect her. My doctor recognized my upset and fear, so he put me in touch with a mental health professional who he thought could be of some crucial help. I had an appointment to see her the following morning.

After meeting the new doctor and telling her what had taken place in the matter of two days, she immediately saw the need to put me on strong antidepressants and anxiety medication. I spent the next two weeks on heavy medication and saw the doctor on a daily basis. Also during this time, I had to seek legal advice and file papers to keep Sandra and me safe; I lived in fear. My close friends kept a constant vigil making sure I was never alone because of the fear my husband would harm me. I was so terrified. My depression seemed to be getting worse, and everything started to sink in about what had happened. A few weeks passed with my therapist increasing the antidepressants. Life continued on but with me always looking over my shoulder.

Two or three months went by and I started feeling better. My energy was increasing and I refused to be unhappy. I got involved with anything and everything I could to keep myself busy. I started a new business selling cosmetics and, before long, I was riding high on cloud nine. Everyone around me was amazed as to how well I was coping. Once again, a pattern developed to where I was everything to everybody, hardly eating or sleeping and carrying on as if I had the greatest life in the world. I took a vacation with John and his family and while on this trip, I spent thousands of dollars on clothes during a four-day trip to Hilton Head, South Carolina. I bought so many things that I had to buy additional luggage to get everything home. This was during the Thanksgiving holidays. As Christmas approached, I spent uncontrollably on everyone I knew assuring them a very good Christmas. I spent, I spent, and I spent. I was also feeling very generous with family; friends, and I also anonymously gave money to many local churches. I adopted many underprivileged children through the Angel Tree campaign and bought numerous toys and other items to brighten up their holiday. As time kept going on, so did my out-of-control spending. I was on the high of all highs and rarely thought about the terrible thing that only months ago happened in my personal life. Little did I know, I was heading for an even more disastrous event in my life, one that would take me a lifetime to recover from.

1-19-2007   **166 lbs.**

Life for me became like living in a fog. I was completely out of control. The worst part of it all was the fact that I was unaware of the trouble I was getting myself into and was oblivious as to what was taking place. It soon became obvious, though. Bills started piling in, but this was not the worst of it. The truth of the matter is, it was not just *my* money I was spending; it was my dad's! I took out numerous credit cards in his name and ran each one of them up to extremely high limits. In a matter of a few weeks, I had spent in excess of twenty-four thousand dollars. Even with me writing this, it still shocks me to realize what I had done.

I remember clearly when my dad placed the first phone call to me after he got the first bill from a credit card company. It was right after Christmas and I was sitting down in front of a mirror putting on my makeup getting ready to leave for a meeting. His voice was shaky on the other end of the phone. He said to me, "We have a problem!" I immediately asked what was wrong and he started the conversation by telling me about an enormous credit card bill he had just received at his mailing address. It was an account he was unfamiliar with that showed numerous charges from Hilton Head at the time I traveled there. As he started reading off some of the charges, a dark reality started to come over me. There is no way for me to explain the fear and helplessness I experienced as my very disappointed father continued to read off charge after charge to store after store I had visited. I wanted to die at that very instance as I tried to make sense of it all. I knew what I had done but yet in another way, I was unaware at the same time. He had the proof right in front of his eyes but I can say, I did not start out to harm him in any way. For someone who has never experienced something so completely devastating, I know there is no way to understand how something like this can happen. I was out of control but it was as if it was not *me* doing it; it was as if I was so caught up in the moments of my craziness, everything was blurting by so rapidly, that there was no time to think of the consequences I would have to face somewhere down the road.

There was no denying what I had done. The shame and guilt totally consumed me. I did not understand why or even how I could have done such a terrible thing to the one person who had always been on my side. How could I have betrayed our trust in this way? What kind of monster had I become? I hated myself. I wanted to crawl under a rock and disappear. I did not want to look my father in the eye and try to explain to him how I could have had carried on such devastating actions which could have destroyed our family as we knew it. The darkness was consuming me from the outside in. The shame was more than I could handle. I fell completely apart.

The next few days were even harder than the first. Each day, a new credit card bill arrived for my dad to open and look at, in shock. He did not even want to make the daily trip to the post office to see what devastation waited in his mail. I isolated myself from everyone as I tried to escape my actions. I knew there were dire consequences for me to face, but my mind was so completely overwhelmed with racing thoughts that I could not focus on anything. It was as if I was watching the rerun of a scary movie every time my father presented me with a new bill I had run up without his knowledge. I felt so horrible about what I had done that I could not face anyone. My dad called my sister Sheri and told her of my actions. She turned her back on me for a while, or so I thought, and told him he needed possibly to press criminal charges against me to protect himself financially. When he told me this, I took it to mean that she hated me for what I had done and truthfully, I could not blame her if she did. At that time, however, I needed her love more than I had ever needed it before. We were so close and with our mother gone, I needed my big sister to tell me we would somehow get through this as a family, together. She, on the other hand, took the tough-love approach and thought I needed to be made accountable for my terrible actions. I could not blame her for her feelings because, believe me, she was being easy on me compared to how I felt about myself. I was the lowest of all low life as far as I was concerned. Only the scum of the earth could betray their families' trust the way I had done. That is right: only the scum of the earth, the lowest of the low. That scum was me.

My shame oozed out from me. Sandra was a teenager and I had to face her daily, knowing she knew what horrible things I had done to her grandpa. I could not look her in the eye. How could I be a mother to her, a role model for her to look up to, when I had just carried on such a betrayal? What had I done to her? How could she ever look up to me again? Again, at this time in my life, I found myself faced with the thought of ending everything and just disappearing off the face of the earth. I knew I would never be able to hold my head up ever again. I knew my family hated my actions and the disappointment they felt in me was horrible, but their disappointment paled to what I was feeling. My father would come over to my house and sit down on my couch and weep, asking me how I could do what I had done. I had no answers for him other than I did not know what I was doing. I know this sounds lame, but not up until several days had passed and the shock was sinking in further did I realize I really was not in control of my actions. I never set out and said, "Gee, I think I'll go out and open up several fraudulent charge accounts in my father's name and see just how long it takes for me to get caught!" I just did it. I had no control of my thoughts, let alone my actions. It was as if I was being flung through a relatively short span of time, racing actions, racing thoughts, never eating, never resting, and never stopping, just existing with everything about *me*, but not really me! I did not know *this Karen,* nor did I even know she existed.

It was time to face facts. I had to get help, once again. I open up the phone book and found an advertisement for the hospital in Clarksville, Tennessee that showed they had psychiatric care, so I placed a call to them. I spoke to a very pleasant woman who shared my name of Karen, and after telling her briefly what was going on in my life, we agreed that I needed to come in for an interview. We set it up for later that afternoon.

When I arrived at the hospital, Karen greeted me and we sat down and talked. After telling her the complete story of my financial disaster, she asked me if I had ever been diagnosed as being bipolar. I told her I had not and that I was not quite sure what bipolar meant. She went on to explain the illness and what several other bipolar patients she knew about had done. After her telling me some of her stories, I felt a certain sense of relief come over me. There were actually others with similar episodes of manic behavior and even some who had done even greater damage than I had done. Financial disaster is not uncommon in people with bipolar disorder. We continued to talk and before long, it was decided that I would enter the program they offered, as an outpatient. This suited me better because of having a teenager at home. All was set and I started the following day.

Outpatient therapy was a revelation for me. I arrived every day by 8:30 in the morning and stayed until three. A psychiatrist as well as a psychologist saw me, and I attended group therapy. They started me on lithium and some other medications. I remained in treatment for three weeks. I learned something every day, and every day I had to forgive myself for my actions. It became obvious within two days that I suffered from bipolar disorder and probably had for a very long time. We also discovered that the Prozac a previous doctor had prescribed for me, had most likely sent me into the tailspin of massive manic behavior. Prozac and bipolar disorder do not mix well, I found out.

After I completed the hospital treatment, I had to try to adjust to all of the new medications and their side effects. Before long, it became obvious that the side effects of the lithium were more than I could handle. I started losing my hair and had other things like a constant upset stomach and loss of appetite. We had to start trying other medications to come up with the right combination for me. Actually, this took several years to master but now, I am doing well with the medications I take to keep me on an even keel. This is not to say that I will not need different ones as time goes on, but for now, I am all right.

After my outpatient treatment, we had to deal with the financial aspect of my mania and, with a very good attorney's help, we were able to settle with the credit card companies for pennies on the dollar. It took a long time, but we finally paid off the debts. A heavy burden was lifted.

Years have passed since the bad episodes I have spoken about in this chapter. I still struggle to maintain some sense of normalcy in my daily life dealing with both bipolar disorder and lupus. You have read about my struggles with the mental disorder, which is an everyday affair. Now at the completion of this chapter, I will send you into another chapter of my life where I am made to deal with a physical illness on an everyday basis. Some experts say the two disorders may go hand in hand. There is still much to learn about both. I learn something new daily and I am sure I will never stop learning how both affect me. Each day is a new experience, there are new aches and pains, and new ways one illness, or the other, affects me. Nevertheless, each day I am thankful to be alive and thankful to be able to share with others my own knowledge of living with two very difficult disorders and making the best of my life. Each day, I thank God for seeing me through and always somehow giving me the strength to persevere when I feel like I cannot go on any longer. I have to "Let go and let God" everyday. This is a constant in my life: not always easy, but something I have learned to trust, by faith. I live by my faith and because so, I know my Savior will care for, me. There is no obstacle to large to handle with Him by my side.

CHAPTER SEVENTEEN

LUPUS: A WOLF IN SHEEP'S CLOTHING!

11-19-2007   **166 lbs.**

Lupus is the Latin word for wolf. For me, it means a range of symptoms including constant fatigue, and it affects my everyday life. I received the diagnosis of my illness in the early nineties. Never hearing of the disease before, I had absolutely no idea what it meant. All I knew was the fact that I had been ill for quite sometime without any reason as to why. At first, I felt my illness still stemmed from all of the problems I had after Jeffrey was born. I had extreme kidney problems for years. I suffered through it and it started affecting my whole being. The fatigue, the aching of my entire body, the low-grade fever accompanied with flu-like symptoms, made no sense. I lived at the doctor's office complaining of massive pain and increasing weakness, only to be given more and more medicine and not a lot of explanation. Before long, I was consumed by fatigue. It was difficult for me to even get out of bed. I felt the medication was making me feel this way but I could not live without it. I did not know where to turn.

It was on a Sunday evening around eight when my phone rang. It was my doctor and he was calling me from his office. He told me he had some test results for me but he did not want to wait until the following morning to discuss them with me, so he asked me to come to his office immediately. Of course, I was scared by his sense of urgency, but I did as he asked and made the two-mile trip to meet with him. Upon arriving, he met me and escorted me back to his lab and then he sat down with me and started going over his findings. Blood work showed a puzzling pattern, and he tried to explain it to me so I could understand. Within minutes, the outlook for my life changed forever.

Lupus is such a mystery. It is not known what causes it nor are there any known cures. It is mysterious in the way it presents itself and each who is afflicted presents many different symptoms. No two patients are alike but yet, most of us suffer from paralyzing fatigue. So many times, we suffer in silence because by looking at us, we may not look like a sick person. Many times we are just considered lazy or faking. How can you look normal, yet be so ill? How do we make family and friends understand what we are going through when we ourselves do not understand? It is hard; trust me, it is hard!

Statistically speaking, lupus affects more women than men and, it seems, African Americans are more likely to have the illness than Caucasians. It has also been shown to affect more young women than older women. There is research ongoing to link hereditary factors. Each day, more and more is learned about this illness and each day, those of us who suffer with lupus await the news of a cure. You can die from this disease or you can live with this disease. As for me, I choose to live! I try doing so using the rule "You have to have a positive attitude!" Sometimes this is very hard to do when I am having an episode and feel like crap! I have to really work on myself to keep my chin up at times but I know by doing so, I feel better in the long run. I believe attitude is more than half the battle! Now don't get me wrong. I have myself some good old fashion pity parties every once in awhile especially when I allow myself to succumb to negativity. When I let my guard down, negativity can rear its ugly head and I then have to give myself a well-deserved attitude adjustment! I know for as long as I am in a negative frame of mind, this illness tries to get one up on me and take over my life; I then have to fight it with everything I am to not let it devour me. This can become a full time job if I let it, but I refuse to let it!

My doctors and I have learned about lupus together. When I first moved to Kentucky, I found a good family doctor in a small town nearby. When I first met him, he took my history. He then told me he was not very familiar with lupus. There were no rheumatoid specialists close by but he agreed to treat me if I wanted him to do so. This is how we learned together. There were many different medications tried and I continued to present many different symptoms. Unfortunately, after a few years of taking care of me, my doctor passed away at a medical conference he was attending. His clinic changed hands several times but the nurse practitioner who worked with him stayed, and she continued my care. Each new doctor who came into the clinic had to learn how to take care of me. I have had great doctors there. My current doctors are wonderful and compassionate and we have an excellent relationship. I am seen monthly so they can monitor my medications and my symptoms. This is an ongoing process.

Lupus is an autoimmune disease, which means the immune system is overactive, causing it to turn on itself. The inflammation is a reaction to this process. Medications, including heavy steroids, are used to reduce the inflammation. There is also chemotherapy as well as immunosuppressive drugs used. As you can imagine, all of these heavy drugs have side effects. Sometimes it is a toss up, whether I prefer the illness or treatment, but nonetheless, treatment has to be undertaken.

There are different kinds of lupus. I have systemic lupus erythematosus, otherwise known as SLE. This form of lupus affects the connective tissue in the body causing inflammation and it can attack any internal organ. It can also affect the skin, causing lesions and scarring. My body is covered with scars from the skin involvement lupus has caused and I have had surgeries to graft and heal severe lesions. One particular lesion caused me to have four different surgeries before it would heal. Coupled with the other symptoms, there are times when I am very ill.

Depression, migraines and memory loss are some other symptoms patients may deal with. I have migraines and take a medication for migraine prevention and I do suffer from some memory loss. The fact I have depression has already been established in the previous chapter but one of my doctors told me if we could cure the lupus, we would probably cure the depression. "From his mouth to God's ears!" That would be wonderful! Anyway, lupus is difficult to deal with, but when you are handed this disorder of the immune system, you learn to cope in your own way. Each person has to find inner peace and deal with what life has given him or her. This disease is crazy in the way it affects each person. Some people are very severe and some have mild forms of the illness. Some lose their fight due to major organ destruction caused by the lupus, while others live their life distracted by more minor forms. I think I fit somewhere in the middle and I am aware of it every day. I am aware of it every time I get up in the morning and my body aches, every time I have to take my many medications, every time I have a doctor's appointment, every time I do not feel like playing with my grandkids and every time someone does not believe me when I tell them I am not feeling well. But the truth of the matter is I refuse to let these things rule my life! Lupus is *not* who I am! I am I, a fifty-year-old woman who has lived half a century of my life, mostly well, with lots of love, spirituality, a beautiful family and a healthy sense of humor! I cannot take myself too seriously and even though I know my illness can be serious, I have to take each day with a grain of salt and look for the positive in that *little grain!* If I do not feel like doing something today, then tomorrow is another day and with it, a new sense of rebirth! I keep telling myself this and re-program any negativity that might slip through the cracks! Yes, it does happen from time to time, honestly, but I am very strong willed and I *will not* let lupus dictate who I am. I want to be an example for others suffering with this. I want all who have the illness to stand up proud, hold their heads up and strive for whatever their dreams are, even if not today, tomorrow or this year. As long as you have dreams, keep them at the forefront in your mind because those dreams will make you feel better and take your mind off the many medications, aches and other annoying issues you have to deal with daily. I do believe you can change your physical day by first adjusting your mental attitude for the day. If you keep those dreams right up at the front in your thoughts, your attitude will be healthier and you will feel better for it. My motto? Make the best of every situation. Take what God has given you and learn from it, deal with it and accept it. Only then, can you experience life to its fullest and teach others along the way.

CHAPTER EIGHTEEN

FINALLY! HOW MANY DAYS HAS IT BEEN?

11-27-2007   **167 lbs.**

It was 331 days and 59 pounds ago that I started this journey. I knew I had to make it to the end but there were times when my energy slacked or busyness got in the way that I felt the pressure of the calendar rapidly sneaking up on me! At the beginning, I scolded myself terribly if I did not write every day! This put an undue amount of pressure on me and I finally had to give myself a break! One side of my brain was saying, "Got to do it, got to do it, got to get it done!" but the other side of my brain, the "smart" side, was lazily contradicting its *other half* with its more reassuring, calming tone: "It's okay girl, you've got plenty of time... relax... sit a spell, take a load off..." As you can tell by the dates of my writing, I took the "smart" side's advice and this took some of the pressure off. Not to say that the last few weeks the less popular side of my brain was screaming, "Got to do it, got to get it done fast, times a runnin' out!" I've felt the pressure daily. This has been especially when I have not devoted the time to finalize this book when I thought I should have! My "due date" for myself has changed at least five or six times in the last two months! This is the beauty of being in control of the situation! Ha! I have come to realize I have no control of anything! Just about the time I think I do, *reality* rears its familiar head, raises that left eyebrow, and emulates my foolish thinking! It is amazing how much I still have to learn!

Here is a tongue twister for you: "How much wood could a woodchuck chuck if a woodchuck could chuck wood?" Heck, do you know the answer? I don't. Who even cares, right? First off, why would a woodchuck be chucking wood and what does "chucking" even mean? As you can see, there are strange times when silly things just pop into my head for no known reason but to make me stop and waste time thinking about it and pondering over it, and here it happened while sitting here writing for you! I don't know why it came to mind, it just did! Sometimes, I have to just go with it and see where it leads! That is how most of this writing experience has been. I have had to just go with thoughts and see where they lead. I am sure people who write silly jokes probably do the same thing! Something silly pops into their head, but they become compelled to go with it and build on it. I am sure some of the funniest things we hear are built on one single silly thought like a woodchuck chucking wood! I do, however, feel there are exceptions to this theory! Some funny things come from certain corny personality traits that we observe in others! Being a blond, and knowing my own intelligence, I find the stereotypical jokes about those with my same hair color quite funny. What is even funnier is being able to actually relate sometimes!

Not to offend anyone, but here's a blond joke for you: How many blonds does it take to write a book? Do you know the answer? In most cases, it takes two! One to hold the book while the other writes "a book" on the front cover. Then there is me. In my case, it took seven blonds: myself, my daughter, Sandra, my adopted daughter Tammy, my son Jeffrey, my grandson Clay, my granddaughter Lily and my deeply missed sister Sheri. With us all being blonds, it took the life experiences of all of us plus one redhead, my mother, and one gray head, my dad, to give me subject matter! Without them, I would have not had much to work with, and even though there is gray creeping into my blondness, I try to tell myself it is "highlights" the Lord has blessed upon me naturally, because I deserve "forever youngness!" At least it sounds good, don't you think? I will let you know in a few more years, or shoot; it could be a few more months, if the Lord continues to *bless m*e!

Exactly one year ago, if someone would have told me I was going to spend 2007 writing my autobiography and venturing on a massive weight loss journey at the same time, I would have probably laughed at them, rolled my eyes and followed with a "Yeah, sure!" In a few days, it will have been a year ago that Jeffrey called me and uttered those famous words, "Mom, I've been thinking!" Yep, I know I responded to him I am sure in the same way, but then his words kept repeating themselves in my head and his direct "You're going to write a book this coming year" approach would not allow me to just sweep it aside and ignore a direct order from my son! He had never done that before when it came and his assertiveness of the matter made me really think about just what exactly he was saying. This is what I was hearing him say: "Mom, your life is worth something special and if you can get your story out there, you will feel better about yourself and help others at the same time." How could I ignore that? His firmness was also his love for me unfolding, so I could really see what he felt inside when it came to his mother. I knew we were about to take a welcome turn in our relationship with each other. I could not tell him no, let him down, nor did I want to listen to what he might have to say if I cowered under the challenge! When was it that the tables turned? When did my "little man" grow up on me and become my biggest fan and at the same time, my biggest critic if I refused to step in line? I know I am far from the age when your children take over the role as the parent and you, the parent, take the role of the child! I am _excessively young,_ as a matter off fact! But suddenly, I was hearing the makings of a future great father if he so chooses, cheering me on to go for it but knowing if I refused to do what he asked, there was going to be great disappointment and yes, heck, to pay!

As I am sure you know by now, I do pray and I do believe in prayer 100%! I have never kept this a secret. To me, to pray is to live! I would have never made it this far in life without lots and lots of prayer, then lots and lots more! However, the praying part is only the first step of my faith. I have to be willing to wait patiently if I am asking for an answer, and then be content with what the Lord sees fit to answer. I do not always get the answer I am hoping for, nor do I think anyone else does all of the time, but He does grant me the answer I need and I have to trust Him to know my needs. For many years, I have been praying to God to make my life mean something to others. I do not mean I prayed to look important in others' eyes, which I cannot in all honesty say I have not wanted from time to time, but what I did mean was I wanted my trials and tribulations to be a learning experience for others on "how not to do things" that have caused me great pain and difficulty. Man, I've pulled some whoppers and told some even bigger whoppers in my 50 years of living, but I'm here, I lived to *tell* about it, and any shame I have gone through, I am now able to release and vow to do better, from now on. Is this not what we all try to do when we say we are reforming, the "vowing to do better from this point on?" The problem is though we usually never cut ourselves some slack and forgive ourselves for past mistakes. This causes us to carry shame upon added shame, which immediately adds self-doubt and builds daily until we can hardly carry around all of the added *"stuff"* we have piled upon ourselves. Of course, others in our lives sometimes feel it necessary to dump on us as well because they see us doing it to our self and figure "why not?" They make themselves feel better for a second or two covering up their own inability to forgive themselves for their own mistakes and if they have to suffer, why not us? Is this not truly sad? I'll say it is! As I see it, if you do not believe there is something out there, bigger and stronger than you are, looking out for you in your times of fallen grace, and granting you forgiveness so you can survive yourself, you are doomed! From mistakes I have made, I've had to know that I could forgive myself and I have been forgiven by something way more powerful than I've seen in this life. Therefore, here is my point: I have had to forgive myself so I could move forward, talk about it, hoping others learn insight from my stories, and possibly recognize something I have talked about in himself or herself or someone else they love. We are all human we all make mistakes. Nevertheless, we need to learn from our mistakes, forgive ourselves, and then, by gosh, move on!

For me, prayer has made this an easier process. I would have never been able to write some of the things I have opened up about in this book if I had not forgiven myself. I have prayed to be able to tell my story with honesty, forgiveness of myself as well as others, sincerity, humbleness, certainty, humor and most of all, *love*. My Creator has seen me through this year and this project and here I am, about to finalize my work and turn it over to others. It is indeed a bittersweet day for me. In some ways, my work is almost over, but in other ways, it is just beginning! The next few weeks will be filled with what I hope to be hustle and bustle as I prepare a "child of mine" to send off to prospective publishers. I know the work in front of me, but I also know I will miss the excitement of sharing my life with you and at the same time, healing myself. I never knew what a true healing experience it would be. I have to say, this is the best therapy I have ever done, by far!

While sitting at this computer and typing these final thoughts, I want each of you to know that I am proud of you! You have made it through these pages with me and you are still reading! There is a lot to be said about "hanging in there" and boy, you have really done that! I hope you kept on reading because you liked the book, but even if it was only because you could not believe any one person could be as messed up as I have been yet had the gall to make you endure my shortcomings just to sell a book, then you are a trooper! You came through it all with flying colors' maybe a little worse for wear, but you did it! I am a happy camper... in advance, that is!

Here we are. My fingers are tired; I have typed most of the day. My eyes are bugging out more than usual and my aching back is tired of sitting. What do we have to show for it? **THE END** is near but not until I have my final thoughts:

Live and laugh a lot! BELIEVE. Never take yourself too seriously! BELIEVE. Trust in something greater than yourself! BELIEVE. Have faith in yourself! BELIEVE. Do not just jump in with both feet, jump in with your WHOLE HEART! BELIEVE. Never look back, before first looking forward! BELIEVE. Those who are unafraid of everything are not human!

My FINAL THOUGHT for you is to LOVE YOURSELF AND LOVE A LOT... MAY ALL YOUR TROUBLES BE FORGOT... LOVE TO LOVE AND LOVE TO LIVE... AND ALWAYS BE WILLING TO FORGIVE!"

THE END

ISBN 142517641-0

9 781425 176419